Instructional Technique

Ivor K. Davies

Indiana University

McGraw-Hill Book Company

New York   St. Louis   San Francisco   Auckland   Bogotá
Düsseldorf   London   Madrid   Mexico
Montreal   New Delhi   Panama   Paris   São Paulo
Singapore   Sydney   Tokyo   Toronto

Library of Congress Cataloging in Publication Data

Davies, Ivor Kevin.
  Instructional technique.

  Bibliography: p.
  Includes indexes.
  1. Teaching—Handbooks, manuals, etc.   I. Title.
LB1025.2.D32   371.1   80-18421
ISBN 0-07-015502-X

Instructional Technique

15 16 17 DOC/DOC 9 9 8 7 6 5 4 3 2 1

This book was set in Souvenir by Creative Production Concepts. The editor was James J. Walsh; the designer was Caliber Design Planning; the cover was designed by Jane Moorman; the production supervisor was Marie Birdsall. The drawings were done by J & R Services, Inc. R. R. Donnelley and Sons was printer and binder.

Foreword

Ivor Davies is a master teacher. And fortunately for those of us who practice the craft of instruction, he is also a prolific writer and documentarian of the skills which can lead us, with hard work and energy, toward the mastery of teaching.

In this practical text, Dr. Davies reminds us that our objective is not instruction—but learning. We can seldom train anyone to do anything through sheer force of will—because skill acquisition and behavior change are self-development phenomena which require the active involvement and consent of the individual learner in a shared enterprise. Our challenge as instructors is to create the environment and facilitating experiences so that learning can happen.

Geniuses are rare in such expressive arts as music and theater, yet there are countless competent practitioners who are highly effective because of their talent to convert the techniques and materials of their profession into exciting and fulfilling events for their audiences. Similarly, successful instruction relies not on genius or extraordinary gifts, but on clear understanding of time-tested principles, dedication to excellence, and conscientious preparation and practice.

Effective training is a practical blend of art and science, tactics and strategy. When all elements are combined in the proper mixture, the result can be dynamic and joyful for learner and instructor alike. But how do we begin to formulate the best possible recipe for our particular style of instruction and content? One good way to start is to turn this page and read on. . . .

Kevin O'Sullivan
Executive Director
American Society for Training
and Development

Washington, D.C.
Spring, 1980

v

*For my daughter Michelle,
who deserves good instruction.*

Preface

This book is about instruction. In recent years, a great deal of attention has been given to the design and development of more efficient and effective training programs. However, if the training process is to work, attention also needs to be given to the techniques of teaching.

The quality of instruction has always been an important concern in training and education. But in the last few years, it has tended to take a back seat. This book sets out to help redress the balance, as renewed interest in instruction begins to show itself among trainers and educators.

A new term has recently been coined to capture this new interest. It is called "direct training." A direct trainer is anyone who, in any shape or form, directly helps someone learn. Direct trainers include not only teachers and instructors, but also coaches, counselors, ministers, managers, supervisors, and lecturers.

There are all kinds of situations in which one person helps another to learn. Parents help their children, and children certainly teach their parents. Children teach other children, and adults teach other adults. Regardless of age and education, everyone is a direct trainer in one form or another. This book sets out to help people exercising that role.

Like many things that take on a character of their own, *Instructional Technique* owes a great deal to other people. Four teachers in particular have had a profound influence upon me—E. Watson-Taylor, "Chris" Morley, M.V.C. Jeffreys, and Julian Steward. All of them were masters of their craft and skilled in the techniques of face-to-face instruction.

Yet, on reflection, I realize that it is unlikely that any of them were *born* good teachers. Like most people, they had to labor at it. They acquired the skill by dint of hard work and perseverance. They were good because they wanted to be good. So they set about obtaining mastery.

Enthusiasm and a sense of humor were two qualities that they all shared. They also shared a willingness to prepare and plan. They identified an aim and then made certain that they maintained it through thick and thin. All four of them had a clear sense of purpose and a willingness to set priorities. They would have made excellent politicians and good generals.

Since all of us may exercise such an influence on people at some time or another, it is important that some of their skills be passed on. This book sets out to do that, in a simple, practical manner.

At times, some of the material appears somewhat "old fashioned." Yet it is mostly based on the findings of recent research. The Biblical advice to "Prove all things; hold fast that which is good," applies as much to instruction as to life in general.

Many people have helped in the preparation of the manuscript, and I am deeply grateful to them for their assistance and advice. In particular, I would like to thank Stephen J. Guynn for his consummate library skills and conscientious assistance in the more arduous aspects of writing, and Eliot Phillips for his help in producing the book. I would also like to acknowledge the assistance, patience, and endurance of my family.

Ivor K. Davies
Bloomington, Indiana
18th June, 1980

Contents

Part Two
Tactics of Instruction

Part Three
Instructional Concerns

Epilogue
Effectiveness and Competence   344

Instructional
Technique

Introduction
Everyone An Instructor

*People in their lives
play many parts.*

FOCUS

"What are the many roles of the instructor and teacher?"

KNOWLEDGE OBJECTIVES

After carefully reading and studying this chapter, you will be able to:

1. realize that everyone is an instructor at some time or another;
2. distinguish between the art of instruction and the science of instruction;
3. appreciate some of the many roles an instructor has to perform when teaching;
4. distinguish between the manager role and the operator role of an instructor or teacher;
5. appreciate the role of decision-making in the instructional process.

ATTITUDE OBJECTIVES

After reading this chapter, the author hopes that you will:

1. value the importance of the many roles an instructor or teacher must play;
2. incorporate the idea of an instructor-manager and an instructor-operator into your style of teaching, so that it becomes characteristic of your instructional technique.

Instruction looms large in our lives. All of us are teachers of one kind or another. Adults and children, people at work and at play, all assume the role of an instructor or teacher.

People in business, government, and the military are called upon to teach. So are managers, supervisors, shop stewards, and ordinary working people. A physician who explains a new diet to a patient is just as much an instructor as is the person teaching a class of apprentices how to weld two pieces of metal. Instruction, after all, simply involves helping another to learn. It is part and parcel of being a person.

Sometimes teaching is well done; often it is not. But we should be glad that it is done at all. Helping others to learn is a time-consuming task. Yet it is also a strangely rewarding one. This is why some people regard teaching as one of the most human of all activities, and one of the most necessary.

If it were not for the help, interest, and enthusiasm of others, few people would acquire the knowledge, skills, and attitudes that make them mature human beings. Good instruction requires much time and effort. Sometimes it involves more time and effort than does learning. A great deal of thought and hard work goes into creating a successful learning experience, although it is often overlooked.

Helping others can be achieved at a nonverbal as well as a verbal level. The spoken and the written word are important in instruction, but learning can occur without them. Knowledge and skill, interest and enthusiasm, can all be communicated by what we do as well as by what we say.

Instruction can also proceed by a variety of methods. Some of these are very old, like the lecture. Some are very new, like computer-assisted instruction. And some that we think are new, like programmed instruction, are as old as the hills.

Learning takes place when one person teaches another. It can also take place in small groups and in a crowd. Some instructional methods do not require the physical presence of an instructor. An instructor, however, is always behind the scenes, intimately involved in the design and production of the materials and hardware.

Television, radio, computers, films, books, and games are all well tried instructional methods. The jigsaw puzzle was invented by a London publisher for classroom use, in order to teach history and scripture through great pictures. Behind every instructional method there is a human presence and a human hand. Instruction is too human an activity to be left entirely to chance.

THE ART AND SCIENCE OF INSTRUCTION

Teaching, Margaret Mead once said, is "an art that has no appeal when it is described only in words." This is the problem of talking about instructional technique. But it is also the problem of talking about any art, such as painting, music, writing, drama, or dance. Instruction is just as much an art as any of these. The spirit of craftsmanship runs deep in teaching, just as it does in the theater. Performance is at the heart of both.

On the other hand, instruction is just as much a science as it is an art. Disciplined thought, systematic preparation, well organized presentations, and good "housekeeping" are all characteristics of good teaching, as they are of scientific discovery.

Behind all great performances, there is a great deal of hard work. Identifying a need, determining appropriate objectives for learning, designing learning experiences, writing instructional materials, evaluating the effectiveness of instruction are all highly dependent on a science of instruction.

But not only is there much for an instructor to know, both about teaching and about the subject to be taught, there is also much for an instructor to *be*. An immature and dogmatic person is unlikely to be a good teacher. A well rounded, experienced, and interesting person, on the other hand, is well on the way to being successful in the classroom or workshop.

Planning and substance are part of any craft, but so are humanity and a concern for others. Science does not need these qualities, although many good scientists possess them. But art does. Instruction without a concern for people simply has no appeal.

The science side of instruction is concerned with the great riddle of teaching and learning. It involves sifting the important from the unimportant. It involves making difficult things easy and complex things understandable. There is a Plan to both instruction and learning, but sometimes it is not readily apparent.

The Plan can be difficult to see when seen from the point of view of the art of teaching. It can be more readily seen, however, when seen from the point of view of the science of teaching. The science side of teaching helps explain to us what must be done. It is concerned with the *how* of instruction. For this reason, the science side of teaching is important to beginners. It helps them to obtain the basic techniques, so that they can get on with doing the job.

Once the basic techniques of instruction have been acquired, it is important to begin looking at the craft from the viewpoint of the artist. Teaching involves seizing *every* opportunity, just as an actor must never pass up an unplanned for situation. At times, as in any art, it is necessary to throw some of the basic techniques out of the window. Every rule in the book, at times, needs to be broken, but always with deliberation.

Before you can do this, though, you have to know what the rules are. You also have to understand why you need to break them. When, regardless of the risks, you break the rules in order to obtain a particular effect, then the art side of instruction has taken over. Only then will you find it possible to exploit unplanned opportunities, and do something that is both exciting and surprisingly effective.

The art side of instruction cannot really be taught. It is gained by experience and by learning from that experience. The science side of instruction can be taught, and that is what this book is all about—hopefully leavened with some of the art. By studying and systematically acquiring the strategies and tactics associated with the science of instruction, almost anyone can become a competent teacher.

Those few who also acquire the art become really good teachers. Even those, however, can further refine their skill by returning once more to the science side of their craft. There is always something to learn, provided one is open minded enough to be willing to make the effort.

THE VARIED ROLES OF AN INSTRUCTOR

In our everyday life, we play many roles. Parent, spouse, offspring, employee, citizen, decision-maker, and instructor are just some of these roles. There are many, many more. In some of the roles we can be quite skilled; in many we can be lacking in experience and motivation. Yet in each one of these roles there are still further roles to be played. So it is with the role of instructor.

An instructor, as Earl Pullias and James Young remind us, is many things. They point out this role includes those attributes of:

- a guide
- a modernizer
- a model
- a searcher
- a counsellor
- a creator
- an authority
- an inspirer of vision
- a doer of routine
- a breaker of camp
- a storyteller
- an actor
- a scene designer
- a builder
- a learner
- a facer of reality
- an emancipator
- an evaluator
- a conserver
- a culminator

But above all, an instructor has to be a person, and also a mature person. Even then this lengthy list of roles is not complete.

There are many more roles that can be added. Roles such as decision-maker, leader, follower, motivator, and thinker must also figure in the list. Similarly, there are matters of style.

An instructor can be an autocrat or benevolent dictator, so that instruction becomes teacher-centered and teacher-directed. At other times an instructor can be consultative and participative, so that instruction becomes learner-centered and learner-directed.

An instructor, ideally, should exercise all of these roles. It is not enough to be just a communicator of knowledge, skill, or attitudes. Nor is it enough to be an autocrat all the time. There is a place for autocracy and a place for a more consultative and participative style. There is even a place for deciding totally to abdicate responsibility for the learning situation, and leaving it all to the student. The important thing is that all these roles have their place. Everything depends upon the needs of the task and the needs of the students.

Of course, it is probably asking too much of anyone to be equally successful in all the possible roles that an instructor should fill. A well balanced, mature person, however, is many of these already. As a teacher, though, it is important to try and do an even better job of filling them. That is why some people believe that good instruction is closely related to good acting. Both are performing arts.

Teaching, like the theater, involves actors, a script of sorts, a stage, and props. Above all, there is a somewhat critical audience, selfishly interested in realizing its own goals and objectives. But students want not only an enjoyable experience; they also want to learn something worthwhile. It is at this point that instruction and the theater diverge.

Also, when people take on the role of instructor, they must act in such a manner that their trainees will take the part seriously. This means that it must be well done. In other words, you have to believe in what you are doing. You also have to work hard at doing it. This involves a lot of preparation and rehearsal, as well as reflecting upon how good or bad you are. Self-improvement is central to good instruction.

Not only must you know what to do and say, but you have to know the subject or skill you are supposed to teach. If you don't know your subject, then you cannot possibly teach it, no matter how good a teacher you are. Indeed, teaching is a humbling experience. All too frequently, it pinpoints gaps in your own knowledge and skill. For this reason, there is a great deal of hard work involved.

Instruction is really nine tenths perspiration and one tenth inspiration. An inborn ability to teach is a great thing to have, but a willingness to labor over it is much more important. Not all actors aspire to be great actors, and not all teachers should expect to become great instructors.

Thorough preparation, a good lesson plan, a well rehearsed teaching method, an effective delivery, and a willingness to evaluate your successes, however, will go a long way to insuring that your instruction is, at the very least, adequate. Confidence in your ability to carry it off will do much to raise the level of your teaching even further. Such confidence, unless it is misplaced, can come only from sound preparation.

THE CONTEXT OF INSTRUCTION

What happens in the classroom, workshop, office, or wherever instruction takes place occurs within a larger scheme of things. All kinds of activities preface the act of instruction, and all kinds of activities follow it. Teaching is not a self-contained activity.

Although this book is concerned only with what happens during the actual teaching or instructional part of the cycle, some understanding of the whole training or educational cycle is obviously important. Fortunately, there are a number of modern books available which deal with the whole process—other than instruction.

Don Michalak and Ed Yager's *Making the Training Process Work* is particularly interesting; attention is also drawn to *Competency-based Learning*. Chris Gane's *Managing the Training Function* is worth referring to, as is Bob Mager and Kenneth Beach's *Developing Vocational Instruction*. All of these books offer a systematic and practical approach to the problems of human performance.

Nature of human performance

Training, by its very nature, contributes to human performance. Business, government, and the military employ people to perform particular tasks, each with its own duties and responsibilities.

Anything that can be done to improve people's performance in their job is an important matter. Not only is production improved, but also safety and protection of the environment. At the same time, people are likely to have a higher morale and greater job satisfaction. Thus, the overall quality of human performance is a key factor.

Published data indicate that almost 50 percent of all the interruptions that directly affect production are due to failings in human performance. Any steps taken to enhance performance are likely to increase both productivity and profitability. While training can be an expensive undertaking, not training can be even more expensive in the long run.

It has been calculated, for instance, that the cost of training in the hotel and restaurant business can be recouped ten times over from the resulting reduction in inefficiencies. Inefficiencies resulting from damaged equipment, breakages, wasted food, poor service, lost customers, and increased labor turnover are very expensive in monetary terms. Excessive staffing, made necessary by the low productivity, adds further to the costs. So do the frustration and dissatisfaction caused by the lack of training.

Similar inefficiencies can occur in other industries. The problems that arose with the Three Mile Island nuclear plant in Pennsylvania are a case in point. It is reported that human error in both the operating and maintenance procedures was a significant factor in the problem that arose with the billion dollar plant.

In a similar way, a major oil spill in the North Sea is reputed to have been caused by a valve being installed upside down. Similarly, an aircraft crashed in the Florida Everglades, seemingly because of a series of errors that started with a burned out light bulb. Human error is a major problem in the world today. It is a last frontier for us to tackle.

All training and education are really founded on the belief that they will contribute to the systematic reduction of human error. If the chances of error on a particular task are low, then there is probably little or no reason to do any training. If the probability of human error is high, then training will probably be essential.

Non-instructional approach

However, error can also be reduced by strategies other than training. Supplying people with incentives to do the job with more care might help. Improving the conditions under which the work is done can also help prevent errors from occurring. If people can't see what they are doing, for instance, a better lighting system is clearly called for so as to improve the job situation.

Redesigning the task is another alternative. For example, complex electronic equipment usually has wires of different colors. People will then know which wire to join to what part. Since some of the colors are very similar, perfect color vision is often required. The job, however, can be changed by numbering the wires rather than color-coding them. Many more people are able to distinguish between numbered wires than wires which are colored. About 8 percent of men and 0.5 percent of women experience some difficulty with color.

Two other noninstructional strategies can help reduce the possibilities of human error. They are: better communication and different patterns of management. If people do not know that they are doing a task poorly, they are unlikely to improve their performance. Feedback of how well one is doing, or how badly, is extremely important.

Some photographers, for instance, were once criticized because their customers didn't like their work. It was suggested that further training was necessary. In fact, the photographers had never been told how their work would be used. Once it was explained that the photographs were not for visual display, but a basis for drawing maps, they started to produce what the customer wanted. Training was not the problem; better communication was needed.

Management problems can also cause errors. Sometimes people are given too much work to do, or are pressured to work too fast. In such environments, errors are almost guaranteed. Autocratic, insensitive managers are sometimes to blame, as are weak ones who abdicate their responsibilities. In some situations, supervision is plainly lacking. Conflict and poor human relationships also contribute to an environment that is "punishing" rather than conducive to productive work.

Instructional approach

The important point to recognize is that not all problems of human performance can be solved by training or education. Training will help only if the people involved lack essential skills, knowledge, or attitudes. If people are not deficient in one or more of these three areas, some other strategy is necessary.

In other words, if people are not performing adequately when they are perfectly capable of doing so, then instruction is not likely to help. Some strategy other than training is clearly called for if the difficulty is to be overcome. As we have seen, such nontraining strategies involve improving the environment in which the work is done. Training and education, after all, are limited strategies. It is unreasonable to expect them to solve every problem.

The simple idea that training and education can reduce the probabilities of human error stemming from deficiencies in knowledge, skill, and attitudes has important consequences. It puts evaluation in a central position. If, after instruction, error is not reduced, then something is wrong. Teaching may have been well done. Training may have been enjoyable. But the simple fact remains: error has not been reduced in any substantial way. Something is wrong with the training.

Some years ago, it was decided to increase the frequency of a well established one-week course. The training was concerned with the setting up, operation, and first line maintenance of a fairly commonplace piece of communications equipment. Learner responses to the course had always been favorable.

The instructor was a skilled and entertaining teacher. Indeed, the course was regarded as a model of its kind. Visitors often sat in on the training, so as to observe the instructional technique. Then someone compared what was taught on the course with what was required on the job.

First, it was found that the probabilities of human error were low. Furthermore, when errors occurred, they were rarely serious. Little could be done by an operator to damage the equipment. As a result of the analysis, it was decided that there was no need for training. Instead of a week of instruction, a small plastic card was placed on the equipment. It detailed a sequence of steps to be followed. A telephone number was also included. The supplier had a twenty-four hour replacement service for malfunctioning equipment: so no real maintenance was necessary.

Steps in the development of a training or educational program

When a training or educational need has been established, there are a number of steps to be followed. Each step is separate but also related; otherwise no coherent program is likely. At every stage, decisions have to be made. Most of them involve money, in one way or another, so it is important to keep asking whether the solution is worth the possible cost. Not every deficiency is worth removing. Not every problem is worth solving.

The steps in the development of a training or educational program include finding answers to the following questions:

- *Identifying the objectives of the program*
  - What is the desired terminal behavior?
  - What skills, knowledge, and attitudes are essential?

- What do the people who will be performing the task already know, what can they already do, and what do they value?
- What, therefore, are the objectives of the program?

- *Designing the program to meet the objectives*
  - What content should the program contain?
  - What student experiences and activities are essential?
  - What instructional methods should be employed?

- *Organizing the program to meet the objectives*
  - What resources (people, accommodation, materials, and support services, etc.) are necessary to the design?
  - When and where should the program be held, and how frequently? How long should the program be?
  - I low can the knowledge, skills, and attitudes acquired on the course be reinforced once training is completed?

- *Evaluation of the program in terms of the objectives*
  - Have the objectives of the program been realized to the standard required?
  - Can the people who have been trained perform the tasks essential to their job or role?
  - How can the program be improved?

Unless the program does its job, it is not worth having.

In the stages which have just been outlined, the role of the instructor has not been emphasized. Indeed, much of the work is often done by people called instructional or curriculum developers. Sometimes, however, an instructor or teacher will do the whole development job, as well as the instruction. Such perfect opportunities don't often occur. Nevertheless, instructors and teachers should *always* have some hand in the development process.

Many of the decisions that have to be made inevitably affect teachers. Also instructors have a fund of experience and knowhow that few developers are likely to possess. If the aim is to develop an effective training or educational program, then the people involved in implementing the program have to be included. They are an essential part of what is going to occur. They are going to manage the learning experience.

THE MANAGEMENT OF LEARNING

There are only two kinds of work in which instructors or teachers can engage. They can either *manage* a learning situation or else *operate* as a learning resource. Of course, instructors can both manage a learning situation and, at the same time, operate within it as one of the resources for learning.

In some situations, instructors might operate more than they manage. On other occasions, they might manage more than they operate. The proportions of operating and managing work can vary enormously, depending upon the situation and the instructor. Bertrand Russell put the whole matter rather nicely when he said:

Work is of two kinds: first, altering the position of matter at or near the earth's surface relative to other such matter; second, telling other people to do so. The first kind is unpleasant and ill paid; the second is pleasant and highly paid.

The moral should not be lost on teachers!

Managing and operating

Let's imagine that an instructor sits down and thinks about planning a training session on "The typical food service employee." The instructor might decide to arrange for two groups of trainees, say five in each group, to list the characteristics of the food service employees they know. The groups could then share their lists. After discussion, a joint list could be obtained, as a basis for a class discussion on morale.

In the above example, the instructor is designing an environment for learning. Decisions are being made, and planning is taking place. The instructor, in effect, is acting as an instructor-manager.

Now let's imagine that instead the instructor decides to give a lecture on the characteristics of the typical food service employee. This decision would still be the work of an instructor-manager, but there is an additional factor. The decision also implies that the instructor will do most of the work. As soon as the lecture begins, and the instructor starts listing the characteristics of food service employees, the instructor becomes an instructor-operator.

Instead of getting the learner to give the points, the instructor lists them for the trainees to copy down. Points such as: not well educated, somewhat emotionally unstable, motivated to work for economic necessity, see their job as temporary until a better opportunity presents itself, basically female, etc. In such circumstances, the instructor is acting as the sole resource.

In effect, the instructor has decided that he or she can do a better job than the trainees. Better than any film, than any book, than any other person. Sometimes this may be true, but not always.

Sometimes decisions are taken on the basis of what the instructor wants to do, and *not* on what the situation requires. The real danger lies less in its happening than in its happening too much. Decisions should be made on the basis of what needs to be done, not solely on the basis of instructor preference.

Because their time is always limited, instructors should concentrate on their unique role as managers of learning. This does not mean that they should never operate. The principle simply emphasizes that managing comes first.

When instructors manage, they do four different types of work. The instructor-manager:

- *Plans*

  This is the work that an instructor does to master the future. It requires thought before action. The work involves such activities as deciding upon the objectives of each training session, and then deciding how they can best be achieved.

  Thorough planning is the hallmark of a successful instructor. Success in teaching is largely the product of work carried out before teaching begins.

- *Organizes*

  This is the work that an instructor does to implement the plans that have been made. It requires action. The work involves such activities as knowing what has to be done, and delegating it to the proper people so that it can be done. Organizing involves a lot of teamwork, and seeing that people work well together.

  People will always find work to do in a training or educational situation. The instructor-manager's job is to make sure that they do the work that needs to be done if the learning objectives are to be realized.

- *Leads*

  An instructor works to motivate, encourage, and inspire trainees to learn. It is an energizing activity. When it is done well it causes trainees to do better than they would ever have thought possible.

  Without it, things may still get done. But with leadership, learning is likely to be enhanced.

- *Evaluates*

  An instructor finds out whether the planning, organizing, and leading have been successful. In other words, have the learning objectives been achieved? Do the plans, organization, and leading need to be adjusted? The temptation to change the objectives must be resisted.

  In order to do the work of evaluating, the instructor-manager must have a clear idea of acceptable performance, not only while training is taking place but also after it is completed.

Although these four functions of the instructor or teacher-manager are quite separate activities, they are also related one to the other.

Taken together these functions define the instructor-manager's role. By implication, they also define the operator's role. When a teacher or instructor is doing something that cannot be classified as planning, organizing, leading, or evaluating, then management work is not being done. Instead, operating work is being carried out.

The instructor as a decision-maker

The concept of an instructor or teacher as a manager, rather than just an operator, emphasizes another point about instruction. All along the way, instructors and teachers are called upon to make decisions. They have to choose between one thing and another. Should this training method be used, or that one? Should this training aid be used, or those two? Should trainees take notes, or should they listen? Should this point be emphasized, or are all the points important? And, where should testing be placed in a program to assure validity?

Sometimes the decisions are easy. At other times they are extremely difficult. Sometimes the decisions are routine. At other times they demand a great deal of creative thinking. Deciding how to lay out the furniture in a classroom might be considered a rather mundane question. But deciding on a series of abnormal conditions with which to challenge an experienced pilot of Boeing 727s, undergoing recurrent training in a flight simulator using a computer-generated image system, would be a challenging task.

The one decision is quite low level, the other is highly sophisticated. Yet regardless of the content of decisions, the process of making them is really much the same. Decision-making is decision-making. Content does not change the way the choice is made. The process of making decisions in the instructional setting is identical to the process used in the boardroom. Only the content is different, and the size of the resources committed.

Peter Drucker puts the matter of decision-making very clearly when he writes:

A decision is a judgment. It is a choice between alternatives. It is rarely a choice between right and wrong. It is at best a choice between "almost right" and "probably wrong"—but much more often a choice between two courses of action neither of which is provably more nearly right than the other.

So it is in the matter of instructional technique. There is *no* best way. Rarely is there any best decision. Teaching and learning are much too complex for that to happen. If the problems of teaching were simple, then all we would need would be a cookbook of instructional recipes. Decisions would rarely have to be made other than to identify the correct recipe for the situation. Because teaching and learning are so complex, some compromise is always involved.

Instructor-managers have to choose *what* is to be done, *who* is to do it, and *how* it is to be accomplished. Inevitably, this leads to a consideration of *why* it should be done at all. Thus, planning a simple training session on the advantages and disadvantages of airline deregulation can result in a whole series of complex decisions.

Some of the issues that would have to be considered include: economic uncertainty, falling traffic, and soaring fuel costs. Consideration would have to be given to the fact that deregulation seems to work well for both airlines and the traveling public during an economic upswing. But will it work as well during an economic downswing? The problems facing the trainer are the same as those facing the industry. They call for high level thought, which is not always recognized as far as training is concerned.

No decisions, of course, are made in isolation. Each decision an instructor or teacher makes affects *every* other decision. Decisions concerned with *what* is done affect *who* is to do it and *how*. Decisions concerning *who* is to do something affect *what* is done and *how*. Decisions concerning *how* something is done affect *who* will do *what*. And so it goes on.

Most people believe that decisions begin with a search for the facts. But in many situations the facts are not readily available. Instead, instructors have to start off with opinions—preferably, well thought out ones. There is nothing wrong with starting in this way. If fact, it is an intelligent way to begin.

It would be very odd if instructors and teachers did not have opinions about teaching. Such a lack would suggest that they had gained very little from their experience. Opinions are as good a starting point in instruction as they are in science. Everyone knows what to do with them. Opinions, which are really nothing more than untested hypotheses, should not be discussed or argued. The only thing to do with them is to test them in the real world.

What facts support each opinion? What facts do not? Once a sort of balance sheet has been drawn up for each of the possible ways to go, a choice can be made. Once the decision is taken, it must be tested in the training room or wherever the instruction is taking place.

Instructors will soon find out whether the decision was a good one or not. Then they can decide whether or not they will need to change their choice the next time they teach the same topic. In this way, instructors can learn from both their successes and their failures, just as the airline will from the decisions they made following deregulation.

CONCLUSION

Instruction and teaching are both an art and a science. The spirit of craftsmanship runs deep in both, as does the need to search out the truth. There is much for an instructor to know and much to be.

Sometimes instruction involves simply telling learners something. More usually, it involves guiding them so that they reach mastery of the skill for themselves. Objectives are the compass in all this activity. The quality of the learning experience, though, is also important, for learning should be both enjoyable and useful. Instruction, after all, is a people-oriented activity.

Since people are of primary importance, instructors must play many roles so as to meet learner needs. Guide, authority, inspirer, actor, storyteller, learner, evaluator, and above all manager are just some of the roles.

The manager role, however, is especially important. Far too many instructors and teachers unthinkingly take on the operator role, so that there is little time left for the management functions. Yet without the decision-making associated with good planning, organizing, leading, and evaluating, instruction can never be more than a time-consuming and irrelevant activity. If it is to be different, situations have to be managed. Only then will learning be both efficient and effective.

Part One
Strategies of Instruction

Strategy shapes our destiny.

All instruction involves a strategy. Sometimes the strategy extends over a number of lessons; sometimes it is specific to a particular lesson. Regardless of the time span, a strategy simply consists of a grand design likely to achieve some broad objective. Tactics, on the other hand, are much more detailed. They fit within the strategic plan.

Most tactical planning occurs within the lesson. It usually takes place while instruction is underway. Strategic planning, on the other hand, must be done beforehand. Unless you know the broad design, detail is bewildering.

Strategies are concerned with the "why" of instruction. Tactics involve the "how." Yet both the "why" and the "how" are dictated by the same considerations. These revolve around the needs of the task and the needs of the people involved in that task. In this sense, strategy and tactics are different aspects of the same thing. When strategy and tactics are separate, they are meaningless.

Inspiration comes from a sense of strategic purpose. Objectives supply the unifying force, evaluation the critical dimension. Seen from the viewpoint of Part One, five aspects of an instructional strategy are critical. All of them, however, relate to the objectives to be realized.

17

The five aspects of instructional strategy are:

- The role of efficiency and effectiveness.
- The choice of instructional methods.
- The structure of a lesson.
- The preparation of a lesson.
- The settings of instruction.

Viewed as a whole, these five topics are the components of the grand strategy necessary to instruction. At every stage decisions are involved, and compromises necessary.

An instructional strategy does not evolve out of thin air. It is the product of innovative minds, the result of dreams and reflections on previous experiences. A creative process is involved, calling for a blend of both the art and the science of instruction. Values, too, enter into the situation, as does the instructional setting.

Sometimes an instructor will have control over the environment within which learning will take place, and can modify it at will. Often a teacher will have little choice, and must use what is available. Regardless of difficulty, teachers and instructors must exploit the possibilities of the situation. Possibilities are always there. But they have to be sought, for it is easy to overlook them. For this reason, instructors need to cultivate a way of searching for alternatives.

Chapter 1
Efficiency and Effectiveness

FOCUS
"What part do efficiency and effectiveness play in the teaching-learning process?"

KNOWLEDGE OBJECTIVES
After carefully reading and studying this chapter, you will be able to:
1. distinguish between education and training;
2. state what is meant by the term "mastery learning";
3. distinguish between efficiency and effectiveness;
4. recognize the skills of effectiveness;
5. use the ABC classification scheme as a way of identifying effectiveness areas and setting priorities.

ATTITUDE OBJECTIVES
After reading this chapter, the author hopes that you will:
1. value the importance of efficiency and effectiveness in the teaching-learning process;
2. incorporate the concepts into your teaching, so that they become characteristic of your instructional technique.

Effectiveness converts effort into results.

The objective of all instruction is knowledge, skills, or attitudes. They must, however, be worthwhile. It is not enough to learn something. What has been acquired should have merit; it should be useful. Learning has to be meaningful to a specific task, job, or role. If the task is not worthwhile, then students and trainees are unlikely to learn.

Training and education

In the case of training, learning should also have an immediate payoff. For instance, in the light of a need in the American wine market, a group of Italian vintners were trained in new ways to manipulate the fermentation process. Italians prefer wine that is dry, light, and fruity. Americans, used to drinking Coke and other sodas with their meals, prefer wine that is bubbly and slightly sweet. The training program, therefore, was geared to producing a new salable product that could be immediately marketed using this knowledge about American and Italian tastes.

Education, on the other hand, is for the longer term. There may be immediate advantages, but the emphasis is on the future. Listening, for instance, is something that is not usually taught to people. Normally, instead of instruction, people are given admonitions to listen like "Pay attention."

Yet listening, like most skills, is teachable. It is difficult to acquire, but it benefits from instruction and guided practice. It is also such an important skill that many companies would benefit from organizing educational programs in effective listening for their employees. Managers and supervisors, particularly, might find the experience rewarding.

Research indicates that most adults listen at about a 25 percent level of efficiency. Furthermore, experience shows that an effective listening program can double listening comprehension in just a few months. But while listening skills can be increased over the short term, the impact in the company may not be discernible for some time. The payoff is not immediate.

A course in effective listening, therefore, is usually classified as educational. The results are likely to be long term, and the skill will be useful regardless of whether jobs change or people are promoted. The fermentation course, on the other hand, is an example of training. A new product was the primary objective. The vintners were trained so as to add to their skills. The new skill gained, however, was specific to a particular time and place. If they change their jobs, knowledge of the new fermentation process might be irrelevant.

20

Once the distinction between training and education has been made, it is probably best put aside. As so often happens, the distinction blurs in the real world. It is not always possible to say something is one thing or the other. The key point is that, regardless of whether education or training is taking place, learning should be meaningful.

Learning has to confer an advantage to learners. Otherwise, why should they bother? Sometimes the advantage is self-evident. More usually, teachers need to point it out. For this reason, teachers have an important responsibility as far as motivation is concerned. But they also have a special responsibility to plan. If instruction is not carefully planned, and irrelevant material is included, then the impact of what is essential can be reduced or lost.

MASTERY LEARNING

If education and training are to confer an advantage on learners, it is essential that skilled performance be acquired. It makes little sense to learn part of a skill, or to know just some of the safety requirements. No one expects trainees to learn everything. However, they should learn enough to be adequate in the task or job. Anything beyond adequacy is a bonus, and one well worth having.

The idea that most people, given the right circumstances, can learn almost anything is a very old one. It is at least two thousand years old. The modern idea of "mastery learning" is founded on the same principle.

The meaning of mastery learning

Good teaching, coupled with remedial assistance for people with learning problems, should insure that interested students learn. But there is one important qualification. Trainees have to be given sufficient time to acquire mastery. Some people require more time than others. People learn at their own particular rate. Forcing everyone to learn at the same speed is counterproductive.

The ultimate goal of education and training is mastery. Everyone should have a reasonable chance of acquiring an adequate level of skilled performance. The purpose of training and education is not for *some* trainees to be successful and for others to fail. Steps need to be taken to insure that the majority of people realize the objectives of satisfactory performance in desired tasks. Equality of opportunity may be less important than an expectation of equality of outcome. People have a right to equal opportunities to be successful.

Mastery, to a very large extent, is an attitude of mind. If instructor and trainees believe that only a few people will be successful, then that is what is likely to happen. A few will do very well, most will come somewhere in the middle, and a few will fail. On the other hand, if instructor and trainees believe that everyone will reach mastery, then that is what will probably occur. We tend to fulfill the prophecies we make. Pygmalion is still with us!

The 90/90/90 criterion

Mastery learning involves realizing the objectives which have been set for a particular task. A typical expectation would be that 90 percent of the students will achieve 90 percent of the objectives 90 percent of the time. This is usually referred to as the 90/90/90 criterion. The specific percentages are not really important. The important point is that people are successful most of the time.

In order to reach the 90/90/90 criteria, learners must be given individual help and guidance when they need it. Remedial help has to be available; otherwise many will fail. If everyone receives exactly the same instruction, some people are going to have problems. Individual needs, as they occur, have to be taken care of in some way or another. Sometimes this can be done on a small group basis, but occasionally individual instruction will be necessary. Teaching at times has to be personalized or customized to handle individual differences.

Just as it is possible to have one standard diet, so it is possible to have common instruction. But, as with diet, individual differences and needs have to be taken care of as they arise. If they are overlooked, mastery will not be achieved.

EFFICIENCY AND EFFECTIVENESS

The principle of mastery learning highlights two words that are often used in training and education: *efficiency* and *effectiveness*. These words are commonly used to describe not only teaching but also learning. An instructor needs to be efficient and effective, just as much as a learner needs to be efficient and effective. Yet the two words are often used without a real appreciation of what they imply.

Efficiency

Efficiency is concerned with doing things right. Effectiveness is concerned with doing the right things. This is shown in Figure 1:1. The name of the game, of course, is to do the right things right. But, surprisingly, many people seem overly concerned with efficiency. Efficiency is important, but effectiveness is the central issue of both teaching and learning.

Instructors are paid to be effective. Efficiency will help, but it will not guarantee that they are effective. Similarly, efficiency will help trainees, but it will not guarantee that they will learn. In each case, effectiveness is the ultimate goal.

Most of us can recognize efficient instructors. They do things right; they do things properly, correctly. Their instruction is likely to be well planned. They prepare their training room and discussion rooms carefully. Efficient teachers develop a good instructional voice and manner. They ask challenging questions, use well thought out instructional methods. They use the right audiovisual aids, practical exercises, and experiences. They know the name and background of all their trainees, and continually assess their progress.

All of this implies that they are well organized. They are efficient, and they should be commended for it. However, none of these things implies that they are effective. That still remains to be demonstrated.

Effectiveness

Effectiveness does not involve an instructor's personality. It is not concerned with the quality of the instructional strategies or the novelty of the experiences. Effectiveness is a function of what instructors and learners do. It is a measure of the extent to which they realize their responsibilities.

If teachers fail to manage learning situations properly, or if learners fail to achieve mastery, then they are ineffective—no matter how efficient they might have been. In each case, instructors and trainees have to be judged by what they accomplish.

Fortunately, effectiveness can be learned. It is rarely a quality that is brought to a situation. Instead, it is something that is done to manage a situation.

This means taking into account both the needs of the task that is to be accomplished and the needs of the learners involved. Both sets of needs, people and task, need to be met and harmonized. Sometimes one set of needs may be more important than the other. Usually, however, both are important, and both must be taken into account. It is a management rather than an operating problem for learner and teacher alike.

FIGURE 1:1. Effectiveness and efficiency in teaching and learning.

The name of the game

Effectiveness	*Efficiency*
is doing	is doing
the right things	things right

doing the right things right

Everyone, of course, wants to be effective. Unfortunately, what is required is not always obvious. Some who know what to do feel unable to make the necessary commitment. Too many instructors and teachers see themselves as knowledge banks—paid for what they know, rather than for what they do. They view themselves, in effect, as operators, rather than primarily as planners, organizers, leaders, and evaluators.

The skills of effectiveness

In order to be effective, a person must make effective decisions. Learning needs must be identified, resources arranged, methods chosen, motivations harnessed, progress monitored, and plans for improvement implemented. These are time-consuming and challenging tasks. It is much easier to get involved in the details of everyday teaching and learning. Effective decisions are then left unmade. Unless they are attended to, there is no guarantee that the teacher is doing the right things.

Four prime skills are involved with effectiveness. Teachers and trainees who seek effectiveness need to become:

- *Sensitive*
  This means becoming sensitive to the needs of the learning task and the needs of the people who are involved in acquiring mastery of that task.

- *Diagnosticians*
  This means being able to determine what is required, and what has to be done if mastery is to be achieved.

- *Expert*
  This means choosing just the right teaching-learning methods, and then putting them into effect without passing up unplanned opportunities.

- *Flexible*
  This means being flexible enough to do what the learning situation requires, and to vary plans accordingly.

All of this, of course, requires dedication and skill. It also means that you need to have a clear idea of the objectives that have to be realized.

Above all, to borrow from Peter Drucker, effective teaching and learning involve a clear understanding of where an instructor's and trainee's time goes. It requires that you know where to gear efforts to results. Often effort is tied to busy work that fills the time available.

Effectiveness also requires that you build upon your own, as well as on other people's strengths. Not on weaknesses. There is little use in pointing out what learners can't do. It is much better to identify what they can do. These strengths can then become the foundations of their learning.

Making effective decisions

Effectiveness also involves making the right decisions. These, as we have seen, need to be based on "dissenting opinions" rather than on a "consensus of the facts." Effectiveness involves focusing upon opportunities, not on difficulties. It is easy to see why something cannot be done. It is more difficult to see how barriers can be overcome. Such an approach is also more useful. Negative thinking is a recipe for failure.

When all of this has been understood and mastered, one final skill of effectiveness remains: to concentrate upon those few key areas that produce outstanding results. It is rarely possible to try to achieve everything. All that is likely to happen is failure through lack of time and energy. Priorities have to be set and, much more difficult, maintained.

For instance, an instructor might organize a discussion on small business systems. A whole wealth of things could be considered. However, it is more efficient and effective to focus the discussion on a specific problem. This might be on "How well are small business systems currently meeting the needs of the users?"

Many things can still be included, so the instructor would be wise to limit the discussion to a few key factors. These would form the priorities for the discussion, although other points could still be considered. Key factors might include: system performance, reliability, ease of use, ease of maintenance, and vendor after-sales support to the customer.

In order to focus the discussion still more, as well as to encourage participation, each trainee could rate each factor on a five-point scale. The ratings could then be averaged, and the results used to determine how far small business systems currently available meet user needs.

Limiting discussions to a few factors and employing a rating scale of some sort or another are simple yet effective instructional techniques. Methods such as these assure that priorities are recognized and maintained. They enable an instructor to manage the teaching-learning process. And they add interest to the proceedings.

EFFECTIVENESS AREAS

There is a well known idea in science, usually referred to as Pareto's Law, sometimes as the 20/80 rule. It states that in any given group of things, a small number of items will account for most of the value, effort, or importance. In other words, applying the rule to the context of a business, a small number of managerial activities have an extraordinary impact on the economic results of the company.

Key effectiveness areas

Once these activities have been recognized, they form key effectiveness areas. For instance, a manufacturer of twelve products found three of them accounted for 81 percent of the total profit. A typical job description of a sales manager might include more than two dozen different types of responsibilities. But not all of them are of equal value. Five are much more important than others.

These five key tasks form effectiveness areas. They include: insuring that the company achieves its budgeted turnover and gross profit; maintaining customer goodwill; obtaining effective cooperation with production and fiscal departments; advising the chief executive on present and future market trends; administering the sales department so as to meet market needs within the agreed margin of expenditures. Training and education would be involved in each of these responsibilities.

Applying Pareto's Law to instruction, a telling generalization can be drawn. Something like 20 percent of the students are likely to cause 80 percent of the problems. Some 20 percent of these problems can absorb 80 percent of the effort an instructor is called upon to make. Finally, some 20 percent of this effort can easily consume 80 percent of the instructor's time. And so on.

It would obviously be neat and tidy, and certainly efficient, to give equal time to all the responsibilities with which an instructor is faced. However, as with the sales manager, it is much more effective to identify key responsibilities. Most of the time and effort can then be spent dealing with these. Any time left over can then be spent on what still remains to be done.

Thus, the simple 20/80 rule can be a guiding concept in both instruction and learning. It helps prevent a person from being overwhelmed by the myriad of things that must be accomplished. By identifying key effectiveness areas, it is possible to separate the forest from the trees. To help in this task, an "ABC" classification of responsibilities can be used.

The ABC classification

From the point of view of teaching and learning, objectives can be classified into three distinct categories. Each category needs to be managed differently by teacher and learner alike. The three categories are:

- The "A" items
  These are of great importance. Either they are critical to mastery, or else they are especially difficult to achieve.

  Generally speaking, there will be relatively few "A" items. They probably make up about 20 percent of the total. However, they are likely to account for 80 percent of the instructional and learning effort.

- The "B" items
  These are of medium importance. They are not of critical nor are they of

FIGURE 1:2. The ABC classification of mastery learning tasks.

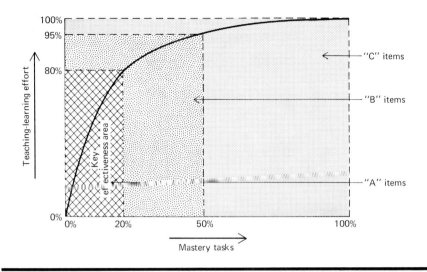

small importance. They occupy a middle position in teaching and learning.

Generally speaking, "B" items make up about 30 percent of the total mastery tasks to be achieved. However, they are likely to account for only about 15 percent of the instructional and learning effort.

- *The "C" items*
  These are of small importance. They are not critical to mastery. They are also likely to be easier to learn.

  Generally speaking, there will be many such items. They probably make up about 50 percent of the total. However, they are likely to account for only about 5 percent of the instructional and learning effort.

Within each one of the three categories, of course, there is a further ABC distribution. In other words, even within the "A" category some items are of greater and some of lesser importance. So it is with the "B" and "C" categories.

This breakdown of learning tasks, for instructional purposes, is an arbitrary one. Nevertheless, the distinctions are exceedingly useful. They enable both instructors and trainees to set priorities by sorting out key tasks. In this way, people are less likely to be overwhelmed by the sheer magnitude of the task.

One large international company, for instance, designed an in-house educational program for supervisors. The course involved almost five hundred objectives. Obviously, something had to be done, if only to communicate which were the most important. The ABC method helped solve the problem. It did so in a way that benefited both instructors and trainees.

Managing priorities

One further advantage of the ABC scheme remains to be discussed. Not only does the method set priorities, it also helps instructors to manage the priorities differently.

For example, instructors can manage "A," "B," and "C" learning tasks in the following manner:

- *The "A" learning tasks receive*
  - highest priority and greatest emphasis in the instruction;
  - close and detailed supervision so as to insure mastery;
  - frequent practice and revision to minimize forgetting;
  - regular assessment so that any necessary remedial action can be taken in good time.

- *The "B" learning tasks receive*
  - second priority and emphasis in the instruction;
  - moderate amounts of supervision to insure mastery;
  - adequate practice and revision so as to minimize forgetting;
  - adequate assessment so that remedial action can be taken.

- *The "C" learning tasks receive*
  - lowest priority and emphasis in the instruction;
  - minimal amounts of supervision conducive to insuring mastery;
  - minimal practice and revision conducive to minimizing forgetting;
  - minimal assessment conducive to identifying emerging needs for remedial action.

In this way learning tasks can be managed differently, according to various instructional priorities.

Low priority tasks, however, must still be mastered. Less time might be given to them *in* the instructional setting. They can also be worked on outside the classroom. Guidance, however, will be necessary. Teachers and instructors will also have to monitor what is happening, in order to insure that progress is being made.

CONCLUSION

Efficiency and effectiveness are important concerns for instructors and teachers. The former is concerned with *how* something is done, and with the best way of doing it. Effectiveness, on the other hand, is concerned both with *why* it is being done in the first place and with whether or not it has been *successfully* accomplished.

This does not mean that efficiency is unimportant. Effective teachers can fail because they are inefficient. On the other hand, no amount of efficiency will help an ineffective instructor succeed. What is needed is an ability to do the right things right.

It is also important to set the right priorities. These are the foundation of success. Effort must be geared to results. If the results are to be achieved, time has to be managed. Recognizing key tasks will assure that the right things are covered in the teaching. This is why a methodology such as the ABC classification is important.

A methodology enables teachers and learners, alike, to manage the situation, and put effort in the right place. In recognizing key effectiveness areas, the first step has been taken toward developing a plan for teaching and learning. An instructional method can be selected from the alternatives that are available.

Chapter 2
Instructional Methods

FOCUS

"What are the advantages and disadvantages of the various instructional methods?"

KNOWLEDGE OBJECTIVES

After carefully reading and studying this chapter, you will be able to:
1. distinguish between telling and asking in the context of teaching and learning;
2. distinguish between the lecture, demonstration, lesson, discussion, and independent study strategies;
3. appreciate why instructors and teachers tend to operate too much and manage too little;
4. choose an instructional method suitable to the learning task and the needs of the learners involved;
5. appreciate the central role of the lesson method in the teaching-learning process.

ATTITUDE OBJECTIVES

After reading this chapter, the author hopes that you will:
1. value the importance of choosing the right instructional method for each teaching-learning situation;
2. incorporate the principles into your teaching, so that they become characteristic of your instructional technique.

It is common sense to choose a method.

The problem with a great deal of instruction is the illusion that learning has taken place. Instruction does not guarantee that people will learn. As any parent will tell you, teaching and learning are not necessarily related. Sometimes, however, we seem to behave as though they are always associated. No wonder we are disappointed when things do not turn out as we imagined.

People can learn without instruction. One hopes, though, that instruction facilitates learning. It increases the probability that mastery will be attained with the minimum of fuss.

Advantages of method

Facilitation begins when a method is identified which gives purpose and direction to the learning task. Method offers a system, a way of going about things in an organized manner. When learning activities become random and haphazard, the resulting inefficiencies indicate an absence of organization. Method is missing.

The skill of reading faster, for instance, is well worth acquiring. Most of us are not as efficient as we could be. Yet the amount of things we are required to read gets ever larger. However, there are two simple methods that will help most people to get through more material without reading every word.

As Bill Cosby points out, the important thing is to get the overall meaning of what has been written, without going through all the detail. If the material is long and heavy going, then previewing is worthwhile. If the material is short and rather simple, it is better just to skim read the document.

The method of previewing involves reading the first two or three paragraphs in detail. This will give you a clear idea of what the paper is about. Then simply read the first sentence of the remaining paragraphs. When you come toward the end of the text, read the last two or three paragraphs in their entirety. This will inform you about any conclusions or recommendations.

Skim reading is even easier. Simply let your eyes sweep over the lines of text, picking out key words or phrases as you go. Sometimes your eyes will move rapidly without seeing anything important. At other times, they will alight on a critical phrase or group of words. Even though you will have skimmed over the material very quickly, you will still have a very good idea about what has been written.

In both examples, previewing and skim reading are two different methods. A choice has to be made between them depending upon the circumstances.

Both facilitate learning from prose materials. Neither is ideal. They simply offer a strategy of dealing with a particular type of situation. So it is with all instructional methods.

TELLING AND ASKING

Strategies consist of a plan to realize worthwhile objectives. They cannot guarantee that the objectives will be achieved. A good plan simply makes it more likely. This is why it is important to spend time selecting just the right instructional method. There is a wide range from which to choose. Everything depends upon what you wish to achieve and the situation with which you are faced.

Methods are our greatest riches, but they can be a source of difficulty. The sheer number and variety of them makes it difficult to choose. As a result, it is hard to resist the temptation of overusing *one* particular way of doing things.

Instructors and teachers often fall into this trap, because one particular instructional method becomes a favorite way of teaching. They feel comfortable with it. They have experienced success with it. But variety is not only the spice of life. It is also essential if different objectives are to be attained. Personal preference does enter into the selection of an appropriate instructional method. However, it is considerably less important than some other factors. So much depends upon the situation.

An example of telling and asking

For instance, suppose you wanted to teach a group of trainee salespeople how to reach a prospective customer. One of the topics you would need to cover would involve the different ways that sales contacts are made.

As an instructor, you could *tell* the trainees what they are. For example, you might list them: sales call, phone call, letter, trade show visit, advertising. Or you could *ask* them to tell you. If you use the latter method, you might be surprised how well the trainees do. Their list will certainly be longer than yours!

The first method, that of telling, involves a more autocratic way of doing things. Learners are reduced to a largely passive role. They have little responsibility, other than to listen and learn. Lecturing is a prime example of the telling method. As such, it is teacher-centered rather than student-centered.

The second method, that of asking, involves a more participative style of teaching. Learners have much more responsibility and freedom. They assume an active role, although they are functioning within quite narrow limits set by the instructor. Discussion is a prime example of the asking method. It involves a great deal of sharing. It is student-centered.

Now suppose that you wanted the trainee salespeople to consider the various costs associated with making different kinds of sales contacts. You could lecture to them. You could tell them that an average sales call costs $96.79; a phone call $3.50 or more; a letter $4.47; a trade show visit $38.99; and an advertisement in a weekly business magazine $0.15 per reader.

Instead of lecturing to the trainees, however, you could ask them. But a discussion is not likely to be useful. They would probably have little idea about the relative costs. However, they could be asked to find out for themselves. This would involve some type of independent study or project.

Once they have researched the costs associated with making sales contacts, discussion might once more be appropriate. Time would certainly need to be given to debating the varying advantages and disadvantages of the different ways of making a contact. Each one arouses customer interest and creates preference for a line of products in a different way.

All that now remains is for the trainees to learn how to make the customer a proposal and close the order. Again, they could be told or lectured. Alternatively, the instructor could arrange for someone to come to the training session and show trainees how it might be done. Such a demonstration would add a degree of realism to the instruction.

Advantages and disadvantages

In every case described above, telling the trainee salespeople would have been more efficient than asking. Telling is quicker and easier. Asking takes much more time and is more difficult to arrange. Furthermore, things are often likely to go wrong. Telling is more straightforward.

There is nothing like autocracy for saving time. It is efficient but *not* often effective. People are not always willing to sit, attend, listen, digest, and then put into effect what you have told them.

People usually want an active role. They prefer to assume some responsibility for their own learning. For this reason, a range of instructional methods needs to be considered. Although there are probably as many methods as people, there are five basic strategies.

As we have seen in the sales training example, these consist of the lecture method, the demonstration method, the discussion method, and the independent study method. A fifth strategy, not mentioned in the example, is the lesson method. These five strategies—lecture, demonstration, lesson, discussion, and independent study—all vary in the amount of telling and asking.

Managing and operating

The five strategies also vary in the amount of managing and operating work an instructor is required to accomplish. Figure 2:1 illustrates this point. The lecture method, because of the amount of telling, involves a great deal of operating work. Although there is still a small amount of managing work to be done, an instructor spends most of the time acting as *the* main learning resource.

In independent study, the reverse is true. Instructors, in this strategy, spend most of their time managing the learning situation. They may still occasionally operate as a learning resource, when it is necessary. But it is not their primary role.

The lesson method occupies an intermediate position. There are almost equal amounts of managing and operating work to be done. It is also a combination of the other four methods, containing a little of each. For this reason, it will be dealt with later in this chapter as *the* base method of most instruction.

In addition to the five basic methods of instruction, there are a number of specialized variations of them that need to be considered. These involve: internships, practicums, simulations, gaming, role playing, and programmed instruction. In each case, teachers and instructors exercise a management rather than an operating role.

Problems arise in instruction when a teacher slips into an operating role without very much thought. This often happens with inexperienced instructors. They sometimes do more operating work than they should. Instead of concentrating on planning, organizing, leading, and evaluating, they fall into the trap of doing too much telling work.

There are a number of reasons for this. Instructors and teachers operate too much because of:

- *A desire to achieve objectives faster*
  Many inexperienced instructors feel that more will be done if they do everything themselves.

FIGURE 2:1. Instructional methods as a function of managing and operating.

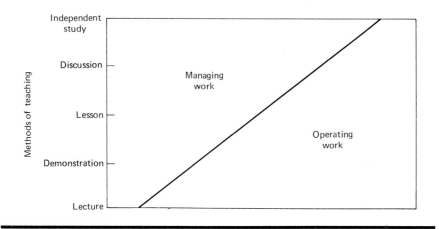

- *Familiarity with the operating side of instruction*
  All instructors have been students. So they are familiar with the operating side of the teaching-learning process. Therefore, it is easy for them to fall back into their old ways.

- *Feelings of underconfidence*
  Underconfident instructors find operating work preferable. It is highly visible, and it is tiring work. They feel they cannot be blamed if *they* have worked hard.

- *Example of other instructors*
  Inexperienced instructors sometimes rely too heavily on the example of "old" hands. Mentors should be chosen carefully. Not everyone is a good example.

These are very real temptations. But if the dangers are recognized, most people are well able to deal with them. They can then choose an appropriate instructional method. Everything depends upon the circumstances of the situation.

SELECTING AN INSTRUCTIONAL METHOD

Selecting an appropriate instructional method depends upon a number of factors. Important in the final choice are two particular considerations. These involve:

- The requirements of the task to be mastered.
- The needs of the students who are to master the task.

There are other factors, like personal preference, but these are the most important when it comes to choosing.

Task requirements

Some tasks can be acquired in a room environment. Others can only be mastered on the job. Sometimes the assistance of a number of people is necessary. The work entails team effort. Sometimes trainees are best left to get on and do it by themselves. On other occasions, the environment for learning has to be a simulated one.

The actual work situation can be a dangerous place for learners. Yet perhaps the classroom is irrelevant for the skills that need to be acquired. Under such circumstances, an artificial environment is necessary. One that looks like the actual job site, but is designed for instruction.

Simulation can be very lifelike. Pilots, at different stages in their training, receive instruction in a simulated aircraft cockpit that looks, smells, and feels like the real thing. Some simulations are less real. For instance, a case study or game involves simulation, but not of the environment. They simulate the decisions that are called for in the real world. They do not attempt to simulate the locations in which the decisions occur.

Needs of the trainees

Just as the nature of the task influences the choice of instructional method, so do the needs of the students concerned. Some people prefer to be taught in large group situations. They find small classes too anxiety-provoking. The anonymity of the crowd is appealing.

Other people much prefer small group situations, or even one to one situations like a tutorial. For them, the intimacy of the small group is a positive factor in their learning. They also appreciate the recognition that comes from being treated on an individual basis.

Many adults, once they have started work, resent being placed in situations reminiscent of a schoolroom. Older people, in particular, who are being retrained for new jobs or careers, prefer instructional methods that deemphasize telling. They benefit from situations that result in discovery learning. Finding out for themselves is much more rewarding. It is also less anxiety-inducing.

Less able students prefer lecturing to be limited. Such situations seem far removed from the reality of the world in which they live and work. Able students, on the other hand, respond more favorably to the lecture method— provided it is not overused.

Trainees who are anxious are often better instructed in environments that approximate the real world. Practical, down to earth people similarly respond well to on-the-job training. It has greater credibility. The instruction they get there means more to them. This is undoubtedly one of the reasons for the long history of apprenticeships. The place of work and the place of instruction are the same.

People who know a great deal about a subject or a skill have different needs from trainees who know very little. Complete beginners usually require a great deal of training room teaching. There is a lot of basic material to be covered and mastered.

More knowledgeable people, on the other hand, usually prefer less formal situations. Independent work assignments and real work experiences, in the form of practicums and internships, are highly regarded.

A practicum, for the most part, involves carrying out a set of tasks or a role in an on-the-job type of situation. Normally, it is done under the close supervision of an instructor or mentor. In fact, it is a form of apprenticeship. An internship, on the other hand, involves carrying out the tasks or role under general supervision. It is a more advanced type of training. Interns carry out the tasks as if all training were finished. Instruction is given only on an occasional basis, as the need arises.

THE PRINCIPAL METHODS OF INSTRUCTION

Instruction can, and does, take place in many situations. It is important, therefore, to beware of stereotypes. A lecture can occur in places other than a lecture room. It can last five minutes, two hours, or more. A discussion does not always have to take place indoors. Nor is it always limited by the clock.

A physician instructing a newly diagnosed diabetic patient how to self-administer insulin is teaching a skill, just as much as someone showing a group of trainees how to rig a vessel or skid a pump. Instruction takes place in all kinds of situations. The five principal methods of instruction are not bound by time or place.

The lecture method

The lecture method is a widely used and well known method of imparting knowledge. In some situations it is called a speech, in others a presentation. Regardless of what it is called, telling is involved. Rarely is an audience given an opportunity to interrupt or ask questions. Interaction, if it occurs, normally takes place at the conclusion of the lecture. Even then it is often limited to asking questions.

Sometimes a lecture involves reading word for word from a prepared script. More usually, the lecturer uses a fairly detailed set of notes or prompts. It is rare for a lecturer to speak extemporaneously. Almost always there has been a great deal of detailed preparation and planning beforehand.

Most lectures are illustrated in one way or another. Indeed, there is often a considerable use of audiovisual aids. In the "old" days, a lecture without lantern slides was no lecture at all. These days, slide projectors are still used, as well as overhead projectors. Flip charts, too, are common, as is television.

Recently more sophisticated media are beginning to be employed. The cost of travel, lost time, and delays in reaching destinations have caused many businesses to use tele-lecturing. Sometimes called tele-conferencing, the presentation is given in a specially wired room. The audience is located in similarly wired rooms around the country. Tele-conferencing can also be used for discussion groups.

Speaker phones, portable conference equipment, and other specialized equipment enable participants to listen to the presentation. They can also ask questions and interact with each other. They may also see any pictures or diagrams that are used to illustrate a key point by means of facsimile machines or closed circuit television.

The recent development of an "electronic blackboard" allows the audience to interact graphically, as well as vocally, with the lecturer. Whatever is drawn on the chalkboards can be seen, via video monitors, in all the locations. Material can also be erased and changed at will.

Types of lectures

Although lectures vary enormously, they normally fall into one of three types. Some lectures are *problem-centered*. A lecture will begin with the presentation of a problem—for instance, the problem of finding sources of energy. The lecturer then presents two or three solutions (coal, oil, natural gas, solar, nuclear) before considering the advantages and disadvantages of each. The lecture typically ends with a solution.

Other lectures present a particular *point of view* or argument: a chief executive speaking to a group of managers, a sales manager briefing a staff meeting. In either case, a goal or a principle would be stated and the supporting data outlined. After considering some of the problems likely to be encountered, a plan or point of view is then stated.

The most common type of lecture involves presenting *a body of knowledge*. Most lectures in higher education are of this type. It is the easiest type of lecture to prepare and deliver. Each point is made one by one, leading up to some sort of conclusion. A typical example would be a lecture describing the benefits of good maintenance: financial, organizational, technical, human, and customer relations.

Advantages and disadvantages

As a method of instruction, the lecture method has a number of advantages and disadvantages. Among the most important of these are:

- *Advantages*
  - A lecture covers a large amount of material in a short time.
  - A lecture is suitable for almost any group size, as long as the lecturer can be seen and heard.
  - A lecture can be used with both beginning and advanced learners, as long as they are well motivated.
  - A lecturer has almost complete control over both the content and the sequencing of the information, without interruption from students.

- *Disadvantages*
  - A lecture involves only one-way communication. There is little or no check that any learning has taken place.
  - Students are largely passive. There is little participation and involvement.
  - Effective lecturing is a difficult skill to acquire. Attention has to be maintained over a long period of time.
  - Lecturing is largely inappropriate for practical subjects, such as the acquisition of skills.

Lecturing is an instructional technique that should be used with discretion. Long lectures are very difficult to sustain. Short ones can often be highly successful, even when the lecturer is not especially skilled. But in every instance, the lecturer must have credibility with the audience.

The way that a lecturer is introduced is a very important matter. Some people try to skimp on the introduction, so as to give the lecturer more time. This is a foolish thing to do. It is most important that the audience appreciate the speaker's qualifications for lecturing on the subject. Someone who has climbed Everest has far greater credibility than someone who is talking about it on the basis of book learning.

The demonstration method

The demonstration method has certain similarities to the lecture method. In both instances, telling plays a large part. In the case of the demonstration method, however, a considerable amount of time is also spent showing trainees how something ought to be done. It is a highly visual as well as an oral method of teaching.

Demonstrating a skill

In the demonstration method, an instructor has to impart not only knowledge but also skill. Understanding is also important. Normally, some sort of procedure is involved. This might include demonstrating the steps involved in replacing a wheel on a car, how to balance a financial ledger, or how to carry out an interview connected with performance appraisal.

The method is based on the idea that skill comes from seeing how something is done, then doing it yourself under the eye of an instructor. Generally speaking, the instruction is prefaced with an explanation of what students should look for when the skill is demonstrated.

As the skill is performed, student attention should be drawn to key points. But this should not be done in a way that detracts from the demonstration itself. As each step of the procedure is shown, it is important to stress its context in the sequence. In this way, the skill will be seen as a whole, and not just a set of separate operations.

Some instructors like to demonstrate the skill slowly, so that trainees can see what is happening. Then they demonstrate it again at the normal speed. It is a good thing for an instructor to recapitulate the main points in words once the procedure is complete. Trainees should then record the main points, as well as highlighting the sequence of operations in their notes.

Once the notes are complete, trainees should practice the skill for themselves. Their performance should be carefully monitored and supervised by the instructor. Errors can then be pointed out and steps taken to eliminate them. If the skill depends upon speed, this should be emphasized right from the beginning of the practice session.

Advantages and disadvantages

As a method of instruction, the demonstration method has a number of advantages and disadvantages. Among the most important of these are:

- *Advantages*
  - The demonstration method, when properly managed, is an arresting and attention-getting form of instruction.
  - The demonstration method relates principles taught in the classroom to real world situations.
  - The demonstration method is challenging and thought-provoking.
  - The pace is flexible, and can easily be altered to fit the needs of trainees. Both demonstration and practice can be repeated as many times as necessary.

- *Disadvantages*
  - The demonstration method demands very careful preparation and organization. If things go wrong, the effect is lost.
  - Unless care is taken, some trainees may not be able to see or hear what is said.
  - Considerable expense and time are often involved in presenting an effective demonstration.
  - Most demonstrations, unless closed circuit television is employed, must be limited to small groups of trainees.

When a demonstration goes well, it arouses a great deal of interest and attention. When things go wrong, however, an instructor can lose a great deal of face.

Although most demonstrations are often associated with motor skills like welding, they should not be restricted to them. Very effective demonstrations of topics like bargaining and negotiating are also possible. Interviewing techniques can be taught. Role playing, which will be discussed in the context of the next method, is a common form of demonstration. It also involves discussion after the demonstration has taken place.

The discussion method

The discussion method is student-oriented. It is participative rather than autocratic. Discussion is an informal strategy, with a great deal of involvement and interaction. For this reason, the method is a particularly popular one with students and trainees alike.

Purposes of the discussion

The discussion strategy is especially useful for solving problems. Discussion groups are also commonly used for exploring issues and making decisions.

Most committees and group meetings are examples of this type of group discussion. The discussion method is also one of the chief ways that an instructor can bring about attitude change. This is done by means of discussion and the careful examination of assumptions.

Discussion groups are an extremely common type of instructional strategy. Three major problems, however, are usually associated with them. Many discussion groups are held with insufficient preparation or planning. Often, too many viewpoints are presented. As the rule of thumb, three opposing points of view are generally sufficient. Finally, far too many discussion groups fail to find and maintain a focal point for the discussion. The solution is obvious for an instructor manager, but more difficult for an instructor operator.

Some discussion groups require the physical presence of the instructor. Other groups do not. When an instructor is present, it is due to a number of reasons.

For instance, the instructor might preface the discussion with a short lecture or demonstration. Alternatively, a film or videotape might be shown. Another reason for the presence of an instructor is leadership. While students often do take on a leadership role, it is sometimes more convenient for a teacher to exercise this responsibility.

Experiential small groups

An instructor can also observe and listen to what is going on in the group. In this way it is possible for the group to get on with the task while the instructor attends to the way in which the participants are working together. This observation and listening role is particularly common for instructors in experiential small group training programs.

Since the 1960's, managers and social workers have been eager to improve their skills with people. Accordingly, there has been a great deal of interest in sensitivity training, encounter groups, T-groups, and other forms of experiential learning.

As in most situations, the line between success and failure in experiential groups is a thin one. Cary Cooper and David Bowles point out that few people appear to exhibit any long-term change. This suggests that the risks associated with such training may not be worth the psychological dangers involved. For this reason alone, some organizations refuse to use such training programs.

Research indicates that people who have benefited from experiential groups generally underwent a particular type of group experience. Trainers were supportive and relaxed, yet somewhat withdrawn from the discussion. Trainees were conservative, a little apprehensive, and self-sufficient. The group had a high degree of structure, so that things appeared organized and controlled. There was little intimacy in the group and very little confrontation between the participants.

Experiential groups in which trainees had adverse effects were generally rather different in character. Trainers were uninhibited and assertive, impulsive and open. Trainees, on the other hand, were self-sufficient, introverted, and serious minded.

In such groups, there was very little structure or organization. Discussion was intimate and confronting. Most of the emphasis was concerned with the here and now of the group situation, rather than with issues external to the group and its immediate environment.

Atmosphere of the discussion group

While this digression on experiential groups has taken us away from the main topic, much the same points can be made about discussion groups in general. The atmosphere of the group *is* important. It should be relaxed, yet planned and organized. There should be a definite beginning, middle, and end to the proceedings.

There should bo a free flow of argument and debate, of questioning and reasoning. If the discussion is to be both efficient and effective, it is important that it be relevant. This means that not only should there be a clear objective, but that the objective be maintained throughout the discussion.

Thus, a discussion has to be prepared for, both by the learners *and* by the instructor. The argument must also be refueled, by posing challenging questions, whenever it appears to be running out of steam or losing direction. The discussion must also be brought to an end or conclusion. It should not be allowed to peter out. This is best done by someone impartially summarizing the major points.

Debates and seminars

The most formal type of discussion group is the debate. This follows rigid rules. Then there is the leaderless group, the most informal of all. In this situation discussion is free flowing, with no one person serving to control the flow of argument.

A seminar, sometimes called a group tutorial, usually involves a semi-structured discussion. It questions, in a critical manner, an argument or approach which has been presented elsewhere. For instance, it may follow a lecture, a reading assignment, or the watching of a videotape. Seminars are particularly useful for developing critical thought. They help trainees to evaluate not only their own thinking but that of other people.

L.B. Curzon suggests that a definite sequence of events should be used in seminars. A seminar should begin with an introduction, which outlines the goal to be achieved. A lecture, demonstration, or assignment should then occur. After initial discussion, there should be a quick summary of the main points that have been made.

After a short break, further and lengthier discussion should occur. The person giving the lecture or demonstration should be given an opportunity to reply. Finally, the seminar should end in a way which allows a conclusion to be reached or a position to be adopted.

An individual tutorial, in contrast to the seminar or group tutorial, usually involves one, or sometimes two, students with one instructor. It is often used for remedial teaching, when a student is in difficulty. More usually, tutorials form part of a guided study package, in which there is also a great deal of independent work. In such a situation, the teacher uses tutorials to question and coach students so that they adopt a more critical frame of mind.

Case studies

Case studies are another variation of the discussion method. They also involve critical examination of subject material. In the case study, however, the material is posed in the form of a real or simulated problem. Sometimes, the problem is presented on videotape or film. More usually, the case is written up in narrative form. The narrative may be a single paragraph or may extend to a large folder containing reports, letters, memos, and numerical data.

Case studies are often associated with business. However, they are widely used in other areas, from medicine to law and social work to safety training. The method lends itself to a wide variety of situations.

As an instructional method, case studies were originally used to develop general decision-making skills. Today, they are usually employed in situations in which there is no one right decision, as well as a great deal of uncertainty.

More recently, they have been used to help students identify underlying principles. Instead of being told the principle, students are forced to discover it for themselves. For instance, instead of telling students that people get more satisfaction from achieving hard objectives than from easy ones, they are caused to discover the principle by discussing a critical incident case study.

There are many types of case study, depending upon the imagination of the instructor. Four varieties, however, can be recognized and used as a source of ideas. They are:

- *Critical incident case*
  Trainees are presented with a blow by blow account of the events leading up to a problem situation—e.g., a labor dispute.

  They are asked: What further information is required before a solution can be identified? How can that information be obtained?

- *Next stage case*
  Trainees are presented with the facts leading up to a problem—e.g., a disagreement over pregnancy benefits.

  They are asked: What is likely to happen now?

- *Live case*
  Trainees are reminded of a well publicized news item in the media—e.g., an incident in a nuclear power station.

  They are asked: What will happen next?

  Then they wait until the next day and check out their prediction. In this way, a whole chain of predictions can be made and then checked out against real world events.

● *Major issue case*
Trainees are presented with a bewildering array of information and statistical data. Some of the data is fact, some opinion. Some is important, some trivial.

They are asked: What is the problem? What solution do you recommend? Why? What other solutions did you consider? Why did you reject them?

All four case study methods can be used to deal with the same topic. For instance, a training program on *Employee compensation and fringe benefit programs* could be built around a company manual and a whole series of case studies, one after another.

Role playing

Role playing is a combination of demonstration and case study. It involves students acting out an incident for themselves, rather than reading about it or watching others act it out on videotape. Role playing can be used for events leading up to a situation. It can also be used to show students how they should deal with the situation. Interviewing, for instance, particularly lends itself to role playing. Incidents in an office, on the factory floor, or outside the work situation all adapt easily to such playlets.

Particularly fruitful in training are *in-basket exercises*. In this instructional method, trainees are given a full in-basket from someone's desk. This contains a whole pile of paperwork. They must then work through all the letters, cables, memos, etc., actioning each one as they go. In some situations, their work goes into the in-basket of another trainee, who must similarly begin actioning the paperwork.

Games

One final method of case study remains to be described. It involves gaming. Instructional games, using two or more players, have become very popular in many training and educational programs. The business game is merely one example; there are many others.

Instructional games can be played on a board, involving chance, as do so many children's games. They can also be played with the help of a computer or word processor. In a very real sense, the board, computer, and processor are merely devices that allow the game to simulate the real world. They also help introduce a competitive element, which adds an important motivating factor to the training.

Some games are extremely complex. Others are "home-made" adaptations of commercially available games. With very little ingenuity, an instructor can take a game designed for entertainment and adapt it for instructional purposes. For instance, the game *Monopoly* can be quickly adapted to a whole range of instructional situations. It can be used to simulate the stock market, skid row, reliability engineering, and any number of other applications. Commercial games are available to teach supervision, negotiation, sales quota attainment, interaction, priorities, leadership, etc.

Advantages and disadvantages

As a method of instruction, discussion has a number of advantages and disadvantages. Among the most important of these are:

- *Advantages*
    - The discussion method permits everyone to participate in the learning situation.
    - The discussion method pools abilities, knowledge, and varying experience in the realization of a common goal.
    - The discussion method is a highly stimulating and motivating experience when properly planned and organized.
    - Group decisions and judgments are often better than individual ones in a problem-solving or decision-making task.
    - The discussion method is a simulation of real world situations. It prepares people for responsibilities they will exercise once training is complete.

- *Disadvantages*
    - The discussion method, unless properly prepared and organized, soon degenerates into an aimless debate.
    - The discussion method places a limitation on the number of people who can effectively take part. Normally, seven is optimal.
    - The discussion method is a time-consuming process. This is especially so if the group contains people from diverse backgrounds.
    - The discussion group can be dominated by an autocratic leader. Highly verbal or dominant trainees can also dominate the proceedings.

Good preparation and a clear focus are the twin keys of effective discussion. But, as many committee meetings indicate, this is easier said than done.

As with all discussion situations, careful briefing and debriefing are essential. Few discussion groups—whether a debate, case study, tutorial, game—have an instructional impact unless the students are adequately briefed beforehand. They need to know not only the rules to be followed but also the learning that can result from the situation. It is essential to identify and maintain the aim of the training session.

Just as learners must be briefed beforehand, so must they be debriefed afterwards. Too many instructors and teachers find that time has run out. So it is not possible to hold a debriefing session. Yet debriefing strikes home the major learning points that have been gained.

Regardless of how enjoyable a discussion or game may be, it must be tailored to allow adequate time for debriefing. Learning must not be sacrificed to amusement and pleasure.

The independent study method

Trainees do not always need to learn in group situations. Nor do they always need the direct assistance of a teacher or instructor. Sometimes it is appropriate for them to learn by themselves, under proper supervision.

Independent study involves learners being given specific assignments. These should be prefaced with a clear statement of the objectives to be achieved. It is important that trainees also have a clear idea of how they will be assessed. In other words, independent study works best when trainees and instructor have a contract or firm understanding of what is expected.

Some people react badly to independent study. They prefer the structure and routine of the training room to the loneliness of working alone. For this reason, it is probably best to limit the duration of independent study to intervals of something like an hour and a half. It can then be alternated with other instructional methods.

Projects and programmed instruction

Programmed instruction gave a great impetus to independent study in the 1960's. Its emphasis on clear objectives and specially designed materials helped to remove many teachers' reservations about the independent study method. The mastery emphasis gave independent study an instructional purpose.

Independent study really involves two quite different types of strategy. One is the project approach. In this version, trainees are given a task to do. For example, they might be asked to design a form for annual performance reviews. Armed with objectives to realize, they are largely left to their own devices. They may be supplied, of course, with a list of readings, people to contact, and other resources.

In the other version of independent study, specially designed instructional materials are involved. Trainees might be given a programmed book to work through. These are written in such a way that the reader has to make continual responses, such as filling in a missing word or phrase. The text is so designed that the learner will be almost always right. This, of course, is particularly reinforcing, and helps to insure mastery.

Slide-tape presentations

Slide-tape presentations are another form of independent study. In this case, trainees sit at a specially designed desk, called a carrel or learning center. There they use a workbook that directs them to a slide projector, which they operate themselves. Tied to the projector is a tape recorder.

Slide-tape presentations are, in effect, an automated form of instruction. Trainees go through the lesson at their own pace. The tapes not only give them instructions as to what they should do next, but also teach them in the real sense of the term. Workbook and slides illustrate the key instructional points. They also offer students a central point of focus while they are listening to the tape recorder.

It has been claimed that able and well motivated trainees can achieve more in nine hours than less able ones can in twenty. Such findings highlight a major problem with all instruction. Able and well motivated students are likely to learn regardless of the instructional method employed. The less able and motivated often require a great deal of skilled help.

In an attempt to meet the needs of every kind of trainee or student, Sam Postlewait has developed an Audio-Tutorial System. This offers not just slide-tape presentations but a multi-dimensional approach to learning. Audiotapes, texts, films, samples, manuals, assignments are all used as part of the audio-tutorial method. Students check out the instructional materials and work through them by themselves in a carrel. They progress at their own pace. When they have questions, or when they get into difficulties, they can obtain help from an instructor, without slowing down the remainder of their group. Lectures, independent study, and quiz sessions are all part of the Audio-Tutorial System.

Personalized system of instruction

Another independent study system that is becoming increasingly popular is the Keller Plan. This is now more usually referred to as the Personalized System of Instruction, or PSI.

The Personalized System of Instruction, or Keller Plan, involves a mastery learning approach. The system divides a training or educational program into a series of modules or learning units. Students and trainees are allocated a module, one at a time. Each module involves an assigned reading, possibly from a programmed textbook. It may also involve working through a chapter in a technical manual or some other type of assignment. An assignment may include questions or problems, exercises and job assignments.

Lectures and demonstrations are used sparingly. They have an inspirational role, and so are designed to be interesting, entertaining, and inspiring. Study guides and review units integrate the material, while assignments and tests probe each person's mastery.

People work through the various assignments at their own speed. Some work quickly, others slowly. When the task is complete, they report to a "Proctor." The Proctor may be an instructor, an advanced student or, perhaps someone such as a secretary in the training department. The Proctor then assigns them a test, to help determine whether or not they have achieved mastery.

Once the test is completed, the trainee discusses the answers with the Proctor in a mini-tutorial situation. A new assignment is then made, or remedial work allocated. In this way the PSI method capitalizes upon some of the better features of programmed instruction. At the same time, it builds in opportunities for social contact with people, as well as a supervisory element.

Advantages and disadvantages

As with all the instructional methods discussed so far, the independent study method has a number of advantages and disadvantages. Among the most important of these are:

- *Advantages*
    - Independent study allows trainees to progress at their own speed. They do not have to proceed at the speed of the class as a whole.
    - Independent study forces people to accept responsibility for their own learning.
    - Independent study focuses on mastery learning, rather than instruction. Learners can take a mastery test whenever they are ready.
    - Independent study enables trainees to receive feedback on how well or badly they are doing. People can thus feel a sense of progress and accomplishment.
- *Disadvantages*
    - Independent study does not work as well with trainees who are not highly able nor highly motivated. Less able people can experience real problems.
    - Independent study is far less effective with trainees who require the presence of other people. Independent study can be very lonely.
    - Assignments cannot always be assessed by means of some written test.
    - Allowing students to progress at their own individual rate poses some logistical problems. What do you do with trainees who are moving ahead quickly? It is not always possible to return them to the job situation.

Independent methods of study have a place in education and training. Usually, they are best used as supplements to more conventional methods of instruction. They are also useful when people have already acquired a working set of skills. Independent study can then be used to build upon what they already know and can do.

THE LESSON METHOD OF INSTRUCTION

The lesson is one of the most versatile and useful of all instructional methods. It can be used for teaching both knowledge and skills. It also has its place in changing attitudes, as in safety training. The lesson can be used with both advanced and beginning trainees.

In effect, a lesson involves presenting material to a group of learners in such a way as to insure maximum group activity. It is not a passive method. There is a great deal of group participation involved. For this reason, attention is readily maintained.

The lesson, as an instructional strategy, involves the main features of every method so far discussed. It typically begins with a short lecture and ends with an independent work assignment. The main body of a lecture includes a great deal of discussion and debate, as well as demonstrations and possibly case studies.

Questioning is used continuously. This serves to sequence the material and also enables an instructor to determine whether or not students are learning. Thus there is a great deal of flexibility. For this reason alone, the lesson is a particularly demanding instructional experience.

An instructor or teacher who has mastered the lesson strategy has also acquired a great deal of skill in the other instructional strategies along the way. For this reason alone, the lesson strategy forms the focus of the remaining part of this section of the book.

Types of lessons

Basically there are two types of lessons. They are the knowledge lesson and the skill lesson. Both have similar structures involving a clear beginning (called an introduction), middle (development), and end (consolidation).

In a skills lesson, something approaching 15 percent of the time is spent in explaining the skill to be acquired. Another 25 percent of the time is spent by an instructor demonstrating the skill. The last 60 percent of the time is spent by trainees engaging in guided practice.

Time allocations in a knowledge lesson are somewhat different. The introduction, which is really a short lecture, usually takes less that 10 percent of the time allocated. The main body of the lesson, called the development, takes about 65 percent of the time available. It is here that the real group activity takes place. Nevertheless, 25 percent of the time is still allocated to the final or consolidation phase of the instruction.

Advantages and disadvantages

As a method of instruction, the lesson method has a number of advantages and disadvantages. Among the most important of these are:

- *Advantages*
  - The lesson method is extremely flexible. It can accommodate to most other instructional methods and is easily adaptable to most instructional situations.
  - The lesson method encourages, demands, and sustains group activity and participation.

FIGURE 2:2. Time allocations in a knowledge and a skill lesson.

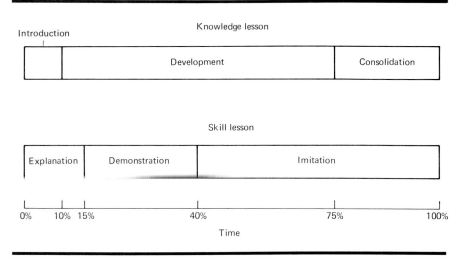

- The lesson method insures that both instructor and trainees cooperate together as members of a teaching-learning team.
- The lesson method lends itself to teaching both knowledge and skills. It also has a role in changing attitudes.
- The lesson method is suitable to both beginning and advanced students. It can also be used for both small and medium sized groups.

- *Disadvantages*
  - The lesson method does not lend itself to subject material which is so detailed that group activity would interfere with the sequencing of information.
  - The lesson method takes more time than a straightforward lecture or demonstration. Telling and showing are quicker than asking and doing.
  - The lesson method is not particularly effective for very small groups (less than five trainees) or very large groups (more than forty).

As a general rule of thumb, the lesson method should be employed in preference to other instructional strategies. However, if special circumstances or conditions occur, one of the other methods should be chosen.

Variety in lessons

The lesson method is the general workhorse of teaching and instructing. No lesson is ever the same. The way trainees participate is so varied, even with the same material, that the lesson is always different. There is, therefore, always a freshness about the instruction.

FIGURE 2:3. Attention profile during the showing of a television module "Pressure makes perfect" [Adapted from Rockman, S., and Auh, T. (1976). *Formative Evaluation of "Self Incorporated" Programs.* Research Report #30. Bloomington, Ind.: Agency For Instructional Television]

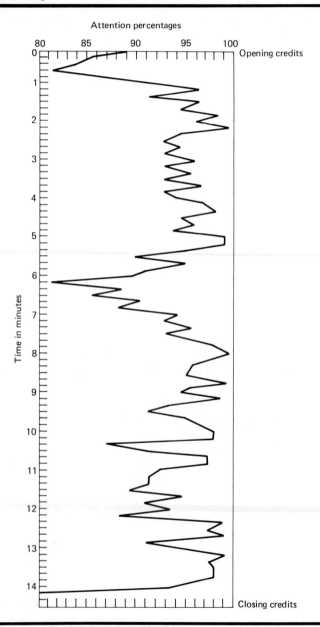

The variety of the lesson is also a very important property. Learner attention is variable. Films and television programs, for example, are generally carefully made by highly skilled professionals to attract and hold audience attention. Indeed, few instructors or teachers can compete with the time and resources available to film producers.

Yet even in the case of a fifteen-minute television training module, the percentage of students attending varied from 80 to 100 percent. Figure 2:3 illustrates an attention profile for the television module *Pressure Makes Perfect.* The attention profile during a lecture on the same topic is likely to be much poorer.

The place and variety of a lesson, however, do confer an advantage. If trainee attention wanders, the lesson method enables teachers and instructors to recapture it quickly. This is doubtless the reason for the method's popularity among teachers and trainees alike.

CONCLUSION

Instructors and teachers are often bewildered by the range and variety of the instructional methods available to them. Although the variety seems endless, there are really only five broad classes of strategy involved. They are the lecture, the demonstration, the lesson, the discussion, and independent study.

Each method has its own advantages and disadvantages. However, the lesson has many advantages, and has become a principal method of teaching and learning. The other instructional methods have important parts to play, but they are not so generally applicable to such a wide range of situations.

Once an instructor has successfully mastered the lesson method, it is relatively easy to experiment with the other alternatives. The lecture involves more instructor talk and less group participation. A discussion, on the other hand, involves less instructor talk and more group involvement. A tutorial has many of the features of a lesson but involves only one or two trainees. The demonstration method highlights the imitation of a skill but does not necessarily challenge learners in the same way as a skills lesson.

The lesson includes ingredients of all the main instructional strategies. This gives it the pace and variety so important to holding trainee interest and attention. Thus the lesson method has a motivating effect, not only from an instructor's viewpoint but also from the point of view of the group itself.

Chapter 3
Structure of a Lesson

FOCUS

"What is an appropriate structure for a lesson?"

KNOWLEDGE OBJECTIVES

After carefully reading and studying this chapter, you will be able to:
1. list the basic characteristics of a lesson;
2. identify the principal "events" of instruction;
3. identify the structure of the basic lesson;
4. distinguish between the tactics associated with the introduction, development, and consolidation parts of a lesson;
5. use an appropriate structure when preparing a lesson to teach knowledge, skill, or attitudes.

ATTITUDE OBJECTIVES

After reading this chapter, the author hopes that you will:
1. value the importance of structure when preparing a lesson or module;
2. incorporate the principles into your teaching, so that they become characteristic of your instructional technique.

An effective lesson has a visible structure.

A lesson, sometimes referred to as a module, embraces one unit of work. Although it is self-contained, it relates to what has gone before and what is to come after. A training program which consists of isolated lessons, each unrelated to the other, is no training program. A program must have an underlying theme, which helps pull the various experiences together.

Lessons vary enormously. Some are very long, some short. They may be geared to advanced trainees or to beginners. Content, too, varies greatly. Sometimes a lesson is knowledge-based. At other times, skills or attitudes may be involved. Often both.

Even the location where a lesson can take place varies. Often it will be held in a room or workshop. Sometimes it will be held in an office, conference room, shop, or on the factory floor.

A great deal of training and education still takes place on locations inside the company or institution. Increasingly, however, they are also being carried out in purpose-built training and conference centers, as well as hotels and nearby colleges. Lessons which have been specially packaged can be taken home for self-study.

A lesson, in other words, is a varied beast. It can vary in duration, location, objectives, content, and audience. Yet despite all of this, there is still one underlying structure to the instruction. This structure gives form to the learning experience.

The structure of a lesson is likely to be more visible in the case of new, inexperienced instructors and teachers. More experienced ones have developed skills that mask the underlying organization. It is still there, but it is more difficult to see. They simply do a better job at hiding it. Even the coarser detail, like the introduction, development, and consolidation, loses some of its sharpness. This gives greater smoothness to the instruction. But it can lessen the impact.

Accumulations over a period of time, as with barnacles on a ship, need to be removed. Each part of a lesson's structure has a function or job to do. Over time these can be lost sight of, so that both efficiency and effectiveness are reduced.

For this reason, experienced as well as beginning instructors need to reflect upon the form of the lesson. Research indicates, in fact, that there is a relationship between lesson structure and trainee evaluations of the quality of instruction.

When lessons have a discernible organization, students and trainees tend to rate instructors as effective. They rate them poorly when their lessons have no obvious form. For this reason alone, the structure of a lesson is well worth attending to and improving.

THE BASIC CHARACTERISTICS OF A LESSON

Although there are many types of lessons, they have a number of characteristics in common. These should be borne in mind when preparing a lesson, as well as when teaching it. The characteristics address issues which are important to the lesson as a unit of work.

Included in the basic characteristics are:

- *A lesson is a self-contained unit of work.*
  Regardless of its length, each lesson should address only one topic. This is a basic property. It gives a lesson integrity.

  A lesson should be able to stand on its own feet. At the same time, it is also part of a larger whole or program. Unless it stands on its own feet, it loses a sense of theme. If a lesson is too long, it loses touch with its objectives and audience.

- *A lesson should be tied to a particular standard of performance.*
  This relates to the objectives of the lesson. It also relates to the expectations that something concrete will come from the experience.

  This does not mean that the results always have to be measurable and observable. It does mean that something worthwhile must be achieved. Mastery is what instruction is about.

- *A lesson should be adapted to the needs of the learners.*
  The objectives of a lesson, and the learning activities necessary to realize the objectives, must be within the capabilities of the trainees and students. They must be reasonable, yet challenging.

  A lesson must be cast at the level of the people involved. Otherwise it is irrelevant to their needs. This includes making sure that the language used is at their level of comprehension.

- *A lesson should have a definite structure.*
  People in a learning situation should understand what is going on. Just as an audience watching a play needs to know which act it is watching, so trainees need to know where they are in the lesson.

  Every lesson needs a framework. The role of instructor and trainees in one part of the lesson is different to their role in other parts of the lesson.

These four characteristics insure that the lesson is a *reasonable* learning experience. They should not be taken for granted.

THE EVENTS OF INSTRUCTION

Whenever instruction takes place, a number of things have to be attended to while the teaching is underway. Unless they are taken care of, learning will be threatened. It might not even take place. Accordingly, these "events" of instruction, as Robert Gagné calls them, are important.

It does not matter what instructional strategy is employed. Effectiveness, as well as efficiency, depends upon them. Since every lesson should have a beginning, a middle, and an end, the "events" are best thought of under these headings.

These are the things that an instructor must attend to:

- *Events in the beginning part of the lesson*
  - Gain the attention of the learners.
  - Tell them what is expected.

- *Events in the body of the lesson*
  - Remind them of what they already know, relevant to the new task
  - Present them with the new knowledge, skill, or attitudes they are to learn.
  - Provide them with encouragement and guidance.
  - Insure that they practice what they have learned.
  - Tell them how they are doing.

- *Events in the last part of the lesson*
  - Consolidate what they have learned.
  - Assess their level of mastery.
  - Assist them to apply what they have learned to new situations.

This is a lot to think about and remember. The main purpose of the lesson structure is to insure that it all gets done. And at the right time, too!

STRUCTURE OF THE BASIC LESSON

In the real world of training and education, there is no such thing as *the* basic lesson. It is a figment of the imagination. Every lesson is different. Every instructor and every teacher instructs in a different way, and few days are the same.

Nevertheless, the concept of the basic lesson serves a useful purpose. It gives instructors a model—something on which they then can pattern their teaching. Such a pattern is a guide rather than a dictate.

A beginning cook will usually follow every instruction in the cookbook. Each recipe is followed exactly. If the cook does not have the right ingredients, the beginner will rush out and buy them. An experienced cook, on the other hand, will be able to make do. A cookbook is still likely to be used as a reference. But every recipe is a springboard for creative action.

So it is with an instructor and the concept of a basic lesson. The structure is a springboard for creative teaching. It is not a straitjacket.

Every lesson should have three basic parts. Each part, of course, should lead naturally to the next. However, each part also needs to have a form of its own. It should be definite and clearcut, with its own beginning, middle, and end.

The three parts of the basic lesson (see Figure 3:1) are:

- *The introduction*
  This should be relatively short in duration. It must lead naturally to the main body of the lesson. As a rule of thumb, it should account for less than 10 percent of the instructional time. However, everything depends upon the specific circumstances of the lesson.

- *The development*
  This is the main body of the lesson. As a rule of thumb, the development will probably account for up to 65 percent of the instructional time in a knowledge lesson. When a skill is involved, this part of the lesson will account for only about 25 percent of the training. This is when the skill is demonstrated.

- *The consolidation*
  This is the end part of the lesson. In a knowledge lesson, it is likely to be relatively short. It will probably account for something like 25 percent of the training. In a skill lesson, however, the consolidation part of the lesson is used to imitate and practice the skill. For this reason, a large chunk of time is normally involved. Sometimes it accounts for up to 60 percent or more of the training.

As we have seen, each of the three parts has a different task to accomplish. Each involves a different set of the "events" of instruction.

THE INTRODUCTION TO THE LESSON

As the name suggests, an introduction leads into the subject of the lesson. As Figure 3:1 indicates, it should be relatively short in duration. Four or five minutes, in a sixty-minute lesson, is adequate. The important thing is to keep it forceful and short.

Many lessons, of course, will be shorter than an hour. Many will be longer. The time actually taken depends upon the topic and the students. In this discussion, for the sake of consistency, we will assume that the basic lesson lasts sixty minutes. Readers can then scale the estimate up or down according to their own circumstances.

The events of instruction

Despite the relatively short duration of the introduction, much needs to be done. Two events of instruction, in particular, have to be taken care of:
- Gain the attention of the learners.

FIGURE 3:1. *Outline of the structure of a basic lesson.*

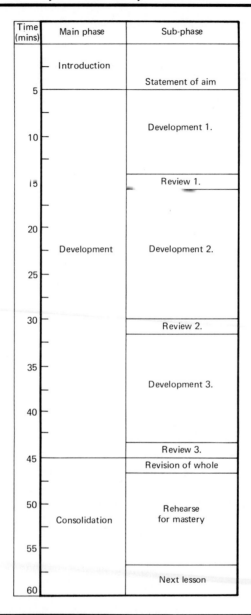

Time (mins)	Main phase	Sub-phase
	Introduction	
5		Statement of aim
10		Development 1.
15		Review 1.
20	Development	Development 2.
25		
30		Review 2.
35		Development 3.
40		
45		Review 3.
		Revision of whole
50	Consolidation	Rehearse for mastery
55		
60		Next lesson

- Tell them what is expected.

The former involves attracting their interest. The latter emphasizes the importance of giving them clear objectives to realize.

In a recent survey of teaching, it was shown that these two events were often overlooked or forgotten. Experienced instructors were as guilty as inexperienced ones.

The introduction to a lesson is one of the more difficult things to arrange. It is hard to think of a suitable introduction, and hard to put it into effect. To some extent, it demands a degree of showmanship or a sense of theater. For this reason, the quality of an introduction can be a good indicator of an instructor's skill. But, like all skills, introductions improve with practice.

The purposes of an introduction

Some introductions to a module or lesson are too involved. Others are too short to serve a useful purpose. No matter how much time you allocate, it is essential that you use it as efficiently and effectively as possible. This means keeping the purposes of the introduction always in mind.

An introduction has a number of jobs to do. It should:

- Concentrate attention and arouse interest.
- Set the scene for the lesson.
- Set the climate or atmosphere for what is to follow.
- Establish links with past lessons and future ones.
- State the aim of the lesson and the objectives to be realized.
- Point out the importance of the task.

This is a lot to do in a short amount of time. But unless it is done, trainees simply will not be motivated. In effect, the six functions serve as a checklist for effective introductions.

There are a number of different ways in which these functions can be achieved. Variety is important. Introductions should not fall into a mold or stereotype. Spontaneity and sparkle are essential.

Sometimes, an introduction can be *too* arresting. A teacher might use an introduction which is so interesting that it becomes distracting. Instead of serving as a link to the development portion of the lesson, the introduction takes on a life of its own. Its power sets loose a chain of distracting thoughts and ideas. Instead of leading the thoughts of the learners to the topic, these ideas head them off in another direction. Showing a centerfold photograph may have this effect, and should be avoided.

Types of introductions

Although there is an endless variety of introductions, many can be classified into one of five types. They are:

- *Review-type introduction*

This type of introduction reviews previous knowledge, skill, or attitudes. Unless care is taken, it can be ordinary, lacking sparkle and interest.

It will often take the form of "In our last lesson, we saw that the three concerns of a business enterprise are: safety, protection of the environment, and profitability. The priorities are in that order. You will remember that many plant managers wrongly imagine that . . . Today, the thrust of . . . results in . . . The purpose of our lesson this morning is to . . ."

Review is important. But unless carefully handled, such introductions can be deadly dull. Of course, they are also the easiest to think of, and the simplest to implement.

- *Topical introduction*
  This type of introduction makes reference to some event currently in the news. It might refer to something that has recently occurred in the company, or something in the community or nation.

It might take the form of "In this week's copy of *Newsweek* there is an article on travel time and travel costs. It says that . . . and points out that . . . One way of putting the lid on the skyrocketing costs of business travel is to . . . There are dozens of creative ways of . . . The purpose of our lesson today is to . . ."

Topical introductions set up strong linkages with the real world. They also help demonstrate how relevant the subject is, and how important. Such introductions are easy to plan and use. They also indicate that the instructor is in touch with what is happening outside the classroom.

- *Anecdotal introduction*
  This type of introduction uses a common experience to illustrate a principle. Sometimes an analogy might be employed. This steals an idea from one field and applies it to another. You might take an idea from magnetism and use it to explain something about people.

For instance, "Watch while I sprinkle some iron filings around a magnet. What do you see? Yes, a field of force around the magnet. Now, Kurt Lewin in the 1930's stole this idea from physics and applied it to people. People have similar fields around them when they interact with other people. You see this when . . . Today, we are . . . The purpose of our lesson today is to consider the role of field force analysis in Organization Development."

Anecdotal introductions can be illuminating. But they are not always easy to think of, unless you really know your subject. The important thing is to be on the lookout for anecdotes and analogies useful to your teaching. File them away for the future.

- *Historical introductions*
  This type of introduction uses an historical incident to introduce a lesson. History is an excellent source of material for introductions. It offers an inexhaustible supply.

It might take the form of "There is a thing called the 'Stockholm Syndrome.' It is named after a group of bank tellers who were locked in a bank vault by armed robbers some years ago. They were kept there by the thieves for a period of time. When finally they were released, they had developed a psychological affinity with the robbers. Indeed, they supported the thieves, and had feelings of loyalty towards them. The tellers felt that society and the bank were in the wrong. All the robbers had been doing was trying to turn society around, by robbing the rich. The Stockholm Syndrome is with us today. The aim of this lesson is to study harmony in work groups such as the shifts in kitchens and restaurants."

Historical introductions can be intriguing. However, they should be used sparingly. When they are overdone, they become a bore.

- *Shock introductions*
  This type of introduction is very dramatic. It sparks interest and concentrates attention. Starting a lesson this way brings the trainees face to face with reality.

  It might take the form of "Last year forty three people were killed and one thousand and sixty two injured in mine explosions. On the basis of last year's statistics your chances of being killed are . . . , and of being injured are . . . You can help reduce the possibility of becoming a statistic by . . . The aim of our lesson today is to consider what can be done to make coal mines safer places by . . . "

  Shock introductions should be used with care. They can frighten people and heighten their levels of anxiety. When this happens they may be unable to cope with the situation.

Personal reminiscences of the instructor and trainees, which can be topical or anecdotal, are also a useful way of beginning a lesson. The trouble is that they may become overly rambling. For this reason, they need to be managed.

Bringing the introduction to an end

Regardless of the type of introduction used, an introduction should be brought to a decisive end. Trainees and students will then know that the development part of the lesson is about to begin. Stating the aim of the lesson is a clear way of signaling that this stage has been reached.

Once the aim has been stated, the instructor should distribute, or draw attention to, the learning objectives of the lesson. Rather than go over them in detail, instructors could "walk" trainees through them.

They should point out which objectives are "A" items, which are "B," and which are "C." At the same time, key points should be emphasized. It is also worth warning learners where difficulties might be encountered, and how they will be helped to overcome them.

Trainees should then read the list of objectives quietly by themselves. While this is going on, the instructor should write the title of the lesson on the chalkboard or flip chart. Trainees should copy it down in their notes for easy reference later on. Anyone who enters the room after the lesson has begun will be able to see what the lesson is about.

A case study is shown in Figure 3:2. Illustrated there is an example of an introduction to a lesson on shoplifters. The lesson, or training module, is for use with sales personnel in a large city store.

THE DEVELOPMENT OF THE LESSON

The development forms the main body of the lesson. As its name suggests, it involves a gradual unfolding of the topic. Inevitably, sequence is a key concern. What should be taught first? What should be taught last? What is logical, and what is not? These are the kinds of decisions that have to be made.

The events of instruction

The development portion of the basic lesson accounts for something like 65 percent of the instructional time. During this time there is a lot to do and a great deal to think about. Planning is essential so that nothing will be overlooked.

Five events of instruction have to be taken care of in the development. The training must:
- Remind trainees what they already know, relevent to the new task.
- Present them with the new knowledge, skill, or attitudes they are to learn.
- Provide them with encouragement and guidance.
- Insure that they practice what they have learned.
- Tell them how they are doing.

The first event will insure that the prerequisites for learning are known. The last event emphasizes the importance of trainees and students receiving appropriate feedback in a timely manner.

The purposes of the development

The development part of the lesson involves a major chunk of training time. For this reason, it is possible for an instructor to lose the thread of things in the cut and thrust of the teaching. The purposes of the development part of the lesson, therefore, should constantly be kept in mind. They can serve as a checklist, to keep instructors on track.

The purposes of the development are to:

FIGURE 3:2. A case study introduction for a lesson on shoplifting.

Let us imagine *you* are the instructor for a training module on shoplifting. The trainees are sales personnel in a large city store. You have four hours for the training session.

Let us think about what you might do in the introduction.

You could begin by showing a short videotape. It could show someone being "arrested" in the store. The tape emphasizes the embarrassment and shame the thief experiences.

You point out that none of this need happen. A nearby salesperson could have prevented it from going so far.

Next you could point out that shoplifting is on the increase. In the store, it is estimated that it is increasing 15 percent a year. It is so serious that the store manager has started a special training program to help reduce it. Salespeople, you point out, have a special responsibility. They can do a lot to make shoplifting difficult. Would-be thieves will then go elsewhere, where it is easier.

You could then bring the introduction to an end by stating the aim of the lesson. Rather than something general, like "Understanding Shoplifting," choose something very specific: "The aim of our training session is to reduce shoplifting in the store 35 percent by the end of the next six months."

After writing the title of the lesson on the flip chart, you are ready to begin the development part of the lesson.

- Develop or unfold the topic in a gradual manner.
- Insure smooth continuity and logical order in the material.
- Provide sufficient periods of class involvement on a group as well as individual basis.
- Insure that there is variety and vividness in the instructional approach.
- Manage time and resources in an efficient and effective manner.

Realizing these objectives casts teachers and instructors in a manager rather than operator role.

Throughout the development, an instructor is faced with the twin problems of priorities and opportunities. Although most of the priorities will have been set before instruction begins, some will emerge during the course of the teaching. Unplanned and unforeseen opportunities, too, will present themselves. Flexibility, therefore, is an essential requirement.

Trainee involvement

The development part of the lesson includes a great deal of telling and asking. It also includes showing and doing. Trainee and student participation is vital. For this reason, instructors must resist the temptation of lecturing. They must not shoulder the whole burden; otherwise, they become teacher-operators. Group activity is the key.

In order to obtain the involvement of trainees, a number of things can be done. These include:

- *Oral questioning*
  Questioning trainees orally insures that they contribute their knowledge and skill, experience and attitudes. Their replies can be used as raw material for the lesson. In this way, the lesson becomes a team effort.

- *Discussion*
  Discussion is another way of drawing things out of the trainees. It is all part of the process of sharing. The instructor can use discussion so that participants analyze, compare, explore, and apply the material with which they are dealing.

- *Assignments*
  Assignments can also be used to keep students and trainees active. They can involve work inside as well as outside class. Some assignments can be made on an individual basis. Others can be given to large or small groups. Such practical activities can involve not only knowledge tasks but also assignments concerned with skill and attitudes. Assignments can also include trainees teaching one another. Peer instruction is useful, and should be encouraged. Role playing, simulations, and games are also important.

- *Note-taking*
  Trainees should be encouraged to take notes during the lesson. This keeps them active. It also serves to focus their attention on the material. Of course, the mere act of writing down key points also helps to reinforce learning. Research clearly shows that trainees who take notes learn and remember more than trainees who don't.

Group participation is an essential characteristic of a successful lesson. Any involvement, however, must be managed.

If there is reason to believe that something is likely to create a commotion, the rule is simple. Don't use it. All distractions must be avoided, no matter what the cost. This is one of the reasons audiovisual aids should be carefully used. Unless their utilization has been carefully planned, they can introduce an element of chaos with beginning instructors. Murphy's Law should be remembered. If anything can go wrong, it will. Pre-class rehearsal with visual aids is a *must*.

The organization of the development

With such a large block of time available for the development part of the lesson, it is easy to lose your way. Irrelevancies creep in and consume time. They also help to hide the underlying thread or theme, which is essential for good continuity.

It is important that the development flows naturally from key point to key point. Thorough preparation is essential. So is timing. It is very easy to find that time has run out before you have covered all your essential material.

In order to guard against running out of time, it is useful to divide the development into a number of parts. The number, obviously, depends upon the task and the trainees. Nevertheless, three is a good number to use as a rule of thumb. These are indicated in Figure 3:3.

Dividing the development in this way makes the whole thing easier to manage. What an instructor does in each part of the development varies. However, it is useful to think of the phases under the headings of examination phase, interpretation phase, and application phase. Alternative sequences will be discussed later in this chapter.

Let us look at each of the parts in detail, in order to get an idea of a sequence of activities during the development of a lesson. The parts are:

- *The examination phase*
  The first phase of a development typically involves examination. Trainees and students are required to think about something, or watch something. For instance, they might read or look at a case study.

  During this phase, the instructor might ask trainees to attend to something. Then to analyze it. Once this has been done, they might be asked to name what they have seen. Any questions that an instructor asks the class will largely be questions of FACT.

  In this phase, trainees actively acquire a body of knowledge. This information will be exploited in the next phase of the development.

- *The interpretation phase*
  The second phase of a development typically involves interpretation. In other words, learners are required to think about what they have examined and explain what it means.

  Discussion is a key activity. Indeed, in the interpretation phase a great deal of class activity and involvement take place. Any questions that an instructor asks will be questions of INTERPRETATION.

  In this phase, trainees are looking for meaning. Their understanding will be exploited in the next phase.

- *The application phase*
  The final phase of the development usually involves application. Trainees and students are required to apply what they have learned to a real world or job situation.

  Practice, encouragement, and correction are key concerns in this part of the training. Any questions that an instructor asks will be questions of EVALUATION.

  In this last phase of the development, trainees put their learning into effect. It is essential that they receive knowledge of their results. Such feedback must be given in a timely manner; otherwise, its impact is lost.

FIGURE 3:3. Structure of the basic lesson.

Time (mins)	Main phase	Sub-phase	Typical concerns
	Introduction		Linkage Motivation Objectives
5		Statement of aim	
10		Development 1. [Examination phase]	Attend Classify Label
15		Review 1.	Recall
20		Development 2. [Interpretation phase]	Identify Explain Conclude
25	Development		
30		Review 2.	Recall
35		Development 3. [Application phase]	Practice Encouragement Correction
40			
45		Review 3.	Recall
		Revision of whole	Retention of whole
50	Consolidation	Rehearse for mastery	a. Reinforce b. Challenge c. Assess mastery
55			
60		Any questions References Next lesson	Linkage

Such a sequence of examination, interpretation, and application should not be followed rigidly. It is useful only as long as it assists trainers and educators and does not hinder them.

As will be seen from Figure 3:3, each of the three phrases of the development ends with a brief period of review. These are sometimes called "recaps" or periods of recapitulation. Webster defines "recapitulation" as a concise summary, and this is precisely what is involved.

The three periods of review have the same purpose. They are designed to:

- Summarize the main points made in the preceding phase of the development.
- Complete the lesson summary on the chalkboard or flip chart.
- Allow trainees to copy down the summary in their notebooks.
- Enable the instructor or teacher to ask questions which revise the material covered.

Generally speaking, it is best to avoid class activity during the review sessions.

An important activity during the development period of the lesson revolves around the chalkboard or flip chart. It is essential that a summary of the lesson be built up as the training proceeds. Hearing and seeing are two important ways of learning. Furthermore, the existence of the lesson summary enables teachers and instructors to review quickly and simply.

Many instructors erase or remove the lesson summary from view once the development is complete. They feel that trainees should be on their own during the consolidation part of the lesson.

Figure 3:4 continues the case study begun in Figure 3:2. Illustrated is an example of a development for a lesson on shoplifting. Study it carefully. Look to see how the points that have been made in the above discussion have been put into practice.

THE CONSOLIDATION OF THE LESSON

The consolidation is the concluding part of the lesson. It involves strengthening what has been learned. For this reason, it should be planned as carefully as the other parts. It is too important to be done hastily.

Unfortunately, due to poor time management, far too many teachers and instructors fail to consolidate. They run out of time. Yet there is little point increasing the amount of time spent on the development if there is going to be little or no opportunity for trainees to consolidate what they have learned.

Instructors must always be willing to be flexible. No matter what they have planned, it is essential to leave out material if time is running away. Such material can either be scrapped or else included in later lessons. Once an opportunity to consolidate has been lost, little can be done. The right moment has passed.

The events of instruction

The development part of the basic lesson accounts for something like 25 percent of the instructional time. During this time, three events of instruction have to be taken care of somehow. All three are important.

FIGURE 3:4. A case study development for a lesson on shoplifting.

Let us imagine that *you* now wish to teach the development part of the training module on shoplifting.

Let us think about what you might do in the development.

In the examination phase of the development, you could deal with two questions: "What is shoplifting?" "How big a problem is it?"

Examination phase

To start, you might ask trainees to think of a specific occasion involving shoplifting. Ask them to think about it. Then ask them to describe it. "What did the person do?"

When you have collected enough examples, they could classify them. Write up the different types of shoplifting on a flip chart. It should include: stealing, changing containers, changing prices, and concealing goods.

Now you are ready to deal with the second topic: "How big a problem is it?" Trainees, when you ask them, will underestimate the size. So give them statistics on a handout or overhead projector.

You could tell them sometting like this. Last year bank robbers stole $25 million; shoplifters $8 billion. Shoplifting is increasing at a rate greater than that of inflation. Veteran shoplifters each walk off with more than $53,000 worth of merchandise a year. The losses add 2 percent to the price of goods. Only one in 1,250 shoplifters ever sees the inside of prison. Even then it is because they illegally possessed drugs or weapons when arrested. It is estimated that one out of three small business bankruptcies are the direct result of shoplifting. Finally, you could tell learners statistics about the store in which they work.

Review the phase.

Instruction, during the consolidation part of the lesson, must do the following:

- Consolidate what trainees have learned.
- Assess their level of mastery.
- Assist them to apply what they have learned to new situations connected with the job or task.

In this way, the knowledge, skill, and attitudes that have been acquired during the learning module will be nurtured and strengthened.

The purpose of the consolidation

The consolidation part of the lesson provides teachers and instructors with a number of opportunities. These should be taken up if learning is to be efficient

Interpretation phase
You could begin this phase by dividing up the trainees into small groups of five or seven people. Give each group a flip chart. Get them to appoint a leader. Ask them to discuss "Why do people steal from our store?" Ask them to come up with a list of ideas. They will be presenting their recommendations, group by group, to the whole class.

As each group reports, you should write down the major points on the main flip chart. Many group presentations will include the same points. You include only the key points. Your list should include: challenge, money, inflation, returning stolen goods for a 100 percent refund, eye to civil lawsuit for false arrest, etc.

Review the phase

Application phase
You could begin this phase by the trainees going back into groups and asking them to come up with a way of reducing shoplifting in their store. This will cause them to apply their knowledge and experience.

As each group gives its presentation, again with the help of flip charts, you list the main points on your flip chart. The list should include: prosecuting all shoplifters as they are caught, advertising that there are security guards and devices, mount dummy cameras and large signs warning shoplifters of penalties, hire actors and stage fake arrests, etc.

When group presentations are complete, point out that they have dealt only with what other people can do. What about the sales floor? Tell them what they can do. They could be more observant, head off trouble off before it occurs, insure that merchandise is not left unattended, lock up valuable items, arrest shoplifters (if the state laws allow) etc.

Review the phase.

---

and effective. The most obvious thing to avoid is making the consolidation little more than a longer period of review.

A period of review and the consolidation period of a lesson are not the same thing. A comparison of the purposes or objectives of the two will highlight the difference. The two thrusts have very little in common.

The main purposes of the consolidation period are to provide opportunities for trainees and students to:

- Rehearse their learning until mastery has been obtained.
- Assimilate and retain their learning.
- Apply their knowledge and understanding to real world situations such as they might meet in their jobs.
- Obtain an assessment of the quality of their performance in real world or simulated situations.
- See their learning as a whole, rather as just a collection of parts.

The best laid plans can go astray. For this reason alone, it is best to have some kind of structure in the consolidation, so that all these things can be taken care of by the instructor or teacher.

The organization of the consolidation

During the consolidation part of the lesson, a sequence of four things is usually employed. This consists of:

- *Overviewing the whole learning task*
  Although learning has been reviewed at least three times during the development, there is no guarantee that the trainees will have pulled all the separate parts together into a whole.

  It is useful, therefore, to start the consolidation off by presenting a complete picture of the task. Remember that the whole is greater than the sum of the parts. A jigsaw puuzle, after all, is more than a box of 1,000 pieces.

- *Providing for further practice*
  Some practice will have taken place during the development part of the lesson. Practice during the consolidation should be designed to reinforce learning.

  Mastery is the major objective of training, and this is the time to provide for it.

- *Providing for mastery*
  No lesson is complete unless trainees have been pushed. For this reason, they should be provided with tasks or problems that test not only what they have learned but also their understanding.

  Challenge occurs when trainees are required to apply their learning to novel situations related to the real world.

- *Assessing mastery*
  Although the consolidation part of the lesson is concerned with practice and challenge, there is another issue to be considered. This is the single issue of competency. Mastery is the name of the game. Human competence, as Tom Gilbert reminds us, is concerned with worthy performance.

  What has to be assessed is whether or not trainees can do the job or task expected. And at the required level.

The consolidation is the time to determine how accomplished the trainees have become as a result of the instruction that they have received.

The lesson summary, which records the key points that have been made, will have been completed before the consolidation begins. For this reason, little use should be made of the flip chart or chalkboard during this part of the lesson.

The time for most learning aids has passed. Learning, if it is to occur, should have taken place by now. This is the time to ram it home. The consolidation period is not the time to start trying to bring it about. Although it may be too early to deal with the real world unsupervised, now is certainly a time for simulations, practicums, and internships.

Before the lesson is complete, three final duties remain. Although they are important in themselves, they also serve to bring the lesson to a conclusion. There is nothing worse than a lesson which just fades away. The three duties are spelled out in Figure 3:3. They are:

- Any further questions?
- References to manuals, books, and other sources.
- The title of the next lesson.

All of these offer the instructor an opportunity of linking learning to past experiences and to future activities.

Ideally, trainees will want to read more about the topic. It is unlikely that you will have covered everything that might interest them. For this reason, it is a good idea to supply learners with references to printed materials that they can follow up by themselves. The readings might possibly include reference to technical manuals, company reference books, operating procedures, safety regulations, etc. The important thing is that trainees are given an opportunity to take the topic further.

One act remains before the lesson is brought to a close. This is to announce the title of the next lesson or module in the sequence. Knowing what is coming up next helps to link today's lesson with the ones that are to follow. It gives trainees a sense of the future—where they are going, and what they expect next. Needless to say, announcing the title of the next lesson is also an extremely good way of tying up the training package.

Figure 3:5 completes the case study on shoplifting. It outlines the steps that might be taken to consolidate the instruction suggested for the introduction and development parts of the lesson. It should be carefully studied to see how the major points made in the discussion on the consolidation part of a lesson have been implemented.

SOME VARIATIONS IN THE BASIC LESSON STRUCTURE

The lesson structure outlined in this chapter applies to a basic lesson. Sometimes, however, variations are necessary, depending upon the circumstances of the training situations. Not all lessons should follow the same sequence of examination, interpretation, and application. Tasks vary in their demands, and variety is important.

Figure 3:6 outlines some of the alternatives possible. They are suggestions, and they should not be taken as dictating how things should be done. They simply represent an additional set of springboards for creative teaching.

FIGURE 3:5.   A case study consolidation for a lesson on shoplifting.

Let us imagine that *you* now wish to teach the consolidation part of the training module on shoplifting.

Let us think about what you might do in the consolidation.

As a first step you should quickly give an overview of all the main points that have been made in the training session. This can be done by reshowing the videotape, then quickly going over the lesson summary. Discussion could then follow.

Now it is time for some role playing. Trainees might act out short playlets, in which they deal with a variety of situations involving shoplifters. Different trainees could play the parts while the rest watch. The class could then debrief their fellow trainees on the adequacy of their performance.

The list of suggestions that were generated for the store should not be forgotten. It might be possible for you to arrange for the trainees to give a short presentation to the store manager or an assistant manager. The fact that they might already know everything they hear is *not* the point. The sales personnel would relish the opportunity of being heard. The presentation would also have a beneficial effect on morale and motivation.

Teaching a skill is very different from teaching a body of knowledge. For one thing, it is a relatively slow process. There are few real shortcuts. As we saw at the end of Chapter Two, the time allocations for a skill lesson are also different from those for a knowledge lesson.

In a skills lesson, something like 15 percent of the time should be spent introducing the topic (compared with less than 10 percent in a knowledge lesson). See again Figure 2:2. About 25 percent of the time should be taken up by an instructor demonstrating the skill. Finally, something like 60 percent of the time should be devoted to trainees imitating the skill under close supervision.

Figure 3:6 indicates that it is often better to give two separate demonstrations.

- *First demonstration*
  The skill ought to be demonstrated in its entirety, with or without a commentary on what is occurring. This demonstration is a demonstration of mastery. Its aim is to show the objective learners are to attain. For this reason, it will be carried out at normal speed.

- *Second demonstration*
  The skill should now be broken down into its constituent parts, and each operation explained and demonstrated. Some instructors like to demonstrate the operations again, either separately or together at a mastery level.

FIGURE 3:6.   Lesson structures for different tasks.

Knowledge	Organizing principle or concept	System, equipment, or component	Skill
Introduction	Introduction	Introduction	Introduction
Development	Development	Development	Development
1. Examination	1. Presentation	1. Purpose	1. Safety
2. Interpretation	2. Comparison	2. Principle	2. Explanation
3. Application	3. Formulation	3. Construction	3. First Demonstration
	4. Application	4. Operation	4. Explanation
		5. Errors	5. Second Demonstration
		6. Maintenance	
Consolidation	Consolidation	Consolidation	Consolidation
1. Review	1. Review	1. Review	1. Imitation
2. Competency	2. Competency	2. Competency	2. Correction
3. Reinforcement	3. Reinforcement	3. Reinforcement	3. Reinforcement

In the second demonstration, each operation should be shown in slow motion. Then the skill should be demonstrated again, as a whole, and at normal speed.

Once the development part of the skill lesson is complete, it is time for trainees to imitate the skill under the watchful eyes of an instructor. Correction should be carried out only after trainees have had an opportunity of getting a feel of what is involved.

There is nothing more annoying to trainees than to be corrected before they have had a real chance of imitating the skill. In any case, the objective is for instructors and teachers to reinforce correct actions. In order to do this, instructors must often bite their tongues, so as to give trainees a chance to learn. It is not an easy thing to do.

The sequences that are used to teach a principle, like Ohm's Law or Affirmative Action and Equal Opportunity, are relatively straightforward. They involve first presenting the problem, then comparing it with related ones. Once the scene has been set in this manner, the principle can be formulated by the class, before they apply it to a range of situations.

In teaching a system (like a chemical process) or a piece of equipment (like a compressor) or even a component (like an aircraft turn and slip indicator), a somewhat different approach is necessary. First, the purpose must be taught. This should lead into a consideration of the principle underlying it.

In some navigational equipment, for instance, the same principle is used as in a child's toy. In this case, having the toy in the classroom or workshop would help explain a gyroscope. Without a gyroscope few of us would be willing to fly, for there would be very little chance of reaching our destination.

Once the purpose and principle have been dealt with, the instructor can move quickly on to the construction of the equipment or system. Errors and tolerances can then be pointed out. The final step involves considering what maintenance is necessary to keep it in good running condition.

CONCLUSION

Order is one of the first steps towards mastery. Without order there is likely to be chaos. This simple rule underlies our whole discussion about the structure of the basic lesson. There are so many things to think of, and so many things to do. An underlying framework or structure gives all of these activities the coherence and continuity that we expect of good instruction.

All lessons sequence activities. The idea of an introduction, development, and consolidation insures that they occur in an appropriate order. Different "events" of instruction have to be arranged. Different objectives have to be attended to if mastery is to be achieved.

While the structure of a basic lesson has been emphasized, it must be kept in perspective. If you follow a map too closely on a journey of exploration, a great deal of the fun can be lost. So it is with a lesson. The suggestions made in this chapter are there to be used or deliberately set aside.

All along the way, choices have to be made. These decisions are necessary acts in the science and art of instruction.

Chapter 4
Lesson Planning

FOCUS

"How do you prepare a lesson?"

KNOWLEDGE OBJECTIVES

After carefully reading and studying this chapter, you will be able to:
1. appreciate the importance of planning in the context of lesson preparation;
2. distinguish among three approaches to lesson planning;
3. appreciate the steps essential to planning a lesson or module;
4. use the steps in your own planning;
5. prepare a lesson or module, using the principles set out in this chapter.

ATTITUDE OBJECTIVES

After reading this chapter, the author hopes that you will:
1. value the importance of lesson planning;
2. incorporate the principles into your teaching, so that they become characteristic of your instructional style.

Success depends upon effective planning.

Effective instructors and teachers plan. They prepare their lesson well in advance of their instruction. There is much to do while teaching is underway, and it is just not possible to think about planning at such a time. For this reason, lesson preparation is something that has to be done beforehand.

Of course, it is possible to overplan, to prepare too much and too rigidly. In such cases, some of the spontaneity will be lost. Good instruction involves seizing unplanned opportunities for learning, just as much as it involves taking steps to insure that opportunities will be created.

Planning, therefore, is a process that has to be kept in perspective. Rigidity in planning is as bad as too little planning. The problem that instructors and teachers face is making certain that they have done enough. Where do you stop? How can you insure spontaneity?

THE NATURE OF PLANNING

Planning involves a concern for the future. It is part and parcel of wise and intelligent behavior. Russel Ackoff put the matter nicely when he said that wisdom is the:

- Ability to see the long-term effects of current activities.
- Willingness to sacrifice short-term advantages for long-term benefits.
- Ability to do what you can, and not to fret over the things that cannot be done.

This is as good a recipe for lesson planning as it is for business.

Good lesson preparation allows an instructor to command the future, rather than allow the future to command the instructor. Unlike a fortune teller who tries to predict the future, a wise teacher attempts to control it. Both teaching and learning benefit from the decisions that are made. They should be recorded in the lesson plan.

The purposes of lesson planning

Planning is anticipatory decision-making. It involves deciding what to do, how to do it, and when to do it. All of these decisions are made before the event.

In this way, nothing is left to chance. Most things have been thought through and decided upon beforehand.

There are many advantages to planning. The more important ones are to insure the following results:

- The aim of the lesson is identified and maintained.
- The lesson material is selected and arranged in a logical manner.
- An instructional method is selected appropriate to the learning task and the needs of the trainees.
- Appropriate trainee participation and experiences have been identified and arranged.
- Instructional time is managed so that the best use is made of it.

All of this involves decisions of one kind or another. Once they have been made, an instructor will have a ready means of keeping on track. The instructor's confidence, too, will be increased, for little has been left to chance.

Many instructors and teachers have feelings of uneasiness about teaching. Sometimes it is because they don't know what to do; sometimes it is because they lack confidence in their ability to do it. In both instances, the solution is careful planning.

In the last resort, some of the real benefits of planning are not to be found in the lesson plan. The process of planning can be more important than the product. In other words, participation in the preparation of the lesson may be more important than the plan that is produced. Having a plan allows you to deal with the expected. The fact that you have spent time thinking about the lesson, to produce a plan, also gives you an advantage when you have to deal with the unexpected.

A common fault to avoid

Frequently, instructors make a fundamental error in their lesson planning. They prepare the material but give little thought to the method. So much of their effort goes into preparing detailed notes on the topic that they fail to complete the job.

A lesson plan must consider three basic questions:

- *What* is to be taught?
- *How* is it to be taught?
- *How* is learning to be assessed?

If any of these three ingredients is missing from the plan, the preparation of the lesson is incomplete. The nature of the learning task, the instructional method, and the means of evaluation must all be decided upon and recorded in the lesson plan. Only then will all bases have been touched.

THREE APPROACHES TO LESSON PLANNING

There are three different ways to set about preparing a lesson or sequence of lessons. The matter is of importance, because some educators and trainers overemphasize one particular approach. There is no "one best way"; it all depends upon the situation. For this reason, a choice has to be made, rather than a dictate unthinkingly followed.

The ends-means question

Planning a lesson involves thinking about ends and means. Decisions have to be made about the ends or objectives that need to be realized, and the means or methods that are available for achieving them.

A problem arises when you have to decide where you are to begin. Should you start your lesson planning by defining the ends? Or should you begin by looking around at the means that are available? Most books on the subject recommend first getting your objectives clear. In the real world, however, this can be a rather idealistic approach.

Resources are not necessarily unlimited. The resources available are not always the ones you want, or would choose. Sometimes, as an instructor, you can obtain what is necessary for the job. At other times, objectives have to be adjusted to real world conditions. Priorities within the company or organization change, and resources are shifted from one program to another.

In some situations, you will get everything you need to do a superior job. In other situations, you will only be able to do a satisfactory job. If you had more time, or more resources, much more would be possible. So you will have to compromise. This is what is meant by the means-ends question. It is a problem of the real world.

Approaches to lesson planning

The three approaches to lesson planning are:

- *The systematic approach*
  This approach to lesson planning involves:
  - First, defining the ends or objectives to be realized.
  - Second, choosing the means or methods of achieving them.
    It is a systematic approach to lesson planning. Once you have a clear idea of what you want to do, everything else follows. The ends define the means.

- *The expedient approach*
  This approach to lesson planning involves:

- First, identifying the means or methods available.
- Second, defining the ends or objectives that can be realistically realized. It is an expedient approach to lesson planning. It enables teachers and instructors to get the job done within the budget available. The means define the ends.

- *The piecemeal approach*
  This approach to lesson planning involves:

  - Seeing the means and ends as interrelated.
  - Successive approximations to lesson planning.
    In other words, the ideal is forsaken for an approach in which means and ends define each other.

    It is a piecemeal approach to lesson planning. First, an instructor might start off by getting a rough idea of the objectives, and then look around at the resources that can be obtained. Once these are known, the objectives can be revised. Additional resources might then become available, which allow the objectives to be changed once more. And so it goes on, as a series of successive approximations.

Instruction is too complex for only one approach to lesson planning.

The systematic approach is ideal. The expedient approach is prudent. The piecemeal approach is realistic. At times, instructors have to choose which approach is appropriate to the occasion. If the lesson is concerned with a basic skill essential to the safety of personnel or equipment, a systematic approach is probably the right way of going. In such circumstances, only the best is good enough.

In the case of a lesson on budget as a control tool, an expedient approach might be satisfactory as long as there is no critical fiscal need. A lesson on communicating through objectives, on the other hand, might be planned by means of a piecemeal approach. The objectives of such a lesson could be rather basic. However, the company might have a number of people who have a great deal of experience in this area. For this reason, more might be attempted than the instructor originally had in mind. Why miss an excellent opportunity?

ESSENTIAL STEPS IN LESSON PREPARATION

The purposes of lesson planning have already been indicated. They can be summarized under the simple idea of exploring alternatives and making decisions. In order to insure that every step has been taken to recognize potential problems, certain essential steps have to be undertaken.

The essential steps in lesson or module planning are:

- *Preliminary steps*
  - Choose the topic of the lesson.

- Take steps to gather material and examples.
- Decide on the aim and the objectives of the lesson.
- Identify what the students know and believe.
- Select the material to be included in the lesson.

- *Main steps*
  - Identify an appropriate instructional method.
  - Arrange the material into a logical sequence.
  - Choose appropriate learning activities and experiences.
  - Decide how learning is to be assessed.

- *Final steps*
  - Write the final version of the lesson plan.
  - Prepare class handouts, audiovisual aids etc.
  - Refer to the lesson plan and refresh your memory.
  - Prepare the room or other instructional setting.

Although the above steps are set out in a list, it is important that they are seen as interrelated activities.

While work is going on gathering material, for example, the first draft of some of the handouts might be designed. Good planning involves preparing things as a whole, rather than treating each step in isolation. The fact that we have to talk about them in a step-by-step fashion does not mean that they have to be planned in that manner.

PRELIMINARY STEPS IN LESSON PLANNING

Before the main activities of lesson planning occur, a number of preliminary steps have to be taken. These steps are:

- Choose the topic of the lesson.
- Take steps to gather material and examples.
- Decide on the aim and the objectives of the lesson.
- Identify what the learners know and believe.
- Select the material to be included in the lesson.

Once all these steps have been done, it is possible to start thinking about *"How is the lesson to be taught?"* The steps are illustrated in Figure 4:1.

Purposes of the preliminary steps

The preliminary steps of lesson planning are all concerned with the content of the lesson. They involve a great deal of work and effort. However, if the work is done well, the benefits to both instructor and trainees can be considerable. If the work is done badly, the lesson will surely fail as a worthwhile learning experience.

FIGURE 4:1. Preliminary steps in lesson planning.

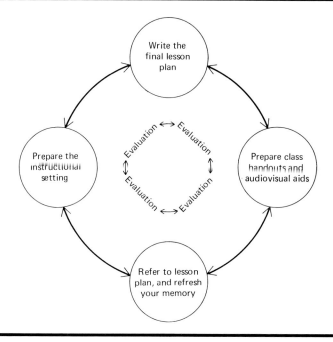

The main purpose of these preliminary steps is to:

- Identify the nature of the task.
- Identify what the learners know already.
- Determine what has to be taught in the lesson.

Sometimes the trainees know a great deal beforehand; sometimes they know very little. It is important, therefore, to find out. The difference between the two answers the question "What has to be taught?" This determines the content of the lesson.

For example, suppose you are to teach a lesson on ultrasonic flow meters and their use to protect the delicate environment around the trans-Alaskan oil pipeline. Since their use represents a new technology, it seems reasonable to assume that trainees would know little or nothing about them.

However, flow meters are a common form of instrumentation. They have been used for many years to measure water flow. For this reason, many trainees in the engineering trades are already familiar with the principle. They would not be familiar with the ultrasonic version, however, and its use to detect breaks or leaks in the pipeline by measuring the flow of oil.

So instead of preparing a lesson that treats the topic as completely new, the prior knowledge of the trainees can be used. In other words, you can use knowledge of the older application to help reduce the learning required to understand the newer one. A topic that might have taken two hours to teach can now be taught in an hour, if the prior experience of the learners is utilized.

Choosing the lesson topic

Instructors and teachers are usually given a syllabus to follow, which sets out the topics to be covered in a training or education program. It is not always possible to cover a whole syllabus in the time allocated for formal instruction. For this reason, the syllabus must be studied, using the ABC classification outlined in Chapter One, so that priorities can be set.

Certain items in the syllabus will belong to the "A" category. More will belong to the "B" category, and the majority to the "C." Once such priorities have been set, decisions can be made about which topics will be covered by the instructor and which left to the trainees.

Often, instructors will not have a syllabus to work from when they plan their lessons. Instead, they must draw one up for themselves. It is not something that they can do without. A syllabus, in effect, is the instructor's job description. It details instructional responsibilities. An example of a syllabus for an educational program on *Equal Opportunity and Affirmative Action Compliance* is shown in Figure 4:2.

Once the syllabus has been studied and the priorities awarded, a *Scheme of Work* can be drawn up. This simply sets out some of the basic decisions that have to be made, in order to choose the topic of the lesson. In some cases, the topic will be exactly as set out in the syllabus, e.g., "The Company's AA plan, and its role in effective manpower planning."

In other cases, the lesson topic may combine a number of the items in the syllabus, so that they can all be dealt with in one training program. More

FIGURE 4:2.   Syllabus for a Program on Equal Opportunity and Affirmative Action Compliance.

Equal Opportunity and Affirmative Action Compliance

Topics to be covered in the basic course include:	Priority Categories
1. Background to Equal Opportunity (EO), and Affirmative Action (AA) regulations.	C.
2. Duties and responsibilities of the EO & AA Officer at the Corporate and Unit Level.	A.
3. Demographics and the Law, both Federal and State.	C.
4. The Company's AA plan, and its role in effective manpower planning.	A.
5. Recruitment and selection within the AA plan, with special attention to the procedures to be followed.	B.
6. Documenting all EO and AA activities, so that a complete record is obtained.	C.
7. Evaluating personnel approaches in light of the law.	B.

frequently, one topic in the syllabus may be broken into a number of lesson topics. There is too much to be covered in one sitting.

For instance, the topic "Evaluating personnel approaches in light of the law" in the syllabus illustrated in Figure 4:2 could be broken down into three lesson topics: initial job placement and lines of progression; training and apprentice programs; and seniority systems in union and nonunion shops. All of this would be recorded in the scheme of work.

A scheme of work would set out answers to such questions as:

- What sequence should be used for topics in the syllabus? (The one in the syllabus? Another?)
- What lesson topics can be identified from the topics in the syllabus? (The same? More? Fewer?)
- What sequence should be used for the lesson topics? (This sequence could be different from the sequence in the syllabus.)
- Which topics must the instructor deal with, and which can be left to the trainees to deal with on their own? (All of them? Some? None?)

Any scheme of work is personal to a particular instructor or teacher. Given the same task, most people would tend to organize it differently. It is a matter of personal preference and instructional style.

Gather material and examples

Once the topic of the lesson has been identified, it is time to begin collecting all the material you will need. Sometimes, you will find that the topic is a familiar one, and that you need to do very little. At other times, the topic which you have separated out is unfamiliar. A great deal of work is going to be involved familiarizing yourself with it.

It is essential that instructors and teachers be complete masters of what they are to teach. It is equally important that they be up to date and acquainted with current techniques and practices. In the case of the Equal Opportunity and Affirmative Action Compliance Program, for instance, recent developments might result in people being out of date unless they took steps to keep in touch.

Once the topic of the lesson is known, it is a good idea to open a folder or file. In this way, material can be added to it, including examples, illustrations, anecdotes, etc. Although you may not use all of this material in your lesson, collecting it enables you to make a more informed decision about what to include. It is better to have too much material than too little.

Decide on the aim and objectives of the lesson

Once the topic of the lesson is known, and sufficient material has been collected so as to make an informed decision, the aim of the lesson can be chosen. The title of the lesson seldom provides more than a hazy indication of the kind of material that will be covered. For this reason, the time has come to tie down the lesson topic in specific terms.

Aims and objectives will be discussed in much more detail in a later chapter. There are a number of specialized techniques that should be used, both to identify them and to state them in words. At this point, it is enough to point out some general principles so that you can get started.

The aim of a lesson should be stated in clear but general terms. It is intended to give more information than the title. It should give learners a sense of direction. An objective, on the other hand, is more specific and detailed. It is intended to communicate what people will be able to *do* once they have gained mastery.

The important thing about an aim is that it offers teachers and trainees a clear orientation. It is a compass, so that everyone can keep on track. For instance, a lesson title might read "Negotiating and Bargaining," while the aim of the lesson might be stated as "The principles of successful negotiating and bargaining." The lesson title simply identifies the topic, the aim clearly spells out the emphases—"principles" and "successful." Other emphases could have been selected.

An aim should be written in such a way that it is:

- expressed simply and clearly;
- written in a positive rather than a negative manner;
- stated in a way that has obvious interest and value to the trainees;
- stated so as to indicate the minimum to be taught.

It is well worth spending time to get the wording of the aim exactly right. Once the aim has been properly identified, the objectives will flow naturally from its definition.

Objectives are written in a much more detailed fashion. In effect, they represent a contract for learning. For this reason, they largely determine:

- the length and importance of the lesson;
- the content of the lesson;
- the instructional strategy;
- the nature of class and individual participation;
- the method of assessment.

So they are not something to be taken lightly. In fact, if there is *one* critical step in lesson preparation, then it is to identify the learning objectives to be achieved through the lesson experience.

When you are trying to decide what the objectives should be, think about what you want the trainees to do and what you do not expect them to do. For instance, you might want them to be able to do something but not to understand it. You don't have to understand how an electronic calculator works in order to be able to use one. Knowing how it works might be interesting, but it is not part of your objective.

In the example used in the discussion on aims, the sequence might be:

- *Lesson title:*
  - *Negotiating and bargaining.*
- *Lesson aim:*
  - *The principles of successful negotiating and bargaining.*
- *Lesson objectives:*
  At the end of this lesson you will be able to:
  - *recognize* effective negotiating and bargaining;
  - *practice* effective negotiating and bargaining;
  - *use* alternative negotiating strategies under different levels of conflict and cooperation;
  - *evaluate* your own skills, and the skills of others, in the same negotiating and bargaining sessions.

The important thing to notice about the illustration is the use of the action verbs.

Objectives begin with a clear statement of what you want people to *do* at the conclusion of training and education. In other words, the verb is a key statement. Do you want them to remember? Understand? Believe? Do? Once this has been decided, all that remains is to determine the last part of the objective. Remember what? Understand what? Believe what? Do what?

Some people will tell you that this is still not enough. They will explain that still greater detail is necessary. However, research does not support their point of view. As is pointed out in *Objectives in Curriculum Design,* adding further detail is a matter of personal preference. It is rarely essential.

Identify what the learners know and believe

Once the title, aim, and objectives of the lesson are clear, it is time to start thinking about the students and trainees. If they know nothing about the topic, you can safely begin at the beginning. In that case, the lesson may involve teaching a great deal of knowledge and skill. If they know a good deal about the topic, starting at the beginning will be a waste of time, as well as being insulting and frustrating to the trainees.

This means that you need prior knowledge about the trainees. Perhaps you have taught them before. Perhaps you can speak to one of your colleagues who has taught them. Their supervisor may be able to give you some information. There may be information in the personnel office that would help you, as well as training records. Annual reports, too, are an important source of information. So is a record of all the jobs they have done, and the experiences they have had.

A more obvious approach is to ask the trainees themselves. You could give them a series of tests. Better still, you could talk to them and find out what they know and believe. There is nothing like knowing your trainees on an individual basis. Then you will cast your lessons at the right level.

Select the lesson content

Although instructors and teachers must know the topic they are going to teach, selecting the subject matter is not always easy. There is always too much. There is never enough time. There is rarely a right time.

A careful sifting of all the subject matter that you have collected is of vital importance. The objectives of the lesson, and your knowledge of the trainees, will serve as your guide. It is a common mistake to teach too much, particularly too much detail. Background information is always useful, but it can get in the way of learning. It is far better to concentrate on the job that has to be done. Concentrate on "need-to-know."

Students can be overwhelmed by an ill-sorted mass of confused detail. Remember, it might not seem like that to you, but it can to them. It is far better to teach a little well than to teach a great deal badly.

In order to overcome the problem of selecting the right material for the lesson, three procedures are helpful. They are:

- Arrange in order all the material that you want to include in your lesson. These are the *teaching points.*
- Relate each teaching point to the objectives of the lesson, and decide whether or not it is outside the scope of the lesson. This will determine what is to be included and excluded.
- Annotate each teaching point as an "A," "B," or "C" task, according to the system of priorities set up in Chapter One.

In order to focus on these three procedures, it is useful to keep the diagram illustrated in Figure 4:3 in mind.

FIGURE 4:3.   The selection target for a lesson.

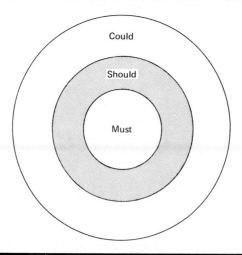

There are certain things that the trainees *must* know. There are others that they *should* know but are not mandatory. They ought to know them, but it is not essential. Finally, there are many things that they *could* know, but it is a matter of inclination. The important thing is to try and hit the center of the target every time.

THE MAIN STEPS IN LESSON PREPARATION

Once the preliminary steps in lesson preparation have been completed, the main steps can be undertaken. These steps are illustrated in Figure 4:4. They include:

- Identify an appropriate instructional method.
- Arrange the teaching points into a logical sequence.
- Choose appropriate learning activities and experiences.
- Decide how learning is to be assessed.

Up to now, the focus of lesson planning has been on "What is to be taught?" The main part of lesson planning focuses on a new issue.

Purposes of the main steps

The preliminary steps of lesson preparation have all been concerned with the content of the lesson. That problem has now been solved. By now you should have a clear idea of what you are going to include and what you are going to leave out. More important, you will know how you came to make those decisions.

The purpose of this part of lesson planning is to:

- Identify how the material is to be taught.
- Identify how the material will be sequenced.
- Determine how learning will be assessed.

Every decision, however, must be made in terms of the objectives of the lesson and the needs of the trainees.

Identify an appropriate instructional method

Identifying a teaching method by now should be largely routine. Certain topics lend themselves naturally to a discussion, others to a lecture. Is telling or asking the major concern? A need for trainees to practice the skill will sometimes be dominant. At other times, students can be largely passive. Is knowing or doing the major concern?

FIGURE 4:4.   The main steps in lesson planning.

These three activities make up the stages of the development part of the lesson.

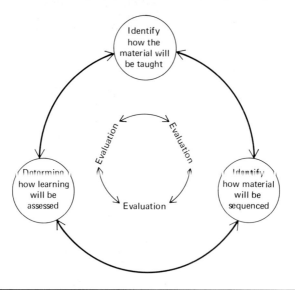

As far as the lesson method is concerned, the decision is already broadly taken. All that remains is to decide where the emphasis will lie. If knowledge is involved, the sequence of instructional tactics will be different than if a principle or a skill is concerned. See Figure 3:6, which was discussed in the last chapter.

In the basic lesson, the instructional method will largely revolve around examination, interpretation, and application.

Identify how the material will be sequenced

Sequencing the teaching points that are to be included in the lesson can sometimes present difficulties. Should this one be placed before that? Should this block of teaching points be after this? Should theory come before practice? It is often a problem to maintain a connected sequence of thought.

In most cases the best sequence will be self-evident, once a common theme has been established. The theme will serve as a link, tying the teaching points together. In such cases, the theme comes directly from the aim of the lesson. Aim and theme are one and the same thing.

If the aim is "How to deal with manipulation and coercion," then that is the theme. The idea of *dealing* can be used to sequence the teaching points and tie them together. If some of the teaching points don't fit into the sequence, perhaps they ought not to be part of the lesson.

In deciding which sequence to employ, Herbert Spencer, many years ago, suggested a way of going. He argued that teaching points could always be arranged in a connected sequence. The important thing was to focus on the relationships between them.

In order to highlight possible relationships, Spencer suggested the following rules for sequencing:

- Proceed from the known to the unknown, or
- Proceed from the simple to the complex, or
- Proceed from the concrete to the abstract, or
- Proceed from the particular to the general, or
- Proceed from observations to reasoning, or
- Proceed from the whole, to the parts, and back again to the whole.

Each one of the sequences highlights a different set of relationships. A lesson built around one sequence will be different from a lesson built around another.

One point about sequencing remains. There is a tendency for some inexperienced instructors to *overemphasize* lower level intellectual tasks. In other words, factual knowledge sometimes becomes the major thrust of the lesson. Higher level tasks like analysis and synthesis, application and evaluation are downplayed.

Teachers, when it is appropriate, need to lift their sights away from just factual knowledge. It is easy to forget that the real world is more concerned with the practical side of things, rather than just the intellectual.

Choose appropriate learning activities and experiences

Teaching and learning involve a transaction. As such, the process is essentially an active one, not only for instructors but also for trainees. Unfortunately, learners are often cast in a passive role, with little to do other than to sit and listen.

One of the key functions of lesson planning is to identify an appropriate set of learning activities and experiences. In this way, trainees can become active partners in the teaching-learning process. Such active participation, however, makes sense only if trainees *understand* what they are learning.

The objectives of the lesson are the key factors to consider when selecting learning experiences. For this reason, it is important to bear in mind three classes of objectives:

- Objectives concerned with knowledge and understanding.
- Objectives concerned with abilities and skills.
- Objectives concerned with feelings, beliefs, attitudes, and values.

Each of these classes suggests different types of learning activities. An activity that might be good for promoting knowledge, for instance, may not be appropriate for a skill or belief.

There are so many different types of activities that it is difficult to classify them. Lois Mossman attempted one scheme more than forty years ago. Broadly speaking, as is shown in Figure 4:5, they can be related to inquiry, people, responsibility, expression, and conforming activities.

In choosing learning activities and experiences, a number of rules may prove helpful. Activities should be:

- Directly related to the objectives of the lesson.
- Comprehensive so that more than one thing may be learned.
- Varied so as to add life and interest to the lesson.
- Suitable to the knowledge and experience of the trainees.
- Balanced so that things do not get out of focus.

An activity or experience that contributes to the achievement of more than one objective is usually more worthwhile than one which contributes to only one objective.

An example of such a multiple activity is questioning. Questions play an important role in the development part of a lesson. Asking and answering questions involves not only knowledge and understanding but also beliefs and skill. Questioning is an inquiry-related activity, and a people- and responsibility-related one as well.

Determine how learning will be assessed

One of the themes running through lesson planning is "What do you want the trainees to be able to do when they leave training?" You don't plan to cover

FIGURE 4:5.   A classification of learning activities and experiences.

- *Inquiry-related activities*
Activities like: examining, questioning, exploring, investigating, planning, organizing, thinking, etc.
- *People-related activities*
Activities like: cooperating, sharing, discussing, disagreeing, caring, helping, participating, talking, etc.
- *Responsibility-related activities*
Activities like: deciding, listening, reporting, judging, challenging, accepting, receiving, affecting, etc.
- *Expression-related activities*
Activities like: communicating, expressing, making, doing, writing, drawing, recording, feeling, valuing, etc.
- *Conforming-related activities*
Activities like: repeating, practicing, drilling, following, ordering, forcing, obeying, etc.

material; you plan to get learning. This is the reason a rigorous approach to objectives is so necessary.

The objectives form a contract with the learners. One of the things that you have to keep in mind, therefore, is "How am I going to determine whether or not they have learned?" This has got very little to do with whether they enjoyed the lesson. The important thing is whether they reached mastery.

In some situations a pen and paper test will be enough. If 90 percent of the trainees answer 90 percent of the questions correctly 90 percent of the time, you can probably assume that they have obtained mastery. This is the 90/90/90 criterion mentioned in Chapter One.

In many situations, however, a pen and paper test will be inappropriate. This is particularly the case with certain skills. The only way to find out whether trainees can interview someone at mastery level is to arrange an interview. Ideally, a real life situation will be used, but a simulated one might be acceptable.

Case studies might be used to assess decision-making and problem-solving. Role-playing could be used to evaluate interpersonal relations or to trigger attitudes and emotions. Games might be used to see how people behave under pressure. Projects and assignments might be used to assess practical skills, such as the ability of a person to weld two pieces of metal together. Always, there is the job that people are going to do.

There are many ways to determine whether or not mastery has been achieved. The difficult thing is to make the right decision. However, as long as the objectives of the lesson are kept in mind, the decision will be easier. The action verb used in the statement of the objective will supply the necessary cue or hint as to what is necessary.

Assessment should always be as realistic as possible. There really is little point in asking trainees to describe in words how they would do something. The realistic test is to get them to do it. This seems a very obvious point. Unfortunately, the rule is frequently broken.

THE FINAL STEPS IN LESSON PLANNING

Once the preliminary and main steps in lesson planning are completed, the principal tasks have been accomplished. Only a small number of final items remain. These steps are illustrated in Figure 4:6. They include:

- Write the final version of the lesson plan.
- Prepare class handouts, audiovisual aids, etc.
- Refer to the lesson plan and refresh your memory.
- Prepare the classroom, or other instructional setting.

Up to now the focus on lesson planning has been "What is to be taught?" and "How should it be taught?" Now a new issue presents itself.

FIGURE 4:6.   The final steps in lesson planning.

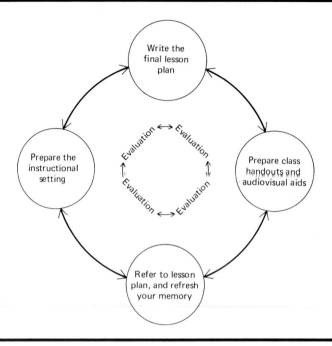

Purposes of the final steps

Most of the creative work has been done. By now instructors and teachers will have a very good idea of their lesson. However, this does not mean that the final steps in lesson preparation are of little importance. If these are not properly carried out, the lesson will be spoiled.

The purpose of these final steps is to:

- Record the final version of the plan on paper, in a form that is usable in the instructional setting.
- Prepare the learning environment and associated instructional aids.

In some ways, it is rather like an actor receiving a script. Instructors, however, often have to write their own script and prepare their own stage. A lesson plan is not always available.

Write the final version of the lesson plan

The lesson plan simply records the decisions in written form. It represents a synthesis of the lesson. Many lesson plans are too detailed. They include not only too much information but too many instructions. The plan should take the form of outline notes rather than continuous prose.

There are many ways of writing lesson plans, and every teacher and instructor has a favorite approach. However, whatever the method employed, the lesson plan should minimally fulfill the following requirements:

- Record the sequence in which the key teaching points will be presented.
- Record the key steps in the instructional method that will be used.
- Record the key features of trainee participation in the lesson.
- Employ a layout that will insure that you can conveniently refer to the lesson plan without interrupting the flow of your teaching.

The outline layout illustrated in Figure 4.7 has been found a practical way of meeting these criteria. It can also be adapted to meet individual needs.

The first part of the plan includes such essential information as lesson title, aim, and objectives. In addition, the type of class and their previous knowledge are indicated. There is also room for details of instructional aids and equipment, as well as the range of time available.

The lesson plan, proper, consists of three vertical columns. They are headed "Keyword," "Treatment," and "Lesson Summary." The keyword column divides the lesson into a number of self-contained parts. Each part is given

FIGURE 4:7. A lesson preparation sheet in outline.

Lesson Preparation Sheet
Title:

Type of class: Aim:
Previous knowledge: Objectives:
Time available:
Equipment required:

Keyword	Treatment	Lesson Summary
Introduction		
Development		
Consolidation		

FIGURE 4:8. Lesson Preparation Sheet.

LESSON PREPARATION SHEET

Title: _____

Aim: _____

Type of class: _____
Previous knowledge: _____
Time available: _____
Equipment required: _____

Objectives:
_____
_____
_____
_____

KEYWORD	TREATMENT	LESSON SUMMARY

KEYWORD	TREATMENT	LESSON SUMMARY

a descriptive title. This insures that instructors will keep their place in the plan, with a minimum of fuss.

The keyword column acts as an index to the lesson. It serves to tell you where you have been, where you are, and where you are going. Keywords should be short and descriptive. For example, in a lesson on skill the appropriate keywords might be: nature of skill, feedback, transfer of training, timing, perception, individual differences, motivation, and practice.

The treatment column sets out the way in which the lesson is to develop. It gives, as it were, the stage directions, as well as an outline of the content to be covered. Subject matter should be indicated in outline form. If questions are to be a key strategy, then the "A" category questions should be written out. This will insure that they are asked in exactly the right manner. Key class activities should also be recorded in the treatment column, particularly those concerned with practice and rehearsal.

The final column of the lesson plan sets out the material that will be included in the lesson summary. In the lesson, this material will be written on flip charts, chalkboard, or overhead projector transparencies. Usually, trainees and students will record this material in their notebooks. As far as learning is concerned, what you hear, see, and write down is more likely to be remembered than material which is simply heard.

Instructors planning their lesson will normally divide the lesson preparation sheets horizontally into three blocks. The first block serves to record the introduction to the lesson, the middle block records the development, and the final block records the consolidation. Figure 4:8 illustrates lesson preparation sheets such as an instructor might use.

Figures 4:9, 4:10, and 4:11 show three examples of lesson plans. One is for a lesson on the problem of shoplifting. Another is on leadership. A final one deals with the simple lubrication system used in turbine engines. It is based on a lesson I used to teach to air force pilots and navigators. The example will help you plan lessons of your own, if you adapt the layout so as to suit your own individual needs.

Prepare class handouts, audiovisual aids, etc.

Once the lesson plan has been written, the time has arrived to think about the aids you will want to use. Some of these might be for your benefit as the instructor; others will be for the benefit of the students and trainees. These, too, need to be planned and organized.

Many of the duties will be mundane. Films need to be ordered, and projection equipment, screens, and projectionists arranged. Some duties will be more onerous. Teaching and learning aids may have to be designed. Perhaps a film or videotape needs to be made. Case studies, perhaps, might have to be written, and games or simulations organized.

FIGURE 4:9. Lesson Preparation Sheet.

LESSON PREPARATION SHEET

Title: Shoplifting

Type of class: Store sales personnel

Previous knowledge: Completed Basic 1 & 2

Time available: 4 hours

Equipment required:

4 flip charts; pens; videotape.

Aim: Reducing the incidence of shoplifting

Objectives:

1. Reduce shoplifting in store 35% by December 31.

KEYWORD	TREATMENT	LESSON SUMMARY
Introduction Videotape	Show videotape of a shoplifter being arrested. Emphasize embarrassment and shame. *Point out* need not have happened. Nearby sales person could have prevented incident. Stress shoplifting on increase: 15% in store, 14% in nation. Store manager has started program to make shoplifting more difficult in store. Write aim on Flip Chart (FC). Distribute objective. Explain goals of the lesson.	*Reducing the incidence of shoplifting in Winyards Store*
10 minutes elapsed		
Development 1. Examination phase	Ask trainees to call to mind a specific occasion involving shoplifting. Think about it for a moment!	
Nature of shoplifting	Q. *What do shoplifters do when they steal from Winyards Store?* *Elicit:* steal goods, change containers, change prices, conceal goods	1. *Shoplifters* • steal goods • change containers • change prices • conceal goods
20 minutes	Write on FC.	
Problem in USA	Q. *How big a problem is shoplifting in the USA?* *Elicit:* magnitude of problem. Students are likely to underestimate the magnitude of the problem. So give small lecture, using overhead projector. Outline facts and figures. Emphasize enormous magnitude of the problem in the country at large.	2. *Shoplifters* • steal $8 billion per year (v. bank robbers $25 million) • earn average $53,000 per year • add 2% to price of goods • rarely are imprisoned (1:1,250) • cause 13 small business bankruptcies • cause jobs to be lost
25 minutes	Write on FC.	
Problem in our store	Q. *How big a problem is shoplifting in Winyards?* *Elicit:* magnitude of the problem. Students are likely to underestimate the magnitude of the problem. So give small lecture, using overhead projector. Outline facts and figures. Emphasize the problem is serious. Write on FC.	3. *Shoplifters at Winyards:* • steal $1.2 million per year • and 2.5% to price of goods • reduce profits 2.2% • rarely are imprisoned (1:1,000) • reduce jobs

30 minutes	
35 minutes	REVIEW
	2. Interpretation phase **Group exercise** Divide class into groups of 5–7 trainees. Give each group a flip chart and pens. Get each group to appoint a leader, who will lead the discussion and make class presentation. Ask them to discuss: *Why do people steal?* Each group to come up with list of ideas. These are to be reported back to the class as a whole.
50 minutes	
	Groups make presentations. You write down major points on FC.
65 minutes	
70 minutes	REVIEW
	3. Application phase **Group exercise** Trainees go back into groups. Ask them to discuss: *How can shoplifting be reduced at Winyards?* Each group to come up with list of ideas. These are to be reported back to the class as a whole.
90 minutes	
	Groups make presentations. You write down major points on FC.
110 minutes	
	Point out groups have *not* dealt with what salespeople can do to reduce shoplifting. Q. *What can you do at Winyards to reduce shoplifting?* *Elicit:* be more observant, head off trouble before it occurs, be sure merchandise is not left unattended, lock up valuable items, arrest shoplifters (if state law allows) Write on FC.
130 minutes	
135 minutes	REVIEW
150 minutes	Coffee break
Consolidation	Overview *all* the main points made during the lesson. Reshow videotape of the arrest. Summarize the main points.
160 minutes	
	Arrange for trainees to role play—sales personnel, customers, and shoplifters. Remainder of class observe. Four role playing: exercises unobservant salesperson; unlocked valuable items; heading off a shoplifter; taking a shoplifter into custody (secondary to state law). Class debrief each "playlet."
200 minutes	
230 minutes	Arrange for trainees to give presentation to store manager of an action plan for the store.
	Any questions? *References:* Shoplifters: store policy, paragraphs 1–7. Write on FC. *Next lesson:* Bringing goods forward.
240 minutes	

4. *People steal because of:*
 • challenge
 • income
 • inflation
 • return goods for 100% refund
 • eye to civil lawsuit for false arrest

5. *Winyards can reduce shoplifting by:*
 • prosecuting all shoplifters as they are caught
 • advertise security guards and devices
 • mount dummy cameras and warning signs
 • have actors and enact "false" arrests

6. *We can reduce shoplifting by:*
 • being more observant
 • heading off trouble
 • seeing that merchandise is not left unattended
 • locking up valuable items
 • arresting shoplifters

Reference: Shoplifters: store policy, paragraphs 1–7.

FIGURE 4:10. Lesson Preparation Sheet.

LESSON PREPARATION SHEET

Title: Leadership in Business Situations

Type of class: Trainee managers (3rd week of training)
Previous knowledge: Minimal
Time available: 4 hours
Equipment required: 3 flip charts, felt pens, two sets of observation sheets for each trainee, videotape LDP 001, and 16 mm training film.

Aim: To understand the role of leadership in management.
Objectives:
1. Define leadership.
2. Distinguish between natural leaders and management leaders.

3. Apply the functions of a management leader to a work group situation.

KEYWORD	TREATMENT	LESSON SUMMARY
Introduction	Explain importance of leadership in society and in business.	*Leadership in management*
	Show class videotape of chief executive talking about the founder of the company.	
10 minutes elapsed.	Write title on flip chart. Hand out objectives.	

Development
Management functions
	Q. *What are the principal functions of a manager?*
	Elicit: Planning, Organizing, Leading, Evaluating
		1. Functions of a manager are:
		  a. Planning
		  b. Organizing
		  c. Leading
		  d. Evaluating

15 minutes	Write on flip chart (FC)	

What?	Q. *What is meant by leading?*
	Elicit: influencing others to achieve organization goals.
	
	Write on FC
		2. Leaders help others achieve organization goals by:
		  a. Maintaining high morale.
		  b. Maintaining high performance standards.

How?	Q. *How is this done?* Elicit: maintain high motivation, maintain high standards Write on FC	
25 minutes		
30 minutes	REVIEW	

Types of Leadership	Explain there are two types of leaders:
	  Natural leaders
	  Management leaders
	  Write on FC
		3. There are two types of leaders:
		  a. Natural leaders
		  b. Management leaders

Natural leaders	Q. *How would you recognize a natural leader?*
	Elicit: sincerity, efficiency, courage, resolution, energy, tact, personality, humor
	
	Write on FC
	Explain that there are many different lists of qualities. Some longer, some shorter. Natural leaders in short supply. So we have to *train* people to become leaders.
		4. Qualities of a natural leader are:
		  a. sincerity e. energy
		  b. efficiency f. tact
		  c. courage g. personality
		  d. resolution h. humor
		
		About 10% of population have these qualities

40 minutes

Management leaders	Explain approach concentrates on what management leaders *do*. Idea of multiple roles. Q. *What do management leaders do when they lead?* Elicit: Achieve task objectives, Maintain group morale, Fulfill personal needs Write on FC
Check list	Point out that each of these three functions separately involve planning, organizing and evaluating. Hand out check list for assessing how well each function achieved. Explain list.
55 minutes	
60 minutes	REVIEW
Class break for coffee	
90 minutes	
Consolidation Film	Tell class they are going to watch a 20-minute film. May take notes. After film has ended, they are to rate the effectiveness of the chairperson as a leader, using checklist. Show film, *"Effective business meetings"* Each trainee completes observation sheet.
120 minutes	
1st Group work	Divide class into groups of 5 trainees. Each group has own flip chart and pens. Get group to appoint chairperson, who will later make presentation to class on group findings using flip chart. *Task:* Each group is to reach a consensus on the effectiveness of the film chairperson, using rating sheet. In their discussions they must *speak to data*. They have one hour.
180 minutes	
Class presentations	Each group makes presentation to class on findings.
200 minutes	Point out differences and similarities of the presentations.
205 minutes	REVIEW
2nd Group work	Reform the same groups. Distribute second set of rating charts. *Task:* Each group is to rate the effectiveness of their own chairperson during discussions and presentation.
230 minutes	
Debrief	Debrief class. Summarize major learning points in the context of the functions of a managerial leader *and* the qualities of a natural leader. Highlight the positive side of the evaluation.
	Any questions? *Reference:* A primer o leadership for managers. Write on FC
240 minutes	*Next lesson:* How to carry out an evaluation of an employee

5. Functions of a management leader:
   a. Achieve task objectives
   b. Maintain group morale
   c. Fulfill personal needs

6. *Reference:* Brown, L. (1979). *A primer of leadership for managers*, pp. –25.

FIGURE 4:11. Lesson Preparation Sheet.

LESSON PREPARATION SHEET

Title: Turbine lubrication system

Type of class: Maintenance engineers (12th week)
Previous knowledge: Elementary
Time available: 45 minutes
Equipment required: Chalkboard, colored chalk, drawing of Faris HT lubrication system

Aim: To understand lubrication systems
Objectives: 1. State two purposes of lubrication system.
2. State functions of filters, oil cooler, relief valves, and pressure gauge in the system.
3. Draw a simple schematic of a lubrication system.
4. Apply the organizing principle behind a simple lubrication system to an appreciation of the specific Faris HT system.

KEYWORD	TREATMENT	LESSON SUMMARY
Introduction Interest Relevance	Stress importance of efficiency. Safety. Tell anecdote of seized turbine. Cost in lost production. *Your life depends on design and efficiency of lubrication system.* Write on chalkboard. Hand out objectives sheet to class. Class to copy Chalkboard Summary as built up.	*Simple Lubrication System*
3 minutes elapsed.		
Development Friction	Q. *What occurs when metal rubs against metal?* Elicit: heat, wear	1. *Purpose of lubrication system:* a. Reduces wear b. Cools
	Q. *How can wear and heat in the bearings of a system be reduced?* Elicit: lubrication system Write on chalkboard (CBS).	2. *Basic lubrication system*
6 minutes	Explain objective is to supply lubricating oil to the turbine bearings.	Draw on Chalkboard Summary (CBS)
Oil Supply	Q. *Where should the oil be stored?* Elicit: lube oil reservoir	
	Q. *How will the oil be delivered from the reservoir to the turbine?* Elicit: oil supply line Explain wish to reuse oil.	Draw on CBS
	Q. *How will the oil be delivered back to the reservoir?*	Draw on CBS
9 minutes	Elicit: return or scavenge line	
Oil pump	Q. *Since gravity is not enough to ensure adequate lubrication of the bearings, what must be added to the system?* Elicit: oil pump	Draw on CBS
	Q. *Where should it be placed?* Elicit: on supply line, after reservoir	Add: pump on CBS, label
12 minutes		
Filters	Oil reduces wear. Dirt acts as an abrasive agent. Q. *What must be the quality of oil?* Elicit: clean Q. *How can the oil in the system be cleaned?* Elicit: filters	

Q. *Where will most of the dirt enter the oil system?*
Elicit: reservoir turbine
Q. *Where should the filters be located?*
Elicit: after reservoir, before pump
after reservoir, after oil pump
after pump, before turbine

Add:
strainer filter,
supply filter
and return
filter to CBS,
and label

14 minutes

Oil cooler
Explain affect of heat on the base soap in oil. Cracking. Loss of lubricating properties.
Q. *Where is the most obvious source of heat in the system?*
Elicit: turbine
Q. *What can be added to the system to cool the oil?*
Elicit: oil cooler
Q. *Where is the best location for the oil cooler?*
Elicit: on return line, before reservoir

Add: oil cooler to CBS,
label

17 minutes

20 minutes
Recap using CBS diagram.

Relief valves
Explain danger of pressure build-up in lubrication system.
Q. *What should be added to the system to reduce the probability of a pressure build-up?*
Elicit: pressure relief valve
Q. *Where should the pressure relief valves be located?*
Elicit: on supply side of turbine on oil reservoir

Add:
pressure relief
valves to CBS and la-
bel

23 minutes

Pressure gauge
Explain need of control room to monitor system. Oil flowing, etc.
Q. *What instrument should be placed in the control room so that control room can monitor lubrication flow?*
Elicit: pressure gauge
Q. *Where should the gauge be located?*
Elicit: on supply line after oil pump, and supply filter

Add:
pressure gauge to
CBS, label

26 minutes

28 minutes
Recap from CBS diagram.

Consolidation
35 minutes
Revise whole system, applying to drawing of specific Faris HT system.
Erase labels on CBS diagram. Check names of parts. Check understanding of functions.
Q. *How soon would the control room know that there was a fractured return line?*
Elicit: after oil reservoir empty
Q. *Can the system shown be drained?*
Elicit: no, need drain at base of reservoir

40 minutes

Any questions?
Reference: Turbine Technical Manual, Chapter 7, pages 101–111
Next Lesson: Lubricating programs

3. Reference:
Turbine Tech ical Manual, Chapter 7, pp.
101–111

Pressure Relief Valve
Oil Supply Line
Bearings
TURBINE
Return Filter
Oil Cooler
Return or Scavenge Line
Pressure Relief Valve
Lube Oil Reservoir
Supply Strainer
Filler Cap
Oil Pump
Supply Filter
Pressure Valve

The important thing is to leave nothing to chance. Planning and organization are twin skills, to the extent that instructor and teacher become both manager and operator at the same time. It is a challenging yet fulfilling responsibility.

Refer to the lesson plan before the lesson

If at all possible, it is essential to prepare for a lesson by rereading the lesson plan to familiarize yourself with it again. Although it is an obvious thing to do, it is something that is not always done. Once the lesson has started, it is extremely difficult for an instructor to refer to any document in detail. The time has passed to remind yourself of what you had in mind. Events are already underway. For this reason, it is important that the lesson be reviewed before the start of class.

Prepare the instructional setting

Most experienced instructors and teachers make it a practice to set up the room before the trainees and students arrive. If you arrive at the same time as the trainees, it is too late to do very much. Ten minutes by yourself are worth thirty minutes when other people are present.

Some of the things you will want to consider include:

- Is the climate of the room appropriate for training?
- Are the seating arrangements for the trainees appropriate to the instructional strategy?
- Is the room neat and tidy, ready for instruction?
- Are all the aids you require available and in operating order?

If you don't have everything you need, do something about it! Either change your lesson plan or obtain what you require.

Sometimes you will have to do the job of the custodian of the building. Clean the chalkboard, get rid of the rubbish, tidy up the room, replace the chairs in a neat and orderly arrangement, etc. A few people have problems doing such work. They feel it is someone else's responsibility. It probably is, but the objective is a simple one. An instructor is obliged to take all the steps necessary to see that the setting for teaching and learning is the best possible one available.

No instructor can expect to walk into a classroom, or any other instructional setting, and find it exactly as required. Just as the lesson has to be prepared, so must the instructional setting. Furthermore, it is essential that such preparation be done beforehand.

CONCLUSION

Efficient and effective lesson planning is undoubtedly one of the keys to successful instruction. The measure of a good instructor or teacher is that person's ability to get the right things done. This requires intelligence, imagination, and knowledge. But these are not enough. Steps must be taken to convert them into results.

Sound and sensitive planning is one thing. Care must also be taken to see that the lesson plan does not become a straitjacket. Spontaneity is essential. An ability to meet emerging opportunities is also necessary. For this reason, the process of planning a lesson is as important as the actual product or plan recorded on the lesson preparation sheets. Process *and* product are both part of the art and science of instruction.

Chapter 5
Instructional Settings

FOCUS

"What steps can I take to obtain an instructional setting suitable for my teaching?"

KNOWLEDGE OBJECTIVES

After carefully reading and studying this chapter, you will be able to:

1. recognize factors in the physical environment conducive to effective teaching and learning;
2. lay out and arrange instructional spaces so that they are suitable for your instructional needs;
3. select a suitable group size for different instructional tasks;
4. manage an instructional group appropriately.

ATTITUDE OBJECTIVES

After reading this chapter, the author hopes that you will:

1. value the importance of instructional settings in the teaching-learning process;
2. incorporate the principles into your teaching, so that they become characteristic of your instructional style.

Instructional settings add a further dimension to the teaching-learning process.

Instruction takes place in many settings. Some have been specially designed and constructed for the purpose. Others have not, and instructors have to make the best of what is available. Regardless of their suitability, physical facilities serve as a stage on which teaching and learning take place.

As in a play, there is a script (the lesson plan). There are also actors (people with varying skill, knowledge, and experience), as well as roles to be played (trainees, instructors, and resource people). The stage has a setting appropriate to the script (decor, furniture, layout), as well as various props (audiovisual aids, class handouts, and other special materials) to be used in the drama of teaching and learning.

Thinking of the instructional setting in these terms highlights the importance of doing the best you can with what you have. Just as a producer will change the stage setting, so must instructors and teachers influence the learning environment. A lot can be done even in the most adverse conditions.

THE PHYSICAL SETTING

The physical setting of instruction influences teaching and learning. It can help, and it can hinder. Indeed, as Keith Wadd points out, the instructional environment is a resource. It contributes to a teacher's personal power. For this reason alone, an instructor should be choosy about the way that space is planned and organized.

This task involves deciding whether the space assigned for instruction is suitable for the job. A number of factors affect this decision. Is the space suitable in terms of:

- Ease and convenience of location?
- Size and shape of the rooms?
- Climate, illumination, and acoustics?
- Availability of furniture and audiovisual aids?
- Seating and viewing patterns?
- Flexibility of arrangements?

In isolation, each one of these factors may do little to affect instruction. In combination, the effects can be considerable.

108

The important thing is to use the instructional setting as an ally. In this way, its potential can be exploited. Sometimes there may be little an instructor can do. If you know what is desirable, however, you will be able to argue for something better next time. There is no point in putting up with adverse conditions.

Even here, however, a word of caution is necessary. An ideal environment for teaching and learning is not *always* an architecturally designed, limestone clad, climate-controlled, carpeted facility isolated from the work environment.

Specially designed facilities are important, often very important. It depends upon the nature of the instructional task. Sometimes it's preferable to carry out instruction where the work will be done. If this is not possible, some sort of simulation may be necessary.

There is a basic rule of thumb. Use a setting for instruction which approximates, as far as possible, the actual setting in which most of the work will be done. Much of cooking is best learned in a kitchen. Learning how to operate the controls of an aircraft is best done in a real or simulated aircraft cockpit. Only a certain amount of information about rigging sails can be learned in a classroom.

Sometimes, teachers and instructors are used to working under "ideal" conditions, from a people point of view. It is then difficult for them to consider other alternatives. For instance, it is better to teach trainee control room operators near the control room than in a comfortable classroom.

Recently a new plant was constructed on the East Coast. It was decided that people would be trained in trailer classrooms *on* the construction site. All kinds of difficulties were presented (absence of utilities, noise, insurance, parking), but all were overcome.

The plant manager recognized the advantages of keeping training on the work site. As a result, the work people became familiar with the plant as it grew. They saw every piece of equipment put into place. They traced every pipeline as it was assembled. By the time construction was complete, they knew the plant completely. Accordingly, start-up was carried out easily and smoothly.

This is an extreme example, but it makes an important point. Instructional settings should be matched to the needs of the teaching-learning process. Sometimes formal settings are appropriate, sometimes informal ones. On some occasions, instruction should be carried on away from the work site. Sometimes room settings are appropriate, sometimes real or simulated work situations are essential. Decisions have to be made, once the alternatives have been identified.

Size and shape

Although many instructors have little to say about the size or shape of the room, it is important to know what is good and what is bad. Then, at least, you will know what is best. The size of the instructional setting is dependent upon two factors:

- The number of trainees involved.
- The instructional activities and experiences planned.

Some physical facilities keep people apart; others bring them together.

Instructional settings generally need to contain both types of space. On occasions, trainees need to work by themselves; at other times, in small or large groups. Whether or not audiovisual aids are going to be used is also important.

There are some guidelines. If media, such as a projector, is going to be used, a rule of thumb would be:

- Lecture room   12 sq.ft. per person (3.7 sq. meters)
- Conference room   20 sq.ft. per person (6.1 sq. meters)
- Instructional room   25 sq.ft. per person (7.6 sq. meters)
- Carrel for independent study   18 sq.ft. per person (5.5 sq. meters)

Most rooms, however, are much smaller than they should be. As a result, trainees are overcrowded.

The results of overcrowding are well documented. People who are aggressive tend to become more aggressive in overcrowded conditions. People who are shy and retiring withdraw into themselves. In the case of a discussion group, this situation would reduce the effectiveness of the instruction.

Shape is important from a number of points of view. The shape of the room can affect the aesthetics of the room, the nature of group interaction, acoustics, and visibility. For these reasons, rectangular rooms are preferable to most other shapes.

Ideally, the sides of a room for instructional purposes should be in the proportion of 1:1.4 (1: $\sqrt{2}$). In other words, if one side of the room is 100 feet (30.5 meters), the other side of the room should be 140 feet (42.6 meters). Rooms in the proportion of 1:1.4 can be divided into two, four, eight, etc., equal areas. Each area has the proportions of the original room.

Rectangular rooms approximating the proportions suggested above will have good visibility. Trainees and students should be able to see the instructor, as well as any flip charts, chalkboard, or screen. There is little worse than not being able to see clearly.

Climatic factors

The climate of the instructional setting is directly related to fatigue. A room that is too hot will cause the class to become sleepy. One that is too cold will cause discomfort. In either case, the efficiency and effectiveness of instruction will be affected.

From the point of view of mental activity, the best temperature is around 68°F (20°C). There is some evidence that trainees can experience a 2 percent reduction in learning efficiency for every degree above 75°F (24°C). Relative humidity, too, should be kept around 50 percent. If the humidity rises above 50 percent, the optimal temperature must be lowered.

The important point, from an instructor's point of view, is to keep instructional rooms cool and well ventilated. There is little point teaching in an overheated, stuffy environment. Opening or shutting windows and doors, turning thermostats up or down, are all within your control. Sometimes this means visiting the room well before time, so that the climate can be adjusted.

Noise

Noise, of one kind or another, is always present. Excessive noise, however, is detrimental to learning and health. In a learning environment, the objective is to be able to hear what you need to hear. Trainees should not be distracted by noise from surrounding areas.

The most significant noise in any situation is *background noise.* This is the noise produced by air conditioning, ventilation fans, distant traffic, clocks, fluorescent light ballasts, people passing by, noise from the rooms next door, etc.

Background noise is acceptable as long as it does not become distracting. Indeed, architects design instructional rooms so that background noise is present, usually around 35 decibels. If they did not do this, there would be nothing to mask the noise of trainees working. Activities like turning the page of a book, foot shuffling, someone talking in another part of the room would become distracting.

People in instructional settings become irritable when the level of background noise changes and becomes distracting. Both stress and fatigue increase. Intellectual performance deteriorates. At the same time, trainees and students work more slowly and tend to make more mistakes.

Sometimes the sounds in the room next door become suddenly annoying. Perhaps that class begins to watch a film. In such circumstances, it is important that instructors do not ignore the distraction. It might be possible to move to a new room. Maybe the volume on the projector can be reduced.

If none of these is possible, there are a number of things an instructor can do. They are:

- Increasing the level of background noise in your work room. This can be done by turning on the air conditioning, the ventilation fans, more fluorescent lights, etc. In this way, it might be possible to mask the distraction.
- Changing the planned activities in your work room. This might involve changing a planned lecture and substituting a discussion group. In this way, trainees might better be able to concentrate.

The important point is not to try to ignore distractions. It is not possible. The situation must be managed, and that means the instructor has to take some corrective action.

Levels of illumination

The lighting of instructional areas should be a matter of concern to teachers and instructors. Most instructional rooms tend to be overilluminated, rather than underilluminated. As a result, there is an increase in fatigue, to an extent that learning is affected.

Also important is the quality of the illumination and the way it is positioned. Hard shadows across table tops should be eliminated. Instead, all working surfaces should be adequately illuminated. The sources of illumination, however, should be outside the line of sight of the trainees.

All forms of glare should be avoided. They can cause fatigue and stress, as well as physiological harm. Trainees should be positioned in such a way as to shield them from reflecting surfaces. Windows, in particular, can be a problem.

Instructors who teach in machine shops should also bear in mind a special condition that occurs with moving equipment. If the shop is illuminated with fluorescent lighting, a rotation or stroboscopic effect can occur. This gives trainees a misleading impression of the motion of machines like lathes.

After a period of unpopularity in some training programs, chalkboards are beginning to reappear once again in modern instructional settings. When they are used, it is important that they be well illuminated and the surface free of glare.

An accumulation of chalk dust on the surface of the board reduces the contrast between chalk and the board surface. As a result, legibility is significantly reduced. Chalkboards, for this reason, should be kept clean. Thorough cleaning at frequent intervals will prevent a build-up of dust.

Color

The effects of color are well known. Indeed, people go to considerable lengths in their personal lives to insure that the environments in which they live are aesthetically pleasing. Color affects the mood of the room.

Some colors appear "cold," others "warm." If there is a choice, research indicates that instructors would do well to choose rooms which are painted:

- In warm colors (yellow, orange, red) for action-oriented spaces like instructional rooms and workshops.
- In cold colors (green and blue) for instructional spaces likely to be used for quiet, study activities.

Personal preferences, of course, should also be taken into account. Not all instructors would choose a red room. Similar care should be taken in the choice of incandescent and fluorescent lamps. Each type has its own color-rendering properties.

THE LAYOUT AND ARRANGEMENT OF LEARNING SPACES

Many of the physical characteristics of instructional settings may be outside the control of instructors. There is, though, always some room to maneuver. In the case of furniture layout, instructors have many more degrees of freedom. They can arrange the room pretty much as they please.

Room layout

Some teachers unthinkingly accept a room as it is from a previous occupant. However, it is very important to decide beforehand what type of layout is appropriate to your objectives. You can then set about getting it. If you can't set up the room in advance, you should have no compunction about using trainees to help you arrange the room before you begin the lesson.

Instructional spaces can be laid out in two broad ways. The furniture can be arranged in a :

- *Formal manner*
  In this case, chairs might be arranged in:
  - Regular rows facing the front of the room, where there would be a chalkboard or flip chart, and perhaps a projector screen and podium. Such an arrangement would be appropriate for a lecture, conference presentation, or formal type of lesson.
  - Regular fashion around a large conference table. In such a case, the chairs would be positioned so that they face the head of the table. Such an arrangement would be appropriate for a lecture, formal meeting, presentation, etc.

- *Informal manner*
  In this case, chairs might be arranged in:
  - Clusters, with perhaps six trainees to each table. Such an arrangement would be appropriate for discussion groups. In the case of seminars, games, case studies, workshops, and committees, work tables are usu-ally larger, and capable of seating up to twelve trainees.
  - Clusters without tables. In the case of tutorials, there might be only two or three chairs. If there is a demonstration, the chairs would be grouped around a table or bench, or even a piece of equipment or TV.
  - Circles of chairs, without tables. Such an arrangement would be appro-priate for discussion groups and case studies. The closer the chairs, the greater the amount of interaction among the trainees in the group.

There are many possible arrangements, and the patterns mentioned above are merely some of the options available.

The most important thing is to use rooms which have easily moved furniture. It is not just a case of setting the room up once during a period of instruction. Sometimes you will want the trainees to go into small groups after you have made a presentation. In such circumstances, more than one arrangement may be necessary during the lesson.

Participation and seating positions

Participation in both large and small groups seems to be strongly affected by location. Trainees and students in the front row of the classroom, and in the center block of the room, tend to participate more than those seated elsewhere. Figure 5:1 illustrates the zone of greatest interaction in a formal situation. The same effect is discernible in more informal settings.

It will be seen that it has the form of a triangle. Students and trainees seated within the triangle are much more likely to participate in a lesson. This probably occurs because people seated in the triangle have easier eye contact with the instructor.

FIGURE 5:1. **Triangle of greatest interaction in the instructional room.**

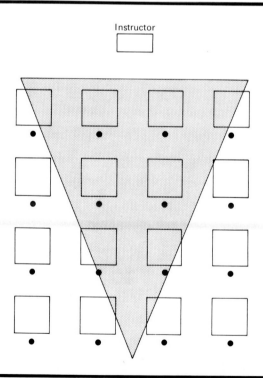

This effect can be made use of by an instructor. Shy and retiring trainees can be seated within the triangle, so as to facilitate their involvement in the lesson. The more extroverted and talkative ones, on the other hand, can be seated outside it, so as to lessen their participation.

Where trainees sit is a matter of concern to instructors and teachers. It is a matter, at least at the beginning of training, that should be decided by the instructor-manager. There is no point in leaving it to chance.

Some people argue that trainees should be seated on an alphabetical basis. They point out that such an arrangement is fair, and easily implemented. It also allows spare seats to be used as buffers. In this way, groups can be separated, and so made more cohesive. Another advantage of this method of allocating places is that the teacher is seen exercising the role of manager.

Whatever the method used, once a place has been allocated, the chair becomes that person's territory. Investigations show that people will rigidly maintain a preference for a particular chair. The preference is maintained in the face of considerable physical discomfort. People like their own seat, and like to keep it.

Alan Lipman, for instance, has found that on sunny days, when certain seats become highly undesirable because of the heat and glare, people will refuse to move. Discomfort is preferable. Chair ownership is important, and deep emotions surface when trainees are moved from one location to another in the same room.

In informal instructional settings, participation within small groups is affected by the placing of chairs. The results of research, conducted by Robert Sommer, are indicated in Figure 5:2. Black circles represent selected positions, and open circles represent empty chairs.

In summary, it will be seen that people in small groups prefer:

- Corner to corner and face to face seating positions for casual type interactions.
- Corner to end and face to face seating positions for competitive type interactions.
- Side by side seating positions for cooperative types of interaction.

It has also been shown that these positions affect the *quality* of the participation. One final point is of interest to instructors. When people are crowded around the table, they become more friendly and talkative. When people are widely spaced, there is a more formal atmosphere in this group, and less trainee participation in the instruction.

Leadership patterns

Seating arrangements affect not only interaction in small groups but also patterns of leadership. It is a common experience, of course, that the person who sits at the head of a table tends to occupy the leadership role in group discussions. Sometimes it is the instructor; sometimes a trainee.

FIGURE 5:2. Patterns of participation in small groups.

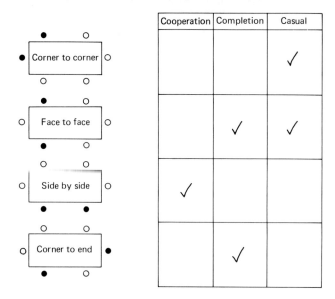

If no one sits at the head of the table, another effect appears. Someone sitting on the side of the table with the fewest number of trainees is likely to take on the leadership of the discussion.

For instance, suppose you have organized a group so that there are three trainees sitting on one side of the table and five on the other. Someone on the side of the table with three trainees is most likely to take over the leadership role.

Such a finding is of practical significance to instructors and teachers. It means that shy and retiring people can be seated in positions that increase their chances of becoming discussion leaders. On the other hand, talkative, dominant people can be seated in other locations. Things don't have to be left to chance.

SELECTING AN APPROPRIATE GROUP SIZE

A common question among trainers and educators is "What is the best size of group for instruction?" Unfortunately, there is no one simple answer. It all depends upon the circumstances of the situation. Nevertheless, most people do have some rather strong opinions about the best group size. People seem to feel that instructional groups tend to be too large.

Generally speaking, small groups are more effective than large ones. In small groups:

- *Learners experience:*
  - A greater sense of recognition as individuals.
  - Greater personal satisfaction and morale.
  - Increased feelings of achievement and progress toward a goal.
  - A more accurate knowledge of results.
  - Increased feelings of cooperation and friendliness.
- *Instructors experience:*
  - Greater personal satisfaction and morale.
  - Increased opportunities to help learners on an individual basis.
  - Greater opportunities to get to know learners as people.
  - Increased opportunities to manage an instructional situation in an efficient and effective manner.

Almost all of these experiences are connected with feelings, attitudes, and values. Others are associated with problems of management and interpersonal relationships.

The relationship between the size of an instructional group and achievement is illustrated in Figure 5:3. It will be seen that a significant change occurs when groups are larger than twenty. In general, as far as achievement is concerned, the Glass-Smith research indicates that:

- In groups larger than twenty, the number of learners in the group does not significantly affect achievement. (Increasing size may, of course, affect attitudes and morale).
- In groups between ten and twenty, increasing the number of learners beyond ten affects achievement.

FIGURE 5:3.   The relationship between group size and achievement, according to the Glass-Smith curve.   (Adapted from *Phi Delta Kappan*, February 1979)

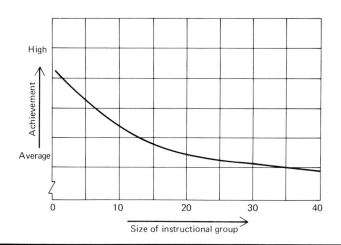

- In groups between one and ten, increasing the number of learners beyond one dramatically affects achievement.

Thus, the size of an instructional group does affect learning. Smaller groups are more efficient than larger ones.

In selecting optimal group sizes, however, a *number* of factors need to be considered. Achievement is one, but there are also such additional factors as:

- The nature of the learning task. Skills and attitudes, for instance, are better acquired in smaller groups than informational type tasks.
- The individual needs of the learners. If there is a degree of anxiety, smaller groups are better. If the group is widely diverse in knowledge, skills, and experience, a small instructional group is optimal.
- The instructional method involved. Tutorials, discussion groups should be small. Lectures can be given to very large groups.

Additional factors, of course, are the resources and time available. If people have to be trained in, say, a crash program on the company's response to increasing inflation or over large inventories, then large groups are inevitable.

As far as instructional methods are concerned, the usual rule of thumb is:

Large group lectures	40 + people
Lectures	10 to 40 people
Lessons	5 to 15 people
Demonstrations	3 to 10 people
Discussion groups	3 to 7 people
Tutorials	1 to 3 people

From an overall point of view, it is best for group size to be limited to less than ten.

If the learners require a great deal of individual attention, the size of the instructional group should be smaller rather than larger. Beginning and advanced trainees can cope with larger groups better than trainees who have progressed beyond the basic phases of training. Older trainees benefit from smaller groups, as do people who have a dependent rather than independent personality.

The nature of the objectives to be realized also affects the choice of group size. Three generalizations can be made:

- Larger groups are not inferior to smaller ones if learning objectives involve the acquisition of facts and basic information.
- Smaller groups are essential if learning objectives involve higher order learning like application, understanding, evaluation, and decision-making.
- Very small groups are essential if learning objectives involve the acquisition of skills and critical thinking.

However, regardless of every factor, both instructors and learners generally prefer smaller to larger instructional groups.

MANAGING THE INSTRUCTIONAL GROUP

Once the lesson has begun, there are still a number of things to be done. Any one of these can affect the atmosphere of the instructional setting, and so facilitate learning. For one thing, it is very important that the instructor and the trainees get acquainted. This is an essential ice-breaking activity.

Getting acquainted

People are always curious about others in the class. Who are they? Why are they here? What do they hope to get out of it? These are all reasonable questions. They are also natural ones. Giving the trainees an opportunity to answer them is an excellent way of getting them involved right from the start of the first lesson.

Name cards and name tags are useful. There is nothing like hearing a name and then also seeing it! Placecards on the tables where people sit serve a double function. They mean that trainees will sit where you want them to sit. In other words, you are managing the situation right from the start of instruction. They also allow trainees to address each other by name.

Placecards can also be used to insure that people from the same company, unit, or department are separated. This prevents people from pairing off together. Pairing can be destructive to class atmosphere. It encourages the formation of cliques.

The simplest and most effective way of getting acquainted is to begin the first lesson with introductions. Simply ask the trainees, in turn, to introduce themselves. Ask them to give their name, where they are from, something of their background, and what they hope to get out of training. Remember, as instructor, to include yourself in this activity.

Setting the stage for instruction

Once introductions are complete, it is important to set the stage. People want to know what is expected of them, and what they will be doing. There is always some anxiety in the first lesson, particularly if they have never met the instructor before.

For this reason, it is essential to put trainees at their ease and to eliminate some of their worries and anxieties. One way of doing this is to "walk" them through the course. Using the timetable and the objectives, simply go over what they will be doing. Point out any special assignments or projects. Indicate when they are due, and how they will be assessed.

It is also important to deal with housekeeping matters. Tell them starting times, finishing times, meal times, and coffee breaks. If it is a residential course, let them know the time the last session will end so that they can confirm their travel arrangements. Mention whether casual clothing can be worn to class.

Finally, as part of setting the stage, arouse the interest of trainees by establishing a need to learn. Point out the relevance of the course and what they will be taking away from it, how mastery will help them in their jobs or tasks.

If it is applicable, point out that what they will learn from the course will be of value to them in their personal lives. If the course is on effective listening, for instance, point out that they will learn something that will make them better spouses and parents.

Remembering trainee names

Some people have no trouble at all learning the names of trainees and students. Others have great difficulty. Yet, regardless of the effort involved, it is most important that instructors learn them, and learn them quickly.

As Dale Carnegie points out, one's name is one of the sweetest and most important sounds in any language. Name cards, name tags, and placecards will all help. Seeing the student, and the student's name, is another positive step toward learning. But when there are twenty or more students, it is still very difficult.

George Bell, a specialist in such matters, offers some practical advice. He suggests that instructors and teachers:

- Pay particular attention to the name when it is given.
- Repeat the name immediately after the trainee gives it. (Bell says that this will increase recall by 30%.)
- Use the name as soon as possible after it has been given.
- Observe the face of the trainee when the name is given. (In this way, name and face will be associated.)
- Try and get a mental picture of the face with a name card behind it. (An active image is important to recall.)

Of course, some names are easier to remember than others. However, much can be done by arriving at class early and talking to the trainees as they come in.

Looking for trouble signs

Not all trainees and students are able to have trouble-free learning. For this reason, be on the lookout for signs that all is not well. In this way, instructors may be able to deal with problems before they take hold.

Observe the behavior of trainees, and listen attentively to them. There are all kinds of signs to look out for, most connected with their body language.

Among the major indicators are:

- Trainees who are not attentive or are daydreaming.
- Trainees who are withdrawn, negative, or hostile.
- Trainees who are bored, uninterested, and tired.
- Trainees who are anxious or critical.
- Trainees who attempt to dominate or take over the class.
- Trainees who talk too much, or talk too little.

Any or all of these symptoms indicate that something is wrong. There are explanations for such behavior. Some of them concern the trainees, some the instruction, and some the environment.

A number of remedies are immediately possible. The important thing is to act fast. Some of the things you might consider include:

- Is the climate of the room conducive to learning or to fatigue?
- Is the material relevant? How can I make it relevant?
- Does the instructional method involve too much listening and not enough doing? Should I change it?
- Do they already know this material or skill?
- How can I use class activity to involve the troublemakers, the shy, the uninterested?
- How can I demonstrate the importance of mastering this task?

As with all matters, flexibility is essential. If things are not going well in class, something must be done to turn the situation around.

Dealing with classroom problems

In the majority of instructional situations, there will be few disciplinary problems. Trainees may get restless, they may get bored, but it is rare for them to become disorderly in the classroom. Nevertheless, it is well to be prepared.

Quite recently, much the same point was made by a training supervisor at a national conference. He went on to claim that adults were far more interested in applying training than in sabotaging it. Very quietly, the person next to him got to her feet and pointed out that her neighbor was indeed fortunate. She worked in another industry, and she had not been so lucky.

The word "discipline" in an instructional setting often implies punishment. To others, it involves good supervision. However it is defined, it revolves around respect for others, as well as for oneself. It implies a respect for reasonable rules, for the property of others, and for the needs of other people.

Discipline assumes reasonable and mature behavior. In the classroom and workshop, it is essential, just as it is in the workplace. Learning and effort are possible only in a disciplined instructional environment.

In a survey of trainees and students, it was found that some teachers and instructors had few disciplinary problems. Others had a great many. When the two groups were compared, it was found that instructors who had the fewest problems shared a particular set of characteristics.

Instructors and teachers had few disciplinary problems if they:

- Interpreted and enforced the rules fairly.
- Knew their subject, and were up to date with current practice.
- Knew the needs of their trainees and students.
- Felt secure in their relationships with trainees.
- Were sincerely interested in people and instruction.
- Behaved in a professional manner as instructors.
- Used persuasion, reason and good interpersonal relationships as the foundation of their leadership style in the classroom.

In other words, successful teachers and instructors were fair, consistent, and competent in their dealings with people. An overbearing use of authority and coercion must be avoided.

Good lesson planning will reduce the probability of behavioral problems. So will group activity and participation. Students and trainees who are occupied and working hard have little opportunity to become a problem. Bored trainees will simply find their own way to get rid of their boredom, and rowdiness is one result.

Figure 5:4 sets out some of the principles important to room management. Embarrassing trainees, ridiculing them and using sarcasm as a means of en-

FIGURE 5:4. Principles of training room control and management.

Reduce the likelihood of disciplinary problems by:
- Thorough lesson preparation.
- Thorough preparation of the instructional setting.
- Making expectations clear to trainees.
- Making certain that instruction is relevant.
- Keeping trainees actively involved.
- Being flexible, and heading off trouble.

Deal with disciplinary problems by:
- Keeping cool, calm, and collected in manner and voice.
- Decide whether or not to ignore what has happened.
- Help trainees to get out of trouble when it occurs.
- Don't overreact. Don't rush; act slowly.
- Keep a sense of proportion.
- Reduce tension and anxiety with humor.
- Help trainees save face.
- Censor the act, not the person.
- Allow trainees to cool off.
- Move physically in the direction of trouble.

forcing discipline, should be avoided. Humiliating trainees is counterproductive. It creates a chain of problems that is difficult to break.

Handle disciplinary problems in a slow, calm, and controlled way. Keep your voice low; do not raise it. Move to where the problem is occurring; this will do a great deal to help. Above all, act as a manager. Gain control of the situation as soon as possible. Don't allow things to go from bad to worse.

CONCLUSION

Preparing the instructional setting is an important activity. There is no point in carefully preparing a lesson and then rushing into a classroom. Instructional space, like the lesson, must also be carefully planned and organized. Teaching and learning depend upon a well prepared stage. Script, people, roles, setting, and props must all be ready.

Preparing the instructional setting, however, involves much more than good housekeeping. The right setting has to be chosen, bearing in mind objectives, trainees, and the activities they will be carrying out. Furniture and audiovisual aids must also be arranged for the patterns of participation that you have in mind.

Finally, there is a whole set of activities concerned with getting acquainted and ice-breaking. Remembering the names of students and trainees is an important part of those activities. Although disciplinary problems are relatively rare with adult trainees, some thought needs to be given to how a situation should be managed. Being prepared is another way of making certain that problems will be avoided.

Part Two
Tactics of Instruction

Tactics are the cutting edge of strategy.

Instructional strategies are concerned with the larger issues of teaching and learning. Tactics, on the other hand, are concerned with the detail. Strategies answer the question "*What* should we do?" Tactics answer the question "*How* can we do it?"

All tactics are linked to objectives. They are the starting point and the yardstick by which success will be measured. Tactics, however, are also concerned with the behavior of instructors and trainees in teaching-learning situations.

For this reason, tactics can range from mundane to highly responsible activities. They involve everything from how to write objectives to audiovisual aids. Despite their range and variety, tactics serve the same objective. Without them nothing would get done.

In Part Two, a number of themes are examined. Each is important to teaching and learning. They include:

- Needs, objectives, and commitment.
- Verbal and nonverbal communication.
- Question techniques.
- Lesson summaries.
- Audiovisual aids.

- Note-taking and class handouts.
- Assessment techniques.

These tactics are at the "cutting edge" of instruction. There are others, but these are the most important.

Strategy gives them purpose, and supplies order to them. Order, however, is meaningless unless there is some larger purpose. In the context of instruction, that larger purpose is concerned with efficient and effective performance in real life situations. Above all, that purpose involves *worthy* performance, which is largely error free.

Instructional skill is not founded on the belief that there is "one best way." Rather it is based on a sensitive awareness of the possibilities. Rules and guidelines are useful, as long as they do not, by themselves, determine action.

What is important is how an instructor or teacher uses rules. Some people are dictated to by rules, and fall into the ruts made by others. Other people use rules to indicate a way, although they may not choose to follow it. The craft of instruction depends upon skill and judgment, just as much as it depends upon order and purpose.

Chapter 6
Needs, Objectives, and Commitment

FOCUS
"What is the role of objectives in the instructional process?"

KNOWLEDGE OBJECTIVES
After carefully reading and studying this chapter, you will be able to:
1. carry out a needs assessment, with a view to identifying a need that can be filled by instruction;
2. identify general and specific objectives, and express them in a clear manner;
3. take steps to obtain management and trainee commitment to the objectives, as well as their active cooperation;
4. determine whether "reality training" is appropriate to the situation with which you are dealing.

ATTITUDE OBJECTIVES
After reading this chapter, the author hopes that you will:
1. value the importance of needs analysis, objectives, obtaining commitment, and reality training in the teaching-learning process;
2. incorporate these principles into your teaching, so that they become characteristic of your instructional style.

Objectives spring from needs.

Teaching and instructing involve meeting the needs of students and trainees. If a lesson fails to meet a learning need, then poor decisions have been made along the way. Time and resources have been wasted. Instructors and trainees have misplaced their effort.

Assessing the need for teaching and learning, therefore, is a key task involving considerable responsibility. It is an essential step in the planning process, which involves identifying needs, setting priorities, and selecting strategies. What? How? When? These are the fundamental questions that must be answered before any instruction can realistically take place.

CARRYING OUT A NEEDS ASSESSMENT

Needs assessment is the basis from which all instruction and learning spring. It involves identifying gaps or deficiencies in everyday performance. If there is a deficiency, there is a need. If there is no deficiency, there is no need to be met. Training is unnecessary.

Steps involved

The procedure itself is not a difficult one, although a mystique has grown up around it. A needs assessment entails:

- Identifying deficiencies in people's performance.
- Determining the costs involved in:
  - Meeting the deficiency.
  - Not meeting the deficiency.
- Deciding which deficiencies to meet, and which to ignore.
- Listing the deficiencies to be met in order of priority.

Deciding upon an appropriate solution is not part of needs assessment. It is part of lesson planning. Nevertheless, a common mistake is to confuse a deficiency with a solution.

Suppose a group of first line supervisors in a key area of a plant are able to deal with all situations except one. They cannot handle aggressive behavior in their work people. When people are cooperative, there are no deficiencies in their supervisory skills.

In crisis situations, however, effective supervision is essential. Crisis situations are also the occasions when aggressive behavior is most likely to occur.

128

The discrepancy between what the supervisors can do (handle cooperative people) and what they cannot do (not handle aggressive people) identifies a learning need. The solution probably involves a short course in assertiveness training, with a lesson or module on supervision in crisis situations.

Identifying a deficiency

A deficiency in people's performance can be identified by asking three questions:

- What must people be able to do?
- What can they do already?
- What can't they do?

In other words, in the context of a specific job is there a gap between what people can do and what they can't do? The supervisors, in the example discussed above, were unable to handle aggressive behavior in crisis situations.

A straightforward way of carrying out an analysis is to make a chart. This should set out what needs to be done. Once such a list has been made, two columns can be used to indicate what people can and cannot do. Figure 6:1 shows a need deficiency chart for people involved in an aspect of industrial engineering, referred to outside the United States as work study.

It will be seen that people in the example can do seven of the ten activities involved in this area of industrial engineering. They are competent procedurally. However, they are unable to carry out three higher level tasks involving aspects of decision-making.

These three areas represent gaps or deficiencies in skill. What now remains to be determined is whether the deficiencies are worth filling. Perhaps it would

FIGURE 6:1. Deficiency chart for industrial engineering.

Responsibilities	Can do	Can't do
1. Select the job to be studied	X	
2. Record details of the present method	X	
3. Examine the details critically		X
4. Develop the best method of doing the job		X
5. Measure the quantity of work	X	
6. Calculate a standard time for the improved method	X	
7. Define the new method and time standard	X	
8. Install the improved method	X	
9. Maintain the improved method	X	
10. Evaluate the success of the project		X

be better to use the people for low level duties. A few highly skilled people could be employed to do the more demanding work. Perhaps it would be better to train everyone in both procedural and decision-making responsibilities. A choice must be made, depending upon the benefits and the costs involved.

Making an inventory of the task or job

In order to determine whether or not people are deficient in knowledge, skills, or attitude, the task or job that they are going to do has to be examined. This entails finding out:

- *The purpose of the task*
- What has to be done? (The aim) Why?
- Who has to do it? (The person) Why?

- *The activities involved*
- How is it done? (The means) Why?
- When is it done? (The sequence) Why?
- Where is it done? (The place) Why?
- What level of skill? (The standard) Why?

Analyzing jobs or tasks in this way is a highly systematic activity, calling for a great deal of time and effort. Once it has been carried out, there is a base of concrete information upon which decisions can be made. Without it there is only speculation.

Continually asking the question "Why?" insures that nothing is taken for granted. In this way, alternatives can be considered and unnecessary activities eliminated. For example, the fact that something is *always* done first needs to be challenged. There may be a good reason, there may not be. Everyday practices need to be justified; nothing should be taken for granted.

Analyzing tasks and jobs is really nothing more than making an inventory of essential knowledge, skills, and attitudes. For instance, an analysis of the task of reading and interpreting financial statements would identify an inventory of three broad classes of activity: working with balance sheets, income statements, and funds statements.

Each one of these activities can be analyzed further. The balance sheet, for example, can be broken out into: working capital, nonrecurrent assets, current liabilities, long-term liabilities, and owner's equity. Current liabilities, in turn, can be broken down into an inventory of: working with accounts payable, notes payable, cash dividends payable, accrued liabilities, and revenues collected in advance. Each one of these can be broken down further. When this is completed you have an analysis of what is involved in reading and interpreting financial statements. This analysis can then serve as a basis for needs assessment.

Sources of information for deficiencies

Once an inventory of the task or job has been obtained, it is time to start collecting information about the trainees' knowledge, skills, and attitudes. Deficiencies or gaps are likely to be found in any number of places. These include gaps in "What?" "Who?" "How?" "When?" "Where?" and "Which?" as well as in the "Why's?"

Some of the information about what people can and cannot do will come from:

- *Observation*
  The easiest and most direct way of finding out what people can and cannot do is to observe them at work. This can be done under either real or simulated conditions. The task inventory should be used as a checklist, as illustrated in Figure 6:1.

- *Critical incidents*
  This method focuses upon collecting information on key tasks, particularly those where problems occur. Data on bottlenecks, poor quality, excessive waste, down time, productivity, highly fatiguing work, excessive overtime, poor layout, excessive absenteeism and sickness, accident rates, errors, lack of cleanliness and good housekeeping, etc., will help signal deficiencies in performance.

- *Interviews*
  Individual or group interviews with the trainees and their supervisors will also help to pinpoint gaps in performance. Often interviewing four or five people is enough, since the process is a time-consuming one. Surveys and questionnaires can be used as a substitute for face to face interviews.

- *Employment and training data*
  A great deal of information is often available. This includes data from: annual assessments, test scores, training and education courses completed, management by objectives records, as well as personal data on previous experience, special abilities, education levels, etc.

As with all information gathering, it is important to use your imagination. There is a great deal of information available, if people have the eyes to see it.

Identifying a learning need

When a deficiency has been identified, it is time to decide whether it represents a learning need. It might be too trivial to justify doing anything about it. Alternatively, the deficiency might be more easily overcome by redesigning or eliminating the task or job.

In order to determine whether the deficiency is important, certain costs and benefits need to be considered. Although costs and benefits are usually reduced to dollars and cents, other terms can be used. They include: safety, lost business opportunities, increased inventory, time in training, possibilities for professional growth, reduced labor turnover and absenteeism, increased productivity, convenience, etc.

The process of identifying a learning need is best carried out in a systematic manner. In order to do this, identify the costs involved in:

- Meeting a deficiency in people's performance.
- Not meeting a deficiency in their performance.

Sometimes, there will be disagreements over the costs involved. These occur because people have different values or attitudes to a situation. Sometimes the disagreement arises because there is not enough information available.

If the problem is one of different attitudes or values, it is best put aside for a moment. It is more productive to get on with the task by collecting additional information. Alternatively, ask for advice from more people. Difficulties will then usually solve themselves.

What was initially seen as a problem sometimes becomes, after further discussion, a symptom of a bigger problem. For instance, absenteeism and high labor turnover may be seen as two separate problems. They may, on the other hand, be symptoms of poor training or poor supervision.

An example of a cost analysis is illustrated in Figure 6:2. In this particular example dollar figures are not employed.
Instead, weightings of "high," "medium," and "low" are used. More specific terms can be employed when necessary.

FIGURE 6:2.   Cost analysis of deficiency in oiling and lubricating equipment in the Crosskeys plant.

Costs to . . .	If deficiency removed	If deficiency not removed
1. Production rate	Low	High
2. Scrap rate	Low	Low
3. Time to do job	Low	Medium
4. Damage to material or equipment	Low	Very high
5. Machine down time	Low	High
6. Absenteeism	Low	Low
7. Labor turnover	Low	Low
8. Sales	Low	High
9. Running costs	Low	High
10. After sales costs	Low	Low

In the case of the example, there is clear evidence that it is worth removing the deficiency in oiling and lubrication procedures at the Crosskey plant. If the deficiency is not removed, the costs to production, damage of equipment, machine down time, sales, and running costs are high.

Not only is there a need, but it is a need that must be filled. The deficiency in oiling and lubrication at the Crosskeys plant cannot be ignored.

Sometimes more than one learning need will be identified. When this happens, it is important to have some method of sorting out high-priority items from low-priority ones. One way of doing this is through the "A," "B," and "C" classification described in Chapter One. Priority can be given, then, to those needs that are important and most urgent.

IDENTIFYING LEARNING OBJECTIVES

Once a need that is worth filling has been established, it should be described as an objective to be realized. Most teachers and instructors agree that identifying objectives is the most critical step in instructional technique.

It assures that teaching is both relevant and responsive to a felt need. In fact, objectives justify teaching and learning. Without clear objectives, instructors and trainees have no map by which they can plan their activities. Objectives, at one point, define the instructional strategy. At another, they are a tactic within it.

The role of objectives

An objective is a statement of what learners will be able to do at the end of a training or education program. Since objectives describe a learning need, they should be written from the point of view of the learner, and not from that of an instructor. They are learning-oriented, not teaching-oriented.

Objectives should be written so that they serve as a:

- Guide to learning.
- Guide to instruction.
- Guide to evaluation.

In this sense, they are an important part of the decision-making process. Since they directly reflect needs that must be filled, objectives serve to light the way to desired performance. Such performance may involve knowledge, skill, or attitudes.

In some ways, objectives identify a destination or goal to be reached. Another way of looking at them is to think of objectives as a target on which to concentrate attention and energy. As soon as one challenge has been met, another one emerges.

Writing general objectives

Since objectives play such an important role, it is essential that they be written in a clear manner. If there is any doubt about what an objective means or implies, teaching and learning will be adversely affected. Clarity is the name of the game.

For this reason, great emphasis is placed upon the verb that is used. Verbs like "to understand," "to learn," "to analyze," and "to test" are ambiguous. They are all right for an aim, but not for the more specific objective. So are verbs like "to discover," "to think," and "to solve." They can be interpreted in a number of different ways.

In fact, such verbs are best avoided. See Figure 6:3. It is better to use a verb that exactly identifies what you want the trainee to do. These are called action verbs. They describe the acts that people will be able to do at the end of training. Action verbs include "to mark," "to name," "to install," "to fix," "to fill out," "to place," "to remove," "to ask," etc. They are clear.

The verb is an important part of an objective, because it identifies part of the performance component of a well written statement. A general objective, at the very least, should identify two things:

- *The desired behavior.* This is a statement of what you want the trainees to be able to do, e.g., "to meet."
- *The content of the task.* This is the subject matter or the object that the behavior affects, e.g., "production schedules."

These two things describe the behavior that you want the trainee to achieve. In the case of the example, the objective is "to meet production schedules." If an attitude is involved, the objective might be "to value meeting production schedules."

FIGURE 6:3. Verbs to avoid and verbs to use.

Vague verbs	Precise verbs
to understand	to mark
to learn	to name
to analyze	to install
to test	to fix
to discover	to place
to think	to move
to solve	to fill out
to determine	to ask
to conclude	to check
to infer	to label
to enjoy	to state
to grasp	to say
to develop	to draw
to deal with	to decide

FIGURE 6:4.   The two essential parts of a general objective.

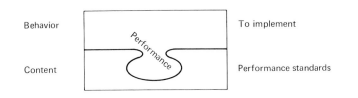

The two parts of the objective are fitted together, as in a jigsaw. (See Figure 6:4.) When this is done the performance required of the trainees is clearly identified. Once mastery has been achieved, the gap or discrepancy will have been filled. The need will have been met.

Usually, objectives are written in lists, numbered for easy reference. This is the method used at the beginning of this chapter. If more than about five objectives are involved, it is useful to draw a chart showing relationships between them.

An example is shown in Figure 6:5 for a lesson on Maslow's Hierarchy of Human Needs. The aim of the lesson is to understand the hierarchy. It will be seen that behavior is listed across the top of the chart, in the form of action verbs.

FIGURE 6:5.   Objectives chart for a lesson on Maslow's Hierarchy of Human Needs.

Content	Recalls	Applies	Recognizes	Appreciates	Evaluates	Accepts	Values	Identifies with
Human nature	A	B	B	C	B	C	A	—
Human needs	A	B	A	C	B	C	B	C
Hierarchy	A	A	B	B	A	C	C	—
Physiological needs	A	B	B	C	C	C	C	—
Safety needs	A	B	B	C	C	C	C	—
Social needs	A	B	B	C	C	C	C	—
Self-esteem needs	A	B	B	C	C	C	C	—
Self-actualization	A	B	B	C	C	C	C	—
Satisfaction of needs	B	B	A	C	C	C	C	—
Usefulness of hierarchy	A	C	A	B	A	C	C	—
Problems of hierarchy	A	C	A	B	A	C	C	—

"A" items are of great importance
"B" items are of moderate importance
"C" items are of little importance
— items not mentioned

Down the side of the chart will be found the content, in the form of key teaching points. In each cell of the chart, where content and behavior intersect, are letters which indicate the emphasis given to each of the objectives. For this purpose, the ABC classification is again employed.

Charting out objectives in this manner has advantages for both trainees and instructors. Trainees are able to see what the objectives are, and the emphases being given them. The chart, in effect, gives students a great deal of guidance. They know where to place their effort.

Instructors, too, find that it is easier to write objectives when they use a chart format. At one glance, they are able to see the whole structure of the lesson, and where its emphases lie. Not all objectives are of equal value or urgency.

Writing specific objectives

In some circumstances, still greater detail is required. Content and behavior do not tie down what is to be done in concrete enough terms. There is a need to restrict performance still further.

In the case of operators at a nuclear power station, it is essential that certain critical actions be done in a regimented manner. Similarly, a surgeon or a pilot needs, at times, to do things exactly as laid down in the manual of procedures. Nothing may be left to chance. No risks can be taken. Anything that involves safety or protection of the environment automatically requires a more detailed type of objective.

Specific objectives have three parts or components. They are:

- *Performance*
  This consists, as we have seen, of:
  - Behavior
  - Content
    Performance identifies what trainees must *do* to demonstrate that mastery has been obtained, and the need filled. It can involve knowledge, skill, or attitude.

- *Conditions*
  These identify special limitations or restrictions that are placed on performance. For instance, can trainees use their own tools? Must they follow the vendor's operating instructions? Can patients break their diet on weekends, or must they follow it at all times?

- *Criterion*
  The criterion states how well a trainee must do before performance is considered acceptable. One set of criteria is concerned with quality, and the other with quantity. For example, a trainee typist might be required to type at a speed of 50 words per minute without error. Mastery for someone

learning shorthand is usually 120 words per minute, with no more than three errors.

Figure 6:6 illustrates the three parts of a specific objective. Other than in special circumstances, there is no evidence that such detail is essential. If safety is a concern, then objectives must be written in this manner.

When writing the conditions part of a specific objective, state the limitations placed on the trainee. Most beginners tend to overuse the word "given." It is a good idea, therefore, to try and think of variations. For instance, the objective could begin with the statement "Field strip and assemble a M-17A1 rifle. . . ." This implies that trainees have been given one to use. Another variation is to identify the conditions under which trainees will be working when they display mastery. For example, "Using an action plan . . ."

The criterion part of an objective normally identifies one or more of four types of standards. These are:

- A reference to a technical manual or a standard operating procedure (e.g., "in correct sequence according to standard procedures").
- A reference to an acceptable level of performance. This includes the number of errors allowed (if any), as well as the degree of accuracy required (e.g., "to the nearest thousandth," "without error").
- A reference to time constraints, if these are important (e.g., "in thirty minutes").
- A reference to production rates of one kind or another (e.g., "at a rate of 150 widgets per minute").

The important thing is that standards are best written in number terms. When this is not possible try to use the most specific verbal terms possible—e.g., "until the engine runs at its smoothest point."

In order to write clear objectives, it is useful to have a list of action verbs in front of you for reference purposes. Figure 6:7 offers such a list. It should be used as a guide, and not as a straitjacket. After a little experience, a vocabulary will be developed that makes the listing unnecessary. Writing objectives, like most skills, is largely a matter of practice and reflection.

FIGURE 6:6. The three parts of a specific objective.

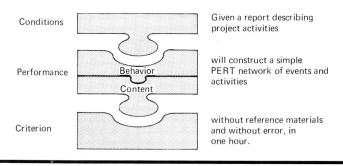

FIGURE 6:7. A list of action verbs for writing objectives.

ACTIVITY	ASSOCIATED ACTION VERBS			
1. *Knowledge*	define	write	underline	relate
	state	recall	select	repeat
	list	recognize	reproduce	describe
	name	label	measure	memorize
2. *Comprehension*	identify	illustrate	explain	classify
	justify	represent	judge	discuss
	select	name	contrast	compare
	indicate	formulate	translate	express
3. *Application*	predict	choose	construct	apply
	select	assess	find	operate
	explain	show	use	demonstrate
	find	perform	practice	illustrate
4. *Analysis*	analyze	select	justify	appraise
	identify	separate	resolve	question
	conclude	compare	contrast	break down
	criticize	examine	distinguish	differentiate
5. *Synthesis*	combine	restate	summarize	precis
	argue	discuss	organize	derive
	select	relate	generalize	conclude
	compose	manage	plan	design
6. *Evaluation*	judge	evaluate	determine	recognize
	support	defend	attack	criticize
	identify	avoid	select	choose
	attach	rate	assess	value
7. *Skills*	grasp	handle	move	position
	operate	reach	relax	tighten
	bend	turn	rotate	start
	act	shorten	stretch	perform
8. *Attitudes*	accept	value	listen	like
	challenge	select	favor	receive
	judge	question	dispute	reject
	praise	attempt	volunteer	decide

Common pitfalls in writing objectives

When writing objectives, a number of pitfalls should be avoided. There are four that cause particular trouble to both experienced and inexperienced instructors and teachers. Badly written:

- Objectives refer to what the instructor is going to do, not the trainee.

  The role of objectives is to describe what *trainees* will be able to do when they have gained mastery.

- Objectives refer to aspects of the teaching strategy, not to what trainees will be able to do.

  Objectives, for instance, should not refer to case studies. Case studies are used to obtain mastery. They are not an end in themselves.

- Objectives sound impressive but mean little. Sometimes objectives are written with such high-sounding words that it is easy to be impressed.

  The best objectives are written in simple, straightforward English.

- Objectives fail to identify performance in clear enough terms. The action verb is ambiguous. The content is badly defined.

  Look at the objective, and decide whether you have defined the performance that is required if the need is to be filled.

A final problem is the temptation to use too many objectives. It is easy to get carried away. The basic rule is to have as few objectives as possible, not as many as possible.

OBTAINING COMMITMENT TO OBJECTIVES

Objectives are a contract. They represent the expectations that instructors have for trainees at the end of training. Since they are clearly written, they can be easily communicated to both trainees and management. In this way, commitment can be obtained, which will help reinforce what occurs in training and education.

Short and long-term success are directly dependent upon instruction being relevant. This means that both management and trainees must *see* teaching filling a work-related need. Success is related to their support. However, it must be earned. For this reason, objectives are a useful vehicle. They are expressions of what trainees have to do in order to overcome a discrepancy in performance.

In order to obtain commitment, Scott Parry recommends that a number of actions should be considered. You might:

- Make sure that people in training are there because instruction is relevant to their needs. Sometimes they are just bodies. They are sent along because they can be spared. Unless instruction fills a need, it is unlikely that they will be motivated.

- Hold a pre-course briefing for supervisors of the people who are to be trained. Discuss the needs that have been identified, and point out how the objectives of the program help fill those needs. Ask the supervisors for their suggestions and cooperation. In this way, you should obtain their active support.

- On the first day of instruction, brief the trainees on the program. Distribute the objectives, and describe the learning need. Point out the relevance of training to their jobs, as well as to their personal lives. (Acquiring better listening skills, for instance, has a payoff outside the job situation.) In this way, you should obtain their commitment to the objectives.
- Arrange for trainees to prepare a written Action Plan. This should be results-oriented, and directly tied to the objectives of the course. The plan should include their personal objectives and expectations, details of possible problems, action steps, time lines, and yardsticks by which they can assess their own progress. If possible, the Action Plan should be discussed with their supervisors and amended as a result of their suggestions. The existence of an Action Plan insures that progress can be monitored and constantly assessed.
- On the last day of instruction, get the trainees to give a series of demonstrations or presentations to their supervisors. Alternatively, debrief supervisors yourself, soon after training has been completed. Follow-up sessions, based on the Action Plans, with both trainees and supervisors, are useful. In this way, learning is reinforced.

It will be impossible, sometimes, to arrange for all of these actions. However, if training is worth doing, it is worth doing everything possible to gain management support.

A measure of the effectiveness of instruction is the caliber of the people who are sent along to be trained. Are you getting key people? Is training a central or peripheral activity in the mind of your company or institution? If a training or education program contributes to the effectiveness of a manager's department, he or she will send along key people.

One way of obtaining the commitment of management is to point out that the goal of instruction is change. If a student or trainee does not change, training has failed. In order to guard against such failure, supervisors must be seen valuing and using the new skills. This is why the pre-course briefing is so important. Once they are committed to what you are doing, success is almost guaranteed.

REALITY TRAINING

Many people tend to think of training as taking place in an artificial environment. However, if instruction is meant to fill a real need, there are times when it is best carried out while the job is being done. Since such instruction fills a need and takes place on the job, it is called "reality training."

Most marketing courses, for instance, take place in the classroom. Instruction, however, can also take place on the job. One large international company has used such an approach in its marketing development activities. A market manager identifies a major business opportunity. A dollar objective is set, and a week is set aside for market development. Appointments are also made for midweek calls on a prospective customer.

A group of four or five people are nominated for the task. The group, in effect, acts as a task force. Normally, it includes someone from field sales, market research, product planning, and production. Their task is to prepare a sales plan. They present the plan to their company's management at the end of the week. It is then critically reviewed and the recommendations assessed for substance.

The first part of the week is used to identify the relevant characteristics of the product. The customer's needs are determined, and a decision is made on whether or not a business opportunity exists that is worth pursuing. By mid-week, when customer interviews are planned, a list of questions has been collected.

Usually, the call on the prospective customer takes a day or a day and half. It is made by the whole task force. The purpose of the visit is to find answers to questions, collect information, and listen to the customer's problems and needs. No attempt is made to sell or promote the product.

Once the visit is complete, the task force returns to base. There it debriefs itself on what it has learned. On the basis of the information gained, the group begins to develop a sales plan. Time is spent preparing an executive presentation, which is given on the Saturday morning.

All the steps described are real world activities. The objectives are concerned with obtaining increased market share, or obtaining a market where none existed before. At every stage, an instructor acts as a "consultant" to the group. When they require help, instruction is given on a need to know basis. Needs, in other words, are identified and dealt with immediately.

What information do they need? How do you carry out a customer analysis? How do you approach and interview a customer? How do you debrief yourself? How do you put together a sales plan? How do you prepare an executive presentation? At the same time, team building activities take place. These help to weld the task force into a more effective work group.

In this way, a business assignment is completed. The presentation is a real one. Decisions are made by the company on whether to commit the resources necessary to put the plan into effect. At the same time, training is taking place in modern marketing methods. Needs are filled as they emerge. Although there are learning objectives, they are dominated by a business opportunity. Work and instruction take on a different dimension. Each is committed to the other.

CONCLUSION

Teaching and instruction are concerned with meeting the needs of students and trainees. Unless instruction fills a need, it has no right to exist. For this reason, care must be taken to insure that a needs assessment is carried out. Once a deficiency in people's performance has been identified, a decision can be made as to whether it is worth filling.

Objectives detail what learners will be able to do once mastery has been obtained. They take the form of learning contracts, in which an instructor's expectations are clearly set out and communicated. Once the objectives have been achieved, gaps in performance will be filled.

Although needs analysis and the identification of objectives are essential steps in lesson planning, they have another role. Since they so clearly communicate the intent of instruction, they can be used to obtain the commitment and cooperation of both trainees and management. Without such commitment, instruction will be unsuccessful.

Chapter 7
Verbal and Nonverbal Communication

FOCUS

"What are the basic principles of verbal and nonverbal communication for instructors and teachers?"

KNOWLEDGE OBJECTIVES

After carefully reading and studying this chapter, you will be able to:

1. make the language of instruction meaningful to your trainees and students;
2. avoid mannerisms and other distracting habits while instructing;
3. employ an effective form of delivery when speaking in instructional situations;
4. match verbal and nonverbal communication so that one reinforces the other in instructional situations.

ATTITUDE OBJECTIVES

After reading this chapter, the author hopes that you will:

1. value the importance of verbal and nonverbal communication in the teaching-learning process;
2. incorporate the principles into your teaching, so that they become characteristic of your instructional style.

Words mean whatever your body language wants them to mean.

Instruction can be looked at from many points of view. One of the most compelng is the perspective of the performing arts. There are many similarities.

Teachers instruct; performers entertain. Both have a role, a script, and an audience. Above all, both use their voice as the chief instrument of their craft. Instructors and performing artists have a responsibility to develop their full potential.

The voice in everyday conversation is used somewhat differently from the voice on the stage. The medium is the same, but the skills involved are not. So it is with teaching.

The bulk of instruction, whether in the training room or on the job, is given through the medium of speech. The voice needs to be trained and cultivated. It is not necessary for instructors to become a Winston Churchill or a Martin Luther King, Jr. However, it is important that they learn some of the underlying principles of speaking in public.

Many instructors fail to attract and maintain the attention of their trainees. They have the necessary vocal equipment. Unfortunately, they have never set about acquiring the art of using it in an efficient and effective manner. Every instructor and teacher must learn to make the best use of whatever gifts they possess.

INSTRUCTIONAL SPEECH IN ACTION

Great orators, from ancient times, have warned against rigid rules. There are only guidelines to effective speaking. Even these should be discarded or adapted, according to the needs of the people involved. What works for one person may not work for another. Nevertheless, a number of general points can be made.

Most of the subjects discussed in the previous chapters are relevant to effective speaking. Careful analysis of learner needs, the identification of objectives, and lesson planning are all prerequisites of effective communication. Good speechmaking is good instructional technique.

Making language meaningful

Speech is not necessarily meaningful. Indeed, some people are unusually skillful in using words that hide meaning. In instructional settings, though, meaning is an essential part of the process. Instructors and teachers must be sure they are understood.

Instructors can take steps to introduce clarity and meaning into their teaching. They should:

- *Select vocabulary with care*
  Vagueness should be avoided. Technical terms and jargon should be used precisely and sparingly. Familiar words and brief statements are the essence of effective speaking. Avoid long words, involved sentences, and flowery language.

- *Use language appropriate to the occasion*
  Clarity is achieved by using language that is right for the task, setting, and trainees. Language appropriate to an executive presentation may not be right in the classroom.

  Sometimes a down to earth approach is useful. Sometimes a more formal approach should be employed. Everything depends upon the occasion.

- *Employ vivid and colorful language*
  Sometimes what is said in a classroom appears boring and dull. Yet vividness is not hard to acquire. Instructors start off with an advantage. They are knowledgeable in the subject matter or skill being taught.

  Similes and metaphors provide vividness. Pointing out that a tribal hunting band is like a sales department gives an insight into the behavior of salespeople. Anecdotes and analogies do the same sort of thing. Relating experiences and examples, using irony and humor, have a similar effect. Some teachers are very skilled at bringing together opposites in a telling way. Others use balanced phrases like, "He came, he saw, and, yes, he conquered General Motors."

- *Use spoken rather than written English*
  Spoken English is not the same as written English. Nothing sounds worse than an instructor reading aloud. The way words and sentences are put together depends upon whether they are going to be read or spoken.

  Preparing good spoken English demands brief notes rather than whole sentences. Spoken English is often ungrammatical. The vocabulary is commonplace. Phrasing and pausing are different, and more deliberate. Notes should be used in preference to a script. See Figure 7:1.

Simply preparing beforehand, using notes rather than a script, and employing colorful and vivid language will do much to improve the quality of your speech.

Plant facts for later use, the way Agatha Christie plants clues in her detective stories. Above all, avoid abstract nouns. Tony Jay points out that they are "the barbiturates of communication; soporific in small doses and lethal in large ones."

FIGURE 7:1. Notes are better than a script when speaking.

NOTES like this . . .	*Not like this . . .*
Use notes, not *written* script.	The best talkers use outline notes rather than fully written scripts, which contain everything that they will be saying to the audience during their verbal presentation; the note format is especially important. If the speaker does not know the information, he or she should not be speaking on it to an audience in a formal setting.
Best talkers:	
natural	
fluent	
friendly	
amusing	
Free from fetters.	
Talks to audience. Personally.	
Just for them.	
Script an insult.	Good speakers have many, many characteristics. There are too many to list here, but four are of particular importance and deserve to be dealt with today in some detail. They are: the best speakers are natural. They are relaxed and composed in their speech, but this only belies the enormous amount of prior planning and preparation that has gone on beforehand. Unless speakers plan, it is impossible to appear natural . . .
Preparation not.	
Know audience:	
What expect?	
What want?	
Why here?	
How can you be good enough?	
Know their *needs*. What? Why?	
Best speakers meet needs *naturally.*	

The simple remark "Now you've put your foot in it" is vivid. More vivid than "The consequences of your verbal interjection are such as to inhibit any further communication on this important matter of mutual concern to both of us."

Mannerisms and distractions

Few people's performance is flawless. Most instructors have some fairly obvious faults. Usually, however, they do not seriously interfere with effectiveness. Meaning still comes across clearly.

Mannerisms, however, are annoying and distracting. They can be mannerisms of:

- Speech.
- Attitude.
- Movement.

The effect is the same. Instructional impact is lost.

Common faults like tossing or rolling sticks of chalk in the hand are irritating. There is little worse than instructors who "conduct" their class with a chalkboard or flip chart pointer. Wringing the hands, playing with coins and keys, and step dancing in front of the trainees should similarly be avoided.

Verbal mannerisms are also annoying. Recurring phrases and words are troublesome. Words like "er," "okay," "don't you know" need to be eradicated. Sexist language and other stereotypes should be shunned. Phrases like "the fair sex" or the "weaker sex" are irritating to some and insulting to others. If you mean women or men, use the words. Anything less is patronizing and offensive.

Job stereotypes also cause problems to some instructors and teachers. Women as well as men should be shown as lawyers, engineers, plumbers, coal miners, managers, and secretaries. When you are teaching do not imply that certain jobs are the preserve of one sex or the other. Women should be spoken of in positions of authority over men and other women.

Certain body positions become distracting. Leaning on a table in front of trainees or constantly looking out of the window are annoying. So is constantly looking at the floor, sitting on the edge of a table and swinging your feet, rocking backward and forward on your heels, and frequently wetting your lips.

Cracking knuckles, looking at the ceiling, folding and unfolding arms, scratching the nose or ear are fairly common mannerisms. It is easy to develop such habits without being aware of what you are doing. Seeing yourself occasionally on videotape, or listening to yourself on audiotape, can be a horrifying experience.

The best recipe is to be sensitive to the dangers. Know the effect of mannerisms and stereotypes upon students and trainees. The problem is then largely solved. It is a simple matter to remove the most offensive ones by monitoring your behavior.

Eliminating all mannerisms, however, is unwise. It can lead to a loss of individuality. A great deal of an instructor's personality depends upon those individual mannerisms that are characteristic of the instructor as a person. Only distracting and annoying mannerisms should be avoided. The others introduce color and interest to your presentations.

Inviting colleagues into your classes is often worthwhile. However, you will have to encourage most of them to point out your most irritating habits. Often a simple remark will help you to improve your performance dramatically.

For instance, a common speech mannerism is constantly to drop the voice at the end of sentences. It has a deadening and boring effect. Once a colleague points it out, it is unlikely that instructors will continue to make a theatrical finale out of the end of every sentence.

EFFECTIVE DELIVERY

The way an instructor enters a room indicates confidence and control. Moving to the front of the class, or to an appropriate position in the group, *before* beginning is a sure sign of an experienced speaker. Once you have taken up your position, pause for a moment. This will allow the class to focus upon you and get ready to listen to what you have to say.

Don't rush into the first part of your lesson too soon. The stance you adopt, your facial expression, and your timing all indicate whether you are in command of the situation or are feeling commanded by it. The best place for your hands is at your side, behind your back, or wherever they feel most natural.

Using the hands to underline a point is an important skill. But it needs to be done naturally and with restraint. You can have too much of a good thing. Gestures are most successful when they are appropriate and unaffected. They should be varied and purposeful. If they become too rehearsed or distracting, don't use them.

Over two thousand years ago, one of the greatest speakers in ancient Greece was asked what was the most important thing in speaking. He thought for a moment and replied, "Delivery." Thereupon he was asked for the second most important thing, to which he replied, "Delivery." And the third, he was asked. "Delivery," he repeated.

So it is today. Delivery is the supreme skill of an effective instructor or teacher. It is made up, however, of four elements:

- Force or volume of the voice.
- Pitch or tone of the voice.
- Quality of the voice.
- Timing or speed of speaking.

Each one of these has consequences for instruction.

Force of the voice

The force or intensity of the voice is an important factor in delivery. Some instructors speak so softly that they can hardly be heard. Others speak with such volume that their voice becomes tiring and annoying to listen to for any length of time.

The aim, of course, is to be heard by everyone. At the same time, it is important to have sufficient range in reserve, so that emphasis can be given to what is said. An instructor may wish to emphasize a point by speaking with slightly more force. At other times, emphasis can be given by speaking quietly.

If everything is spoken with the same force, nothing will stand out as important. Nothing will be emphasized in teaching. Variety in volume gives color and texture to the voice. Without such color, interest and impact are lost.

Fortunately, vocal contrast is an easy skill for instructors and teachers to acquire. The important thing to remember is that vowels have more force than consonants. However, consonants, not vowels, are a key to intelligible speech.

Increasing volume increases the force of the vowels more than the consonants. Speaking more loudly, therefore, will reduce clarity. If people cannot hear, control the force of what is being said. Simply speaking more loudly is counterproductive. Pay attention to the clarity of consonants at the beginning and end of key words. People, then, will be able to hear more clearly.

Carefully managing the force of the voice has other effects. One way of gaining control of a noisy group is to *decrease* the volume of your voice. Students and trainees will then have to strain in order to hear what is being said. Trying to speak above the hubbub of a noisy group of trainees only leads to an increase in the general volume.

Incidentally, it is a good rule to allow only one person to speak at a time. Any falling away from this rule will usually result in noisy classes and problems of instructor control. Only when one person has finished speaking should another be allowed to begin. The only exception to this rule should be when an instructor wishes to cut short a student who has become too verbose or repetitious.

Pitch of the voice

The general level of the voice, on a musical scale, is referred to as "pitch." Everyone has a characteristic pitch to their voice. Moving away from it can become extremely tiring. Indeed, one common mistake is for new instructors to change the pitch of their voice to accommodate to workroom conditions.

As a result, their voice becomes harsh and gravelly if they move down the scale. If they move up the scale, their voice becomes sharp and thin. In either case, the result is artificial. Speaking becomes tiring, if not painful.

If you have any doubt as to the best pitch to use, try a simple procedure. Use your fingers to stop your ears. Then hum first up the scale, and then down the scale. The loudest tone that you hear is *your* optimal pitch. Once having identified it, an effective speaker will temporarily shift away from it, to convey emotion and meaning.

Such variation is called *melody*. A voice without melody is tiring and monotonous. Experienced instructors vary their pitch over a wide range, sometimes as much as one and a half octaves. But it is done deliberately. Anyone who constantly shifts up and down the scale, without relation to what is being said, loses effectiveness.

For example, an instructor who ends every sentence with an upward inflection appears indecisive and lacking in confidence. A teacher, on the other hand, who ends every sentence with a downward inflection appears dogmatic and aggressive. The trick is to use pitch with purpose. In this way, the voice takes on a melody, which is related to the libretto of the lesson plan.

Quality of the voice

The quality of the voice is a sensitive indicator of emotions and feelings. Some voices, like some musical instruments, can be harsh and shrill. Others are sweet and pleasant to listen to for long periods of time.

The main defects for instructors to avoid are:
- Hoarseness—rough or husky voice.
- Stridency—loud and harsh voice.
- Huskiness—dry in the throat.
- Nasality—spoken through the nose.
- Breathiness—voice which has the sound of breathing in it.

Nervousness, faulty breathing, tension, and catarrhal conditions can, singly or in combination, produce such defects. Voice quality is then diminished.

A pleasant voice is helpful to good instruction. Pleasantness, however, is largely a product of the muscles used in voice production. Such muscles are greatly affected by the emotions of the speaker. Instructors and teachers who are anxious and nervous, perhaps because of poor lesson preparation, affect the quality of their voices.

Teachers can take steps to improve the quality of their voices by improving their breath control. Breathlessness is a common flaw in speaking. A great deal can be done to improve this condition by exercising the muscles in the stomach and diaphragm. Controlled movement of the lips, jaw, and tongue will also help. Critically listening to your instructional voice on a tape recorder is another good idea.

Timing of the voice

Most people speak at the rate of 120 to 130 words per minute. However, there is an enormous variation from one person to another. Some extremely quick thinkers speak very rapidly, perhaps over 200 words per minute. More deliberate people may speak much more slowly.

The important thing is for people to speak at a rate which they find comfortable and not too tiring. Obviously the needs of the situation, the emotions of the moment, and the needs of the audience have to be taken into account. However, it is rare for good speakers to exceed 160 words per minute for any lengthy period of time.

Since it is useful to know how it "feels" when speaking at different speeds, try the exercise in Figure 7:2. The passage contains exactly 100 words. Try to read it in just one minute. Most people will find this difficult. It "feels" so slow. Try reading continuously for one minute, and see how many words you have read. This exercise will involve reading the passage more than once.

More useful than the average speed of speaking is the way that variations in speed are used to give emphasis, color, and texture to what is being said. A point can be emphasized by slowing down and speaking more deliberately. When material is unimportant or trivial, speed up the rate of delivery.

Pauses, too, are used to separate ideas. They can be used to signal an important point or to provide time to marshal thoughts. Gaiety, excitement, and enthusiasm can be indicated by a change in pace. Boredom and monotony are usually signaled by an unvarying rhythm.

Increasing tempo will also help an instructor to prepare a class for a climax or finale to the lesson. Knowingly or unknowingly, a teacher communicates

FIGURE 7:2.   Speed of speaking exercise.

Read the following passage, which contains exactly 100 words, so that you speak for one full minute.

Design of any kind involves sensitivity and craftsmanship, labor and discipline, spirit and matter. Good teaching, too, involves more than assembling the right parts in the right order, just as art involves something more than painting by numbers. Paolo Soleri, the Italian philosopher-poet, argues that "Performance is to creation what structure is to form. When one performs, one produces. When one creates, one becomes." So it is with instruction. To argue, as some people do, that it is expecting too much of harassed instructors and teachers to generate their own objectives, is to misunderstand the whole spirit of training and education.

attitudes and motives to trainees. This is done by the way things are said. Delivery, after all, is the most important media at an instructor's command.

Figure 7:3 outlines some of the more important "do's and don'ts." These form the basic principles of effective speaking. As such, they are of importance to instructors and teachers alike. They can be used as a checklist when assessing effective and efficient presentations.

FIGURE 7:3.   Some of the do's and don't's of effective speaking.

Some basic principles of effective speaking

- Select and maintain the objectives of your presentation.
- Prepare and plan what you are going to say.
- Burn off anxiety and nervousness with enthusiasm and good eye contact with the audience.
- Think in ideas, *not* in words.
- Lend authority to what you are saying by lowering your pitch. Also speak more slowly than in everyday conversation.
- Abandon detailed notes or scripts. Use only outlines marked with the emphases you wish to make.
- Give an audience something to look at. This might include material projected onto a screen or written on a flip chart or chalkboard.
- Eliminate distracting mannerisms. Keep anything that makes you an individual—as long as it is not distracting.
- Beware of too much preparation. Slickness dilutes credibility and authority.
- Give an audience something to do besides listen. Handing out detailed data or drawings gives them something to focus on and something to write or doodle on.
- People like to take things away with them when they leave. Prepare material, such as notes or bibliographies.
- Be concrete and specific. Support key points with examples and anecdotes.

NONVERBAL COMMUNICATION

People communicate in many different ways. One way is through words or numbers. Another is through pictures or objects. Still another involves body language. This nonverbal method includes:

- Variations in the pitch, force, timing, and quality of the voice.
- Groans, laughter, and sighs.
- Facial expressions and body movement.

All of these communicate as well, if not better, than words. This is especially true in communicating moods, attitudes, emotions, and feelings.

Indeed, Albert Mehrabian has estimated that only about 7 percent of the emotional impact of a person's message comes from words. Vocal elements contribute something like 38 percent of the message. Facial expressions, on the other hand, contribute 55 percent. Thus, nonverbal communication is an important part of instructional technique.

An instructor, for instance, may speak in an animated or excited manner. This indicates enthusiasm or interest in what is being said. Alternatively, an instructor may use a monotonous, detached, or drawling voice. This indicates boredom and lack of interest.

Hesitancy and lack of assurance are also readily communicated, perhaps unknowingly. This is most often done when an instructor speaks in a hesitant and halting manner. The message is reinforced if the same instructor sits tensely on the edge of a desk or chair. Something is obviously wrong.

The written word can mask such things. The spoken word, as well as the unspoken ones, betray feelings and attitudes. For this reason, it is important that instructors and teachers be sensitive to nonverbal communication. They will then be able to exploit its potential in their everyday teaching.

When instructors and trainees interact, they rarely keep still. Sometimes they will move toward each other, or else away from one another. They also engage in body movements like gestures, shuffling their feet, shrugging their shoulders, or shaking their head.

Movement, in effect, serves a number of purposes. It can:

- Emphasize a key point.
- Show solidarity or comradeship.
- Indicate that you are *really* listening.
- Signal a desire to interrupt.
- Call attention to the passage of time.
- Demonstrate boredom or fatigue.

Such movements, of course, are a key not only to the feelings of instructors and teachers, but also to those of trainees and students.

Distances between people

The distance between people is an important key to inner feelings. It has been studied by a number of people. The most famous of them is Edward Hall, whose book *The Hidden Dimension* has become one of the classics of non-verbal communication.

When people talk to one another, they maintain distance between themselves. This distance varies surprisingly little between different people. Generally speaking, four zones are of interest to instructors and teachers.

Edward Hall recognizes zones of:

- *Intimate distance*
  This extends from touching to 1½ feet (0–0.46 meters). In such a space, the presence of another person is unmistakable, if not overpowering.

  Unless people are on intimate terms, such close proximity can be embarrassing. Indeed, when people are accidentally brought into such close contact, as on a bus or in a crowd, they will hold themselves stiffly. They will try not to touch each other.

  This is not a zone that teachers and instructors should enter. It is important that they be aware of it, so that they can avoid it.

- *Personal distance*
  This zone extends from 1½ feet to 4 feet (0.75–1.25 meters). In such a space, the presence of other people is personal but not intimate.

  The distance is far enough to offer people protection and privacy. But close enough to allow personal conversation and discussion.

  This is a zone for people who are on a friendly basis. As such, it is an area which instructors and teachers can enter. They should know their trainees and students well, however, if everyone is to be at ease.

- *Social distance*
  This zone extends from 4 feet to 12 feet (1.25–3.70 meters). In this zone, a normal speaking voice is appropriate.

  To a very large extent, this is the zone of the group, as well as the zone of most instruction.

  That part of the zone nearer to personal distance is suitable for most discussions and conversations in teaching, as well as business. The part of the zone nearer public distance is appropriate for meetings and classes.

- *Public distance*
  This zone extends from 12 feet to 25 feet (3.70–7.6 meters). It is the largest of the four zones.

  In that part of the zone nearer to social distance, there is a careful choice of words. Grammar tends to be more formal. A louder voice is also necessary, as in the large classroom or lecture room. In the outer parts of the public zone, body language becomes more exaggerated. People speak louder but more slowly. The outer part of the zone is the area of stage performances. It is an area for actors and politicians.

The inner part of the public zone, nearest social distance, is suitable for large lectures. The outer part of the zone is not commonly used for instruction. Examples of its use would be very large public lectures and general sessions in conferences.

Space is a matter of importance. Accordingly, it is something that instructors and teachers should be aware of when dealing with trainees and students.

Trainees are likely to feel uncomfortable if an instructor unthinkingly moves too close. For example, if a teacher moves from the zone of personal distance into the zone of intimate distance, most trainees will step back. This reestablishes "proper" distance.

Reducing the distance between people indicates growing friendship or intimacy. Sometimes this will not be welcome. As a result, people will either attempt to establish the former distance or will leave the situation.

The setting of the interaction, of course, is important. Comfortable social distance in the street is likely to be closer than in a room. Similarly, roles affect distance. Learners, for instance, will usually permit instructors to approach more closely than instructors allow learners.

Posture

Posture is important to good speech. For this reason, instructors should stand upright, and not appear to cower behind a table or lectern. An upright pose conveys confidence and assurance. It also suggests that you are well prepared and have something to say.

The important thing is to convey self-assurance. This comes from a positive attitude toward instruction. Indeed, a great deal is communicated by posture. For example:

- A negative attitude is suggested by shoulders that are turned to one side, away from the learners.
- A positive attitude is conveyed by an instructor leaning forward, rather than backward, while a trainee is asking a question.

If you are interested, your posture shows it.

A recent study at Yale University suggests that posture influences thinking and reasoning. For example, it was found that people concentrate better when they are reclining. When they stand upright, concentration is more difficult. Their thoughts begin to wander. Sitting down showed an intermediate effect on mental ability. It came between standing and reclining in its effect on thinking.

Facial and eye expressions

The effects of changing eye and facial expressions are well known. Subtle changes that come over people's faces are better indicators of true feelings than words. Unfortunately, some people are not sensitive to such changes. They have never learned to notice.

The eyes are powerful cues in communication. In fact, people have little control over the muscles around their eyes. They have much greater control of the muscles in the lower part of their face. Thus, it is harder to lie with the eyes than with the mouth and chin.

Michael Argyle estimates that in group situations people spend from 30 to 60 percent of the time in eye contact with other people. However, only about 10 to 30 percent of the looks last longer than ten seconds.

One of the most important techniques of eye management is the stare Basically there are two rules:

- People do not stare at people when they think of them as people.
- People stare at people when they think of them as nonpeople.

In other words, you can glance at people with impunity. Staring at someone, however, is seen as a sign that the person is considered as an object rather than a person.

Michael Argyle offers a number of rules about eye contact that are of interest to instructors and teachers. They are:

- People who seek frequent eye contact are regarded as friendly, earnest, and believable.
- People who are friends have more mutual eye contact than people who are not. (Thus, the amount of mutual eye contact can be used as a measure of friendship.)
- Short, intermittent gazes during speech are seen by an audience as a sign that the task is more important than personal relationships. Gazes of longer duration are seen as a sign that personal relationships are more important than the task.
- People can invite interaction by staring at someone. People reject the request by averting their gaze.

These four simple rules can be used in teaching. They allow instructors to become more believable and friendly. Furthermore, they help teachers to increase the amount of interaction in their classes. They allow them to treat people as people.

From an instructional point of view, a telling piece of research on eye contact was carried out by Jon Blubaugh. His work suggests that a person will become:

- Less fluent, and present material less effectively, when the audience responds with poor eye contact.

- More fluent, and present material more effectively, when the audience responds with good eye contact.

Eye contact, however, has to be earned. Once obtained, good eye contact is rewarding to an instructor. Poor eye contact is threatening to good instructional technique.

Body movements and gestures

Careful analysis of people in communication indicates that there are more than sixty body movements and gestures. More than half of them involve the head and the face. The rest are scattered over the remainder of the body.

Body movements and gestures work in different ways to underscore communication. Some of the movements help to:

- Regulate the speaker-listener relationship (e.g., nodding the head).
- Emphasize or underline a point or argument (e.g., gestures with the hand).
- Replace speech completely (e.g., a shrug of the shoulders).
- Combine with words to make up the complete communication (e.g., a future tense can be indicated by accompanying the verb with a movement of the hands toward the front of the body; a past tense can be indicated by accompanying the verb with a movement of the hands toward the rear of the body).

There is, therefore, a great range of movements and gestures involved in good communication.

Few body movements, by themselves, have meaning. Meaning comes from the context in which they are employed. In other words, it is simply not true that a body action in isolation means anything. It depends upon the situation, the intention, and the people involved.

If the circumstances are appropriate, it is probably true that:

- Rubbing the nose implies disapproval.
- Steepling the fingers into the form of a church roof implies superiority.
- Patting the hair implies approval.
- Pulling an ear implies a desire to interrupt.
- Resting the head in the palm of the hand implies critical evaluation of what is being said.

Everything, however, depends upon the situation. By themselves they indicate little or nothing. In the context of what is being said, they suggest a great deal. See Figure 7:4.

When an instructor interviews a trainee, a great deal can be indicated by body language. If the instructor sits well back in the chair, feet on the desk, it is reasonable to assume that there is a degree of arrogance in the teacher's attitude. The arrogance would be reinforced if the instructor stared at a learner for prolonged periods of time.

FIGURE 7:4.   Examples of body language in instructional settings.

In appropriate circumstances, trainees and instructors may be expressing:

1. Willingness to listen when they:

rub hands together;
lean head or body forward;
rest chin on the palm of hand.

2. Friendly feelings when they:

smile frequently;
unbutton their jacket or shirt;
maintain good eye contact;
keep hands and fingers still;
uncross legs or arms.

3. Approval when they:

pat someone's hair;
touch a shoulder.

4. Deep thought when they:

pinch the bridge of their nose.

5. Desire to interrupt when they:

tug their ear;
raise their index finger to their lips;
flick their hand upward a few inches;
place their hand on the speaker's arm.

6. Frustration when they:

give a karate-like chop to their other hand;
pound their clenched fist on the table or palm.

7. Disapproval or rejection when they:

rub or touch their nose with a finger;
button their jacket or shirt.

8. Defensive feelings when they:

cross their arms across their chest;
cross their legs.

9. Superiority when they:

steeple their fingers;
hold both coat lapels;
point to a person with a finger;
cross one leg over the arm of a chair.

10. Procrastination when they:

idly mouth a pencil or pen;
clean their eyeglasses.

11. Stay away, don't bother me when they:

place their hand on their brow;
lower their head;
place their feet on their desk or table.

12. Interaction is finished when they:

shift posture so that they are no longer facing the person they are talking to;
raise their head;
stand up with papers or personal belongings.

If an instructor, on the other hand, leans slightly forward toward a trainee who is speaking, genuine interest is communicated. This will further be reinforced if the instructor's head is tilted to one side while the head rests on the tips of the fingers.

Teachers who fold their arms across their chests, hands knotted into fists, while gazing past the trainee appear to be on the defensive. The body language is even more vivid if the trainee is questioning or arguing a point in class.

Sequences of body language

In nonverbal communication, movements of the body are not body language in the technical sense of the term. They are "points." A sequence of points is called a "position," which can last up to five minutes.

Most people run through a number of different positions when they interact with other people. In a casual conversation, they may run through two to four. In a lesson, an instructor may run through eight to ten positions—repeating many of them a number of times.

For example, an instructor may speak in an animated way. What is being said may be punctuated with deliberate movements of the hands, while the instructor is standing in the center of the room. Once the teaching point has been made, the instructor may lean back against the wall, arms and legs crossed, while listening to a verbose and irrelevant discussion from two trainees.

In order to refute the argument, the instructor may raise one hand with the forefinger pointed. Once done, frustration with the progress of the lesson might be indicated by making a karate-like chop with one hand or fist to the palm of the other hand. At the same time, the instructor belies the situation by speaking soothing and encouraging words.

The four positions described make up part of the lesson. Each position indicates a different emotional state, from enthusiasm to frustration. Instructors and teachers who are able to use such body language have an enormous resource at their command. Actions really do speak louder than words. Of course, trainees who are sensitive enough to "read" the instructor also have an advantage over their classmates.

CONCLUSION

Effective communication is a foundation skill of good instruction. Words, however, are not enough, no matter how skillfully they may be chosen. So many things are transmitted in a nonverbal manner that it is essential for teachers and instructors to be sensitive to the problem.

A great deal is involved in good communication. Much depends upon the quality of the delivery. This is largely a matter of the force, pitch, quality, and timing of the voice. At the same time, there are other "hidden dimensions," including the distances that people keep between themselves when talking to each other.

The language of the eyes is especially revealing. Facial expressions, glances, posture, and body movements and gestures all serve to make communication effective and efficient. They betray innermost feelings, including attitudes, values, beliefs, and motivations. Sometimes they will reinforce what is being spoken; sometimes they will contradict the words used.

Instructors and teachers will want to use these means of communication with advantage. As managers of a learning situation, it is important that they be controlled. This means that mastery must be gained over the skills of both verbal and nonverbal communication. Together they make up one of the essential tactics of sound instructional technique.

Chapter 8
Question Technique

FOCUS

"How should questions be framed and managed?"

KNOWLEDGE OBJECTIVES

After reading and studying this chapter, you will be able to:

1. identify the purpose of oral questions in a lesson;
2. frame and manage oral questions in an effective manner;
3. ask penetrating and probing questions;
4. integrate oral questions into your instruction.

ATTITUDE OBJECTIVES

After reading this chapter, the author hopes that you will:

1. value the importance of oral questions in the teaching-learning process;
2. incorporate the principles into your teaching, so that they become characteristic of your instructional style.

Good instruction is more a matter of drawing out than of putting in.

A survey was recently carried out asking instructors to identify the five most important skills of good instruction. Aspects of question technique occupied first, third, and fourth place in the list of responses. Such a finding serves to emphasize the central role of questions in instructional technique.

Indeed, the planned use of questions distinguishes the lesson from other teaching methods. A lesson, as we have seen, is a method in which material is planned so as to insure the active participation of trainees. Such participation is largely obtained by a question and answer technique.

In this way, both instructors and trainees obtain feedback. Trainees learn whether their response was correct. Instructors learn whether the material is understood. If necessary, they can take remedial action, so that the difficulty is quickly overcome.

THE TYPES OF ORAL QUESTIONS

Since question technique occupies a central role, it is important that teachers and instructors master the art. This chapter deals with the art of question technique in the context of a lesson. The more specialized role of questioning as an aid to assessing trainee performance is dealt with in a later chapter.

Questions vary enormously in content but *not* in form. Since questions rarely have the same content, their variety is probably endless. Fortunately for instructors who are eager to master the technique, there are relatively few ways of asking them.

Once the different types of questions are understood, it is a simple matter to extend the skill. Variations on the same type of question can be used. This increases the number of options available. Introducing such variations also prevents an instructor from becoming stereotyped by asking the same type of question all the time.

Purposes of oral questions

Questions serve many purposes. A question in the introduction to the lesson may have one purpose; the same question in the consolidation may have another. Everything depends upon the reason for asking it.

162

The reason is determined by the lesson strategy recorded in the lesson plan. This is why it is so important to include key questions, and the information they hope to elicit, on the lesson preparation sheets.

Basically, there are four reasons for asking questions during the course of a lesson. They are to:

- Motivate trainees by gaining their interest and attention.
- Promote mental activity.
- Involve trainees as partners in the instructional process.
- Obtain feedback on the trainee's ability to recall, understand, and apply what they have learned.

People have become used to using questions for testing and examining. As a result, the power of effective questioning as an aid to learning is sometimes overlooked.

Good question technique will keep a class on its toes. It will assure that they are alert and mentally active. Equally important, questioning will demonstrate that trainees know more than they imagine.

Few trainees, for example, would claim that they knew anything about "cavitation," a technique for detecting underwater submarines. Yet anyone who has ever cooked knows a great deal about the underlying principle. Careful questioning could elicit what happens when a batter is beaten at high speed in a blender. This is an example of the principle at work in an everyday setting.

Figure 8:1 outlines some of the ways that questions can be used. It will be seen that there is a great variety of applications. New instructors will find that it is useful to have such a chart in front of them when they prepare to teach a lesson. The chart will serve as a checklist. It will also insure that they do not fall into the trap of always asking the same kind of question.

Open and closed questions

A common distinction is made between two types of questions. They are called "open" and "closed." The difference is an important one in instruction:

- *Closed questions*
  Closed questions are restricting. They are of two types:
  - *Questions which ask for confirmation or denial*
    These can be answered with either "Yes" or "No."
    Can you weld?
    Will you show us how you balance?
    Do you know the four functions of a supervisor?
  - *Questions which ask for a specific piece of information*
    These can usually be answered with a single word response. They test memory.
    What is the capital of France?

FIGURE 8:1. **Purposes and types of oral questions.**

- *Motivate trainees by asking questions that:*
  - Stimulate curiosity
  - Stimulate interest
  - Confound
  - Puzzle
  - Challenge
  - Intrigue

- *Promote mental activity by asking questions that obtain:*
  - Breadth
  - Organization
  - Interaction
  - Analysis
  - Synthesis
  - Evaluation
  - Creativity
  - Action
  - Information
  - Feelings

- *Involve trainees by asking questions that elicit:*
  - Information
  - Observation
  - Prediction
  - Explanation
  - Evaluation
  - Reasoning
  - Application
  - Analysis
  - Synthesis
  - Evaluation
  - Feelings

- *Obtain feedback on the trainee's progress by asking questions that determine:*
  - Ability
  - Understanding
  - Recall
  - Recognition
  - Application
  - Evaluation
  - Analysis
  - Synthesis
  - Skill
  - Attitude
  - Belief
  - Values

How many centimeters are there in a meter?
When do I use a wood or steel clamp?

- *Open questions*
Open questions are not restricting. They are thought-provoking and challenging. They are of one type:

  - *Questions which offer a variety of possible responses*
  These normally begin with "What?" "Why?" "When?" "How?"
  "Where?" "Who?" and "Which?"
  Why is wool warmer than cotton?
  Why do magnetic disks give quicker access to information?
  How does correct tire pressure save gas?

Generally speaking, open questions should be employed in preference to closed ones. Closed questions add little to the learning process. They have a role, however, in evaluation and assessment. For this reason, they are commonly used in tests and examinations.

Interestingly enough, inexperienced instructors often fall into the trap of beginning questions with the phrase "Can you tell me . . . ?" The only possible answer to such a question is either "Yes" or "No."

In effect, they change an open question into a closed one. Prefacing a question with "Can you . . . ?" changes a thought-provoking question into one asking only for confirmation or denial. Remove the preface, and you have a much better question.

FRAMING AND MANAGING ORAL QUESTIONS

The hallmark of a skilled instructor or teacher is the seeming ease with which just the right information is elicited from the class.

Micro-teaching

Good questions are questions that have been properly framed. Indeed, a great part of the skill comes from paying attention to the way that questions are worded. Since skill is involved, practice and critical review are essential.

For this reason, many teachers and instructors benefit by hearing themselves on a tape recorder. A video recorder is better. Then you can both hear and see yourself at work.

Some instructors favor using a "micro-teaching" approach to develop their question technique. This is a scaled down version of real instruction. Normally, micro-teaching involves practicing a particular skill like framing oral questions. Instead of using a real class, two or three trainees or colleagues are used.

The session, which is usually about ten minutes long, is recorded on videotape. Once the mini-lesson is complete, the tape is observed in private. In this way, instructors can debrief themselves on their successes and failures. If necessary, they can practice the skill once more, using the feedback obtained.

Framing questions

A good question should be carefully worded or framed. Particular attention should be paid to the fact that questions are:

- *Simply worded*
  Questions should test knowledge, skill, or attitude. They should not test the trainee's language skills.

  Simple, direct questions are better than complex, obscure ones. They are more likely to be understood.

- *Well defined*
  Questions should be crystal clear. Avoid ambiguity.

  Each question should contain only one problem, for which only one response is required. Be concise.

- *Reasonable*
  Trainees must have a reasonable chance of answering the question.

  If the answer lies outside the limits of their knowledge or experience, the question is unfair.

- *Relevant*
  Questions should be relevant to the matter being discussed. They should make a contribution toward realizing the objectives of the lesson.

  Relevancy is achieved by insuring that questions spring from the key teaching points of the lesson.

- *Demanding*
  Questions should be thought-provoking. They should challenge trainees and students.

  They must not be too obvious. Instead, they should call for knowledge and understanding.

Questions that fulfill these five requirements are likely to elicit good responses.

Trick and elliptical questions

Even when care is taken in the framing of questions, a number of faults creep into instructional technique. Two types of questions should be avoided, since they serve no instructional purpose. Indeed, their presence usually indicates a fault in technique.

The questions to be avoided are:

- *Trick questions*
  Trick questions serve only to show off the knowledge and skill of the instructor or teacher. They are designed to make a fool of the trainee or student.

- *Elliptical questions*
  Elliptical questions take the form of incomplete sentences. For example, "The purpose of affirmative action is to . . . ?" Trainees are expected to fill in the missing words or phrases.

Elliptical questions encourage guessing or single-word replies. Apart from their use in quizzes, or for revision, there is little to be said in their favor. Examples of poor and better questions will be found in Figure 8:2.

Overhead and directed questions

Instructors often distinguish between two classes of questions. They are called:

- *Overhead questions*

FIGURE 8:2. Some examples of poor and better questions.

Poor questions

"The purpose of evaluation is to . . ."

"Can you tell me the name of this tool?"

"What's the difference between wool and cotton in warmth?"

"Tell me about needs analysis. What is it?"

"Eight different types of data about other employees should be considered in salary appraisal. Some are concerned with salary increases, some with employees, some with performance ratings, and some with salary actions. What are they?"

"What do you know about work program negotiations?"

Better questions

"What is the purpose of evaluation?"

"What is the name of this tool?"

"Why is wool warmer than cotton?"

"What is needs analysis?"

"What data should be considered in salary appraisal?"

"How do you negotiate a work program?"

Overhead questions are asked of the class or group as a whole. Anyone can answer them.

Advantages

Overhead questions can be used to:

- Encourage free discussion.
- Challenge the group as a whole.
- Avoid putting someone on the spot.
- Elicit a range of responses.

Disadvantages

Overhead questions:

- Make for noisy classes.
- Are difficult to control.
- Favor talkative trainees.

- *Directed questions*

Directed questions are asked of individual trainees. Only the person named can answer them.

Advantages

Directed questions can be used to:

- Assure easy group management.
- Involve quiet trainees.
- Distribute discussion around the class.
- Draw on everyone's knowledge and skill.
- Insure a more even pattern of class participation.

Disadvantages

Directed questions:

- Can limit group involvement.
- Can introduce a note of autocracy.

Generally speaking, overhead questions are best employed in seminars, group discussions, or workshop sessions. Free discussion, and a wide range of responses, are then appropriate. Directed questions, on the other hand, are better used in lectures, lessons, case studies, simulations, tutorials, and quizzes.

Managing directed questions

Question technique serves an instructional purpose. For this reason, questions need to be carefully managed. Motivating trainees, promoting mental activity, involving them, and obtaining feedback on their progress are comprehensive activities. Things should not be left to chance.

There are, of course, many ways of asking directed questions. Nevertheless, there is a basic technique available. While it would be foolish to follow it rigidly, it has an advantage for new instructors. It enables them to acquire an effective question technique, with very little effort.

When asking directed questions, there are five things to be done. They are:

- *Address the question to the group as a whole.*
  Don't look at any trainee in particular. Get everyone thinking. This insures that they all prepare themselves for giving a response, if asked.

- *Allow a reasonable period of time to elapse.*
  Once the question is asked, say nothing for two or three seconds. (You might sometimes ask the group to jot down their responses on a piece of paper. In such circumstances, it is a good thing for the instructor to move around the class, and see what different people have jotted down. This will help identify who should be asked to answer the question.)

- *Call on a specific trainee by name.*
  Discourage trainees who have not been named from answering. Avoid group answers. Avoid always asking the same trainees. Distribute opportunities to answer questions around the group. Ask difficult questions of able trainees, and easy questions of the less able trainees.

- *Establish and maintain eye contact with the trainee while the response is made.*
  This personalizes the response. It also encourages the trainee to give fuller information—particularly if unsure of the adequacy of the reply. Maintaining eye contact is proof that you are listening.

- *Deal with the trainee's response.*
  Responses from weak trainees can be improved with judicious prompting. If a response is inadequate, ask for further clarification. You might even rephrase the question. If the response is incorrect, refocus it by turning it into an appropriate reply. Alternatively, you can give the question to another trainee.

  When you have got a correct answer, repeat it. Repetition helps learning. Also indicate that it was correct. You might say something like, "Yes, that's right, the . . ."

Sometimes trainee answers will be rambling or incoherent. In these circumstances, it is a good idea to summarize the reply.

This simple technique of question, pause, name the trainee, maintain eye contact, repeat and reinforce the reply is a powerful one. It requires very little practice to master. Yet the results, in terms of the effectiveness of instruction, can be very great indeed. Inexperienced instructors and teachers appear to be in charge of the situation.

In terms of general question management, a number of cautions can be made. Try to resist the habit of repeating questions. They make for a lazy group of trainees. There is no reason for them to listen to you the first time. Also try to resist the temptation of answering your own question. If a stalemate has occurred, it might be appropriate. Sometimes, however, in the first flush of enthusiasm, it is difficult to resist.

Sometimes trainees will ask a question that interferes with the development of your theme. Answer it as briefly as possible, if you feel it is not too distracting. Otherwise, tell them that you will deal with it at the end of the session or outside the room.

It is always possible that you will be asked a question that you cannot answer. In such circumstances, honesty pays. Simply say that you do not know but will find out. However, make absolutely certain that you do; otherwise you will lose face. It is unreasonable to feel that you should know everything. But it is also unreasonable, in an educational or training situation, for a teacher or instructor to be unwilling to learn.

Relay and reverse questions

Two types of questions involve particular management techniques. They are called relay and reverse questions.

- *Relay questions*
  These are questions that trainees ask the instructor. Instead of answering them, the instructor turns the question back on to the group or trainees.

  They help insure further group participation, and serve to take the focus away from the trainer. In this way, the instructor is also given time to think of the answer, should the class fail.

- *Reverse questions*
  These are questions which a trainee asks the instructor to answer. Instead of answering the question, the trainer fields the question back to the person who asked it.

  In this way, trainees are helped to think for themselves. It is too easy to ask an instructor.

The important thing to bear in mind is not to embarrass trainees and students. It is a good rule of thumb to avoid embarrassing people, regardless of the cost. If necessary, simply answer the question yourself.

ASKING PENETRATING AND PROBING QUESTIONS

Superficial questions should be avoided. They make little demand on trainees and students, and serve little purpose. Superficial questions lead to superficial answers. Careful framing will do a great deal to avoid this trap, but not everything.

Probing trainee responses is important. Too often answers are accepted rather than examined. It is essential that trainees learn to follow through and to examine the information they have offered. This is the only way that superficial reasoning will be avoided.

Four particular techniques of probing are commonly used in instructional situations. They involve instructors and teachers:

- *Seeking further clarification of the answer offered*
  This is done by asking the trainee for further information.
  Another way is to ask for an explanation.

  For example, "What do you mean by saying that?"
  "Put it another way."
  "Show me."
  "Give me an example."

- *Asking trainees to be more critical in their replies*
  This is done by assuring that responses are justified.

  For example, "How would you defend that remark?"
  "Give us another example."
  "What assumptions have you made?"

- *Prompting trainees to go further*
  Sometimes, a trainee will begin to give a reason for answering a question in a particular way. It is often worthwhile encouraging the learner to go further.

  For example, "Tell me more."
  "I'm not certain what you mean by that."
  "And . . ."
  "I'm sorry, I missed that."

- *Refocusing trainee answers to questions*
  Occasionally, a trainee will give a usable answer, but you expected better. In such circumstances, try to redirect the reply.

  For example, "What would this mean if . . . ?"
  "Tell me more."
  "Go on."

Even when trainees give good answers, it is still worthwhile to probe. If trainees realize they will be challenged, they will stop giving superficial answers.

INTEGRATING ORAL QUESTIONS INTO YOUR INSTRUCTION

Some of the questions will be incidental to your teaching. Others will be central to the development of the lesson. Some questions will be unplanned. Others, written out in the lesson plan, will be carefully prepared beforehand. All have a part to play in the instructional process.

Planned questions must be written down beforehand, in the lesson plan. Even after they have been written, go back to them. Reread them, and decide how trainees might misinterpret them. It is important to get them right. In this way, they will ring the responses that you want and need.

Unplanned questions emerge spontaneously during the course of the lesson. Instructors and teachers have to learn to recognize unplanned opportunities as they emerge. Exploiting them is part of the craft of teaching. However, it is important to realize that the role questions play depends upon which part of the lesson is involved.

Questions during the introduction

Many instructors and teachers prefer not to use questions during this part of the lesson. Some instructors disagree. They argue that no opportunity for trainee involvement should be overlooked or lost.

If questions are used during the introduction, they should achieve a specific purpose. Questions can be used to:

- Review knowledge, skill, or attitudes.
- Relate material to work or everyday experience.
- Assess trainee readiness, as well as prior knowledge, skill, and attitudes.
- Arouse interest in the topic of the lesson.
- Challenge trainees with a problem.

However questions are used, they must lead naturally into a statement of the lesson's aim and objectives.

Questions during the development

This stage of the lesson is as much concerned with "drawing out" as with "putting in." Questions during the development of the lesson, therefore, should be used to develop or unfold the topic.

This is best done by encouraging learners to observe and use their powers of deduction. Questioning them, challenging them, is an excellent way of doing this. Many questions will be asked. Some, however, will be key development items. For this reason, they are called *key development questions*. These are the ones that are written out in full in the lesson plan.

Key development questions do not occur in isolation. Each key question is prefaced by a short sequence of subsidiary questions. In order to focus thought and mental set, it is usual for each key question to start with a lead-in statement.

Lessons are built up in this way: lead-in statement, subsidiary question or questions, building up to the key development question, etc. The effect is that of a number of short chains, which together make up the development. Such a sequence is illustrated in Figure 8:3, for part of a lesson on Ohm's Law.

It will be seen that each question in the sequence relates to a simple but important key point. This is concerned with the idea that the electron is an

FIGURE 8:3. A sequence of questions in the development part of the lesson.

Lead-in 1

"Suppose I rub this glass rod with dry silk. Watch."

Subsidiary Question

"What will happen when I place it near these small pieces of paper? . . . Kevin."

Answer

"The paper will be attracted to the glass."

Load in 2

"Yes, you can see it happening now."

Subsidiary question

"What causes the attraction between the glass and the paper? . . . Bill."

Answer

"I suppose it must be electricity."

Lead-in 3

"We call it an electric charge."

Subsidiary Question

"But what did we do to produce the electric charge? . . . Simon."

Answer

"We rubbed the rod with silk. It could have been the friction."

Lead-in 4

"Very good, Simon. Rubbing caused friction. Friction produced an electric charge. OK, suppose someone wears a nylon shirt."

Subsidiary Question

"What will the friction between the shirt and the person's body produce? . . . Nancy."

Answer

"An electric charge."

Lead-in 5

"Yes, an electric charge. Now the smallest charge that can exist is an *electron*. Suppose you wanted to measure the size of the charge of electricity the shirt has produced."

Subsidiary Question

"What unit of measurement could we use? . . . Frank."

Answer

"Numbers of electrons."

*Lead-in 6

"Yes, numbers of electrons. But the charge produced on the shirt would be something like 10^{17} electrons. That is a very large number. Look (writing it on the chalkboard or flip chart), 100,000,000,000,000,000 electrons. Now think of the size of the electric charge of this lamp measured in electrons."

Subsidiary Question

"Would it be very much larger, or very much smaller? . . . Martha."

Answer

"A very much larger number of electrons."

*Lead-in 7

"Yes, in fact an astronomical number. Too large to write on the flip chart. You can see, therefore, that the electron is not a useful form of measurement. The electron is the basic unit of electric charge, but it is impractical. For this reason another unit is used. It is called a *coulomb*."

KEY DEVELOPMENT QUESTION

"What is the basic unit of charge? What is the practical unit of charge? . . . Shirley."

KEY ANSWER

"The electron is the basic unit, and the coulomb is the practical unit."

---

impractical, and the coulomb a practical, unit of charge. Everything in the sequence is related to achieving this single objective. All other things are subservient to it.

In fact, the sequence would take little time. Only the key development question would be written out in the lesson plan. All the lead-ins and subsidiary questions would be built up as the lesson developed. In this sense they would be unplanned.

Questions during the consolidation

Questions play a different role during the consolidation part of a lesson. During this part of the instruction, the aim is to consolidate what has been learned. At the same time, steps will be taken to determine whether trainees and students have obtained mastery.

Questions play an important part in this process. They are to:

- Revise knowledge, skills, and attitudes acquired during the lesson.
- Reinforce and consolidate learning.
- Apply learning to challenging problems.
- Assess whether mastery has been obtained.

Such questions serve two purposes. They help instructors and teachers determine the success of their instruction. At the same time, they supply trainees and students with feedback on the progress they are making.

CONCLUSION

Effective question technique is an indication of good instruction. Questioning is a skill, and like all skills it must be practiced and evaluated. It is particularly easy to fall into bad habits. For this reason, the skill must be renewed and constantly updated.

Acquiring the skill of good question technique, however, is not enough. Trainees and students tend to be asked questions that demand little more than simple recall. Questions are used primarily during the lesson for an instructional purpose.

They must be used, therefore, to introduce, develop, and consolidate the lesson topic. This demands questions that are thought-provoking and challenging, rather than tests of memory. Good question technique insures that all mental levels are involved in effective instruction.

Chapter 9
Lesson Summaries

FOCUS

"How can lesson summaries be made more effective?"

KNOWLEDGE OBJECTIVES

After reading and studying this chapter, you will be able to:
1. recognize the importance of lesson summaries in the instructional process;
2. prepare an effective lesson summary as part of your lesson preparation;
3. choose an appropriate medium in which your lesson summary can be drawn and written;
4. use chalkboards and flip charts effectively.

ATTITUDE OBJECTIVES

After reading this chapter, the author hopes that you will:
1. value the importance of lesson summaries in the teaching-learning process;
2. incorporate the principles into your teaching, so that they become characteristic of your instructional style.

Lesson summaries boost clear mental pictures.

Learning is a complex process. Although it is part of everyday living, there is still much to discover. A number of things, however, are known to be important. Wise teachers and instructors use them as a foundation of their instruction.

Included in the foundation are two recurring themes. Just as job aids are important in a work environment, so are learning aids important in an instructional situation. Such job and learning aids include notes, checklists, diagrams, and flow charts. Displays such as these focus attention during learning. They insure that key points are attended to in a disciplined way.

The second theme adds to this. It is concerned with the fact that people learn effectively if all their senses are involved. Seeing and hearing are especially important. If trainees and students hear a key point, see it, and copy it down, they are much more likely to remember it.

From the point of view of instruction, one other thing can be said. It is useful to have some means of tying together the separate points that are made in the course of a lesson or discussion. In this way, it is possible to revise what has been said or decided. Such a summary enables trainees to see the lesson as a whole. It ties it together.

THE ROLE OF LESSON SUMMARIES

An essential part of a lesson is the gradual building of a lesson summary. This records the key points that are made during the development stage of the instruction. The summary is usually recorded on a chalkboard or flip chart located at the front of the room. It must be visible to the whole class.

Sometimes an overhead projector is used. In these circumstances, the lesson summary is written on clear sheets of plastic, with fine felt-tipped pens. The ink can be either water-based, so that it can be erased with a damp cloth, or permanent. What is written on the transparencies is projected onto a screen or wall *behind* the instructor.

More specialized forms of display are also possible. These include flannel boards, magnetic boards, hook and loop boards, as well as plastigraphs. Occasionally a slide projector will be used. All of these techniques are described in the next chapter.

The importance of preparation

Although a variety of methods are available, most lesson summaries use flip charts or a chalkboard. Both are simple to use and demand minimal skill. As with all media, however, previous planning is necessary.

Nothing should be left to chance. If things can go wrong, they will. That is the fundamental problem with media. Either there will be no chalk, or the chalkboard eraser will be missing. A new paper pad might be needed for the flip chart, there are no felt-tipped pens, or one of the legs of the easel is broken.

The only solution is to prepare for every possibility. Visit the room beforehand. Never expect to walk into a classroom and start teaching. It is an open invitation to disaster. Lessons that begin badly rarely recover. Both you and the trainees will be unsettled, and the advantages of a good beginning are lost.

Purposes of a lesson summary

A lesson summary is an essential part of the instructional strategy. It assists not only instructors and teachers but also trainees and students. Lessons that do not include a summary are incomplete. Part of the effectiveness has been eroded.

The purpose of a lesson summary

Help instructors and teachers to:
- Record the title of the lesson.
- Record key teaching points as the lesson *develops*.
- Display the points in the form of a connected theme.
- Illustrate the lesson with a key diagram or chart that is *built up* as the lesson unfolds.
- Review each stage of the lesson at frequent intervals.

Help trainees and students to:
- Focus attention and stimulate interest.
- Feel a sense of involvement and participation.
- Experience a sense of progress as they see the material unfold and the theme emerge.
- Visualize the material; seeing and hearing reinforce each other.
- Record key points in their notebooks or ring binders; writing helps people remember.

Lesson plans that record the contributions of trainees, rather than those of the instructor, have added effectiveness. Examples of lesson summaries will be found in Figures 4:9, 4:10, and 4:11.

Characteristics of lesson summaries

Lesson summaries are most effective if they are simple. Resist any temptation to make them lengthy. The most effective ones:

- Are concise and to the point.
- Contain only key points.
- Record information in the form of notes or graphics.
- Are built up as the lesson unfolds.
- Use color sparingly for emphasis.
- Are attractive and legible.

A surprising number of lesson summaries are illegible. Either the handwriting is poor, or else the material cannot be read from the back of the class or discussion group.

In some situations, the trainees themselves will build up the summary. This will occur most often when small group discussion is employed. As points are made, one of the students writes them up for all to see.

Usually a flip chart, rather than a chalkboard, is employed. Flip charts have the advantage of being transportable. When the discussion is complete, groups can move with their summaries to one central location. There, they report on their findings. Since time, under such circumstances, is limited, the points listed above are important.

RECORDING A LESSON SUMMARY

When writing on a flip chart or chalkboard, remember that what you write should be legible from the back of the room. What is legible to an instructor may not be legible to the rest of the class.

As a general rule, lower case letters can be read from a greater distance than upper case ones. So keep upper case for headings, and use lower case for important material. Instructors who use only capital letters reduce the legibility of what they have written.

Writing on a chalkboard or flip chart

Lesson summaries should be written in an open, upright style. Flourishes should be avoided. Write from the shoulder, rather than from the wrist. This will reduce fatigue. In order to keep your writing on a level, walk as you write. Do not stand in one place.

If you are using a chalkboard, divide the board into two or three vertical columns. This can be done either with chalk, or more permanently with ½" (13 millimeter) wide colored tape. Dividing the board surface in this manner will improve the way the chalkboard space is managed. You will also be less likely to run out of space before the end of the lesson.

When writing on a flip chart or chalkboard, bear the following points in mind:

- Draw *on* the board. Do not push the pen or chalk *across* the board.
- Use short pieces of chalk or short pens. Avoid long ones. They are tiring to use.
- Write from the shoulder, not from the wrist.
- Walk as you write. Use a plain, upright style.
- Use 2–2½" (50–65 millimeters) high letters. Smaller letters will not be easy to read from the back of a 32 ft. (10 meters) long room.
- Use numbered paragraphs or phrases, and indent material to indicate the structure of the material.
- Stand to one side when you have finished writing. Avoid blocking the view of the trainees.

Some people advise new instructors not to talk as they write. Just as many give the opposite advice. It is a matter of personal preference.

Drawing on the chalkboard or flip chart

Graphic work should be bold, clear, and simple. Highly complicated drawings should be avoided. Instead, a projector should be used, or a wall chart or class handout. Chalkboards and flip charts are meant for simple schematics. They are not the place for works of art.

In carrying out graphic work for a lesson summary, the following rules will be helpful:

- Use firm outlines and bold lettering.
- Labeling should be horizontal. Keep it to the side of the diagram.
- Use color with restraint.
- Use special drawing equipment designed for chalkboard and flip chart use.
- Hold, or tape, two pens or sticks of chalk together, if you wish to draw tubes, pipelines, roads, etc.

Faint blue guidelines, drawn prior to class, will help the drawing of a diagram during a lesson. Trainees will see you drawing the diagram. Actually, you will be tracing it.

Drawing equipment

Depending upon the nature of the subject, a room or workshop should be equipped with a range of templates for use with flip chart or chalkboard. Basic equipment includes: a rule, set square, T-square, protractor, and compass.

For certain specialized uses a template of a retort, test tube, circle, outline, or engine part, etc. is helpful. Although commercially produced templates are available, home-made versions can be produced. Thick cardboard or plywood can be used.

A cardboard tube (such as is used for rolling fabrics, maps, or carpets) is useful for drawing parallel lines. Faint, straight lines can also be drawn by impregnating string with chalk dust. The string should be stretched tightly across the chalkboard or flip chart, then plucked like a musical instrument.

In the absence of a compass, a strip of cardboard can be used. A hole should be pierced for the chalk. A string loop held in contact with the board or chart by a finger can also be used for drawing circles. A stick of chalk, held in the free end of the loop, should be revolved around the pivot of the finger pressing on the board.

Pointers can be made out of a three-foot (one meter) length of wooden dowel. A piece of taut curtain wire across the top of the chalkboard or the front wall of the room, makes an ideal track. It can be used to hang drawings, charts, maps, wall charts, and posters. They can be suspended from the wire with bulldog paper clips. The drawings can then be slid along the wire.

Partly prepared drawings

If you lack artistic skill, prepare the drawing beforehand. Since the learners are not present, help can be obtained. The job can also be done without time pressures.

Three techniques are commonly used. They are:

- *Semi-erased drawings*
  A drawing can be drawn on a chalkboard or flip chart before the start of class. It is then carefully erased, so that it is faintly visible to the instructor but not to the class. When the right moment arrives, it can be drawn (really traced).

- *Projector drawings*
  Complicated drawings can be projected onto the board or flip chart, and traced prior to the arrival of the trainees. If it is not possible to use a slide or overhead projector transparency, an original drawing can be projected with an opaque projector. See the next chapter.

- *Pounce drawings*
  If a drawing is likely to be needed a number of times, a "pounce" technique is helpful. Make a drawing on stiff paper or window shade material. Prick holes with a leather punch (an ice pick or nail will do) along the lines of the drawing. Hold the chart up to the chalkboard or flip chart and pat a chalkboard eraser over the diagram. If the eraser is heavily charged with chalk dust, the pattern of holes will appear. These can then be joined to make a drawing.

The use of color

Legibility and attractiveness are important properties for lesson and discussion summaries. Color, accordingly, needs to be used with care. Lavish use dilutes the visual impact. Color should only be used to emphasize key information.

At the same time, certain colors are more legible than others. If the group is large, legibility can become a problem. There are two matters of concern here:

- The color of the surface on which the lesson summary is written
- The color of the writing or drawing materials, including chalk, crayons, pens, etc.

Sometimes an instructor will have no choice in the color of surface. Nevertheless, an instructor has control over the color of the writing materials used.

Most people think of chalkboards as black or dark green, and flip charts as white. But these are stereotypes. They can have dark surfaces, so that light colored chalks or pens are used. They can have light surfaces, so that dark colored pens and chalks are necessary.

The optimal color for chalkboards and flip charts is primrose yellow. In such circumstances, the chalk or felt pens should be dark blue. Research in 1937, and again in 1968, indicates that:

- Adults and children read dark blue letters on a pale yellow surface 15% faster than white letters on a black surface.
- People copy down material written on a yellow surface in 10% less time.
- Material written on a light colored surface can be read at a greater distance than material written on dark colored surfaces.

Since time and legibility are important, the results are telling. Light colored chalkboards are better than dark ones.

Just as the color of the flip chart paper or the chalkboard is important, so is the color of the writing in the lesson summary. Figure 9:1 ranks colors in descending order of legibility, depending on the color of the background surface. The figure is based on research findings in instructional situations.

It will be seen that if the chalkboard or flip chart pad is black or dark green, yellow is more advantageous than white for any writing or drawing. Light blue, brown, purple, or dark blue should not be used on dark surfaces. Yellow and pink are better colors from the viewpoint of legibility.

If the flip chart or chalkboard surface is white or yellow, dark blue is the preferable color to use for a lesson summary. Purple and brown are also very good. Legibility is important enough for instructors to choose color with care.

MAKING A LESSON SUMMARY

Ideally, there should be two information display areas in a workroom. There should be a main board or flip chart for the lesson summary. This should be fairly large in size. And a subsidiary board or flip chart for incidental work

FIGURE 9:1. Legibility of different chalks and pens according to the color of the background surface.

From the point of view of legibility, the following colors in descending order of preference are preferred:

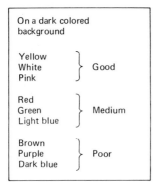

On a dark colored background

Yellow
White } Good
Pink

Red
Green } Medium
Light blue

Brown
Purple } Poor
Dark blue

On a light colored background

Dark blue
Purple } Very good
Brown

Light blue
Green } Good
Red

Pink
White } Very poor
Yellow

connected with the lesson. This can be smaller in size. The subsidiary board is used for supplementary material that does not form part of the lesson summary.

In effect, the subsidiary board or flip chart acts as a "scratch" pad. It might be used to show the spelling of a word. Sometimes, you will want to draw a quick sketch, or perhaps a schematic. Once used, the drawing is erased, or the page turned, so that the material does not become a distraction.

Care must be exercised, so that there is always enough space on the main board for the whole of the lesson summary. If space is not managed, part of the summary will have to be erased. This must be avoided, since it makes review difficult. At the end of the development stage, the complete lesson summary should be there for trainees and students to see.

Generally speaking, the main board or flip chart will be minimally used during the introduction. Similarly, it will be little used during the consolidation. The major use of the board, as we have seen, comes during the development.

Instructors then set out the major points as they emerge, in the form of a progressive lesson summary. This will most likely be included in the trainees's notes. Once the review is complete at the end of the development, the lesson summary is usually erased or removed from sight. This insures that trainees do not refer to it when they are being assessed for mastery.

Types of lesson summary

A lesson summary should follow the logical development of the lesson. For this reason, its layout is dependent on the nature of the objectives to be realized. Different layouts should be used to achieve different objectives.

Five types of lesson summary are commonly used:

- Written lesson summary
- Diagrammatic lesson summary
- Tabulated lesson summary
- Tree lesson summary
- Schematic lesson summary

Three examples of lesson summaries are illustrated in Figure 9:2. The top diagram shows a written summary, with diagrammatic and tabulated elements.

FIGURE 9:2. **Examples of lesson summaries.**

Reactor systems

1. Definition

   ollonry> ullollo >ddl> loll norlo olly orluollu
   onry> ul ollo odll>

2. Simple system

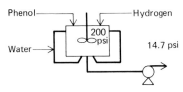

3. System components

   a. olkonry>   b. odll> loll norlo
   c. ullollo   d. ollonry>
   e. odll> I II   f. loll norlo olly

4. Functions of the system

   a. norlo olly orluollu ollonry>
   b. onry> ullolk>
   c. no lo olly orluollu

5. Types of reactor processing

Features	Batch	Continuous
1. norlo	orluollu	ullollo
2. ullollo	olly orluollu	ullollo oddl>
3. olly	ullollo	oliony>
4. norlo	oddl>	loll norlo olly

6. Reference

   ollonry> ullollo oddl> lol

Sales evaluation program:

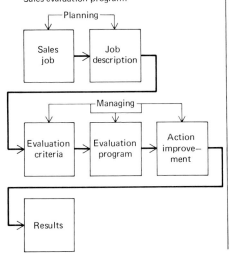

Methods to improve relationships

- Getting acquainted
- Listening
- Giving positive feedback
- Making expectations public
- Likes and dislikes
- Non-verbal encounters
- Role playing

The lesson summary on the bottom left illustrates a schematic layout. On the bottom right is a tabulated one.

A written lesson summary

is probably the most common. Material is set out in a systematic manner. Wordy summaries should be avoided. In order to illustrate the structure of the information, paragraphs and subparagraphs are used. Usually they are numbered and indented, as in the top diagram in Figure 9:2.

Tabulated lesson summaries

are useful when a list of points needs to be made. They are often employed by discussion groups. The format is economical in space and words. Lengthy lists should be avoided. They become tiresome and boring. Tabulated summaries are rarely self-explanatory. Some sort of presentation is necessary if outsiders are to understand them.

A family-tree lesson summary

is advantageous when a classification is involved. It is commonly used to illustrate organizational structures and hierarchies. Engineers use it frequently, as do people in sales.

Diagrammatic lesson summaries

are particularly effective when teaching systems and components. An annotated sketch or diagram acts as an effective record of a lesson. Since the aim is to be as clear as possible, all unnecessary detail should be eliminated.

Three types of diagrammatic summary are used in instruction. They are:

- *Progressively built-up diagrams*
  In this case, the diagram is built up step by step in front of the class. This method permits class participation. It also makes it possible to concentrate on key points, one at a time.

- *Partly prepared diagrams*
  In this case, the diagram is partly drawn prior to the beginning of class. Detail is added as the lesson proceeds. This method is appropriate when time is short, or when the instructor lacks artistic skill. It should also be used when there is a compelling need for accuracy. This would be the case when teaching the isometrics of pipeline layout in a chemical plant.

- *Fully prepared diagrams*
  In this case, the whole diagram is drawn before the arrival of the class. This is usually not a good idea, unless the trainees are already familiar with it. In which case, a fully prepared diagram might be useful for review purposes.

Generally speaking, progressive and partly prepared diagrams are the most common in lesson summaries. Fully prepared diagrams are most often used as wall charts or class handouts.

Schematic lesson summaries

are quite common. They are easy to draw and are visually interesting. The most common use of schematics is to illustrate relationships. They are also used to show a sequence or flow of responsibilities.

Some loss of class contact is inevitable while an instructor or teacher is working on the lesson summary. In order to keep this to a minimum, periods spent writing or drawing should be kept as brief as possible. When a lengthy period of writing or drawing is necessary, give the class something to do. This will keep them occupied while you get on with the lesson summary.

CHALKBOARDS AND FLIP CHARTS

Most lesson summaries, as we have seen, use either a chalkboard or a flip chart. Sometimes, instructors and teachers use both, in combination. Each one, however, has its own characteristics. These should be taken into account when using them.

Chalkboards

Chalkboard surfaces vary enormously. They range from slate through wood to specially treated fabric. Some boards even have a porcelain or other special surface, which require special treatment. Usually they are white and can be used for projection. In such circumstances, liquid chalk or special pens are used. They wipe clean with cloth or erasers, some of which are dry and others wet with cleaning fluids.

Regardless of the surface, the size of the display area of the board is important. There must be sufficient working area for laying out lesson summaries in their entirety.

From the point of view of adequacy, a wall mounted chalkboard should minimally be four feet high and six feet wide (120×180 centimeters). Two boards of this size can be used with advantage. The bottom of the working surface of the board should be more than 3 ft (90 centimeters) from the floor.

The legibility of writing on a chalkboard can be improved by frequent cleaning and washing. Usually the vendor will give instructions on any special procedures. If there are none, use Fuller's earth to remove grease stains. Two coats of a thin type of chalkboard paint or renovator will then restore the surface.

Just as a new board must have its surface prepared, so must a repainted one. Lightly cover the whole surface of the board with a layer of chalk dust. Rub the chalk sideways across the surface. You should use chalk of the same color that you will be employing for everyday work.

Once a layer of chalk has been established, lightly clean the board with an eraser. If the surface is not prepared in this way, serious damage can be done to the chalkboard when it is written or drawn upon.

It is always advisable to use the best quality chalk or markers available. Better quality materials require less pressure, and so are less tiring to use. They also contain fewer impurities and yield more vivid colors.

So-called "dust-free" chalk is available. It is expensive, but is less messy as well as longer lasting. Equally important, "dust-free" chalk will produce finer and clearer lines than everyday chalk.

Although it is a matter of personal convenience, felt block erasers are cleaner than sponge erasers. Chalkboards are best cleaned with broad horizontal strokes, and then finished off with vertical ones. Cleaning them in this manner will yield a better surface to work upon.

Flip charts

Strictly speaking, there are two types of flip charts. It is important to distinguish between:

- *Paper pads or chart paks*
  These are blank pads of paper, usually newsprint. They vary in size from 8½ × 11" (22 × 28 centimeters) to 27 × 34" (68 × 86 centimeters).

- *Flip charts*
  These are pads of paper on which material has been prepared in advance of the lesson. As each page is used, the next is flipped into sight. This makes for a well prepared, slick presentation. In order to insure that students and trainees will not see material before time, write on every other page. This allows you to flip to a blank page.

In this book, both paper pads and flip charts are referred to by the family name of flip chart. Sometimes they are blank, sometimes they have the lesson summary already written out.

The selection of an easel for flip charts is important. Most easels tend to be flimsy and lacking in rigidity. This makes the pad difficult to write on properly. Chalk, crayons, felt-tipped pens can all be used. Water-based pens do not "bleed" through the paper and on to the next sheet of the pad. Since pens dry up, leave the tops on until you need to use them.

As each page is completed, a choice has to be made. You either tear it off and discard it, or simply turn the page over out of sight. An alternative method is to tear off the sheets and post them around the room, using masking tape as an adhesive. Most other tapes and pins will damage the walls.

Just as a chalkboard can be prepared in advance, so can a flip chart. Notes can be written in pencil beforehand, but so lightly that the trainees cannot see them. However, be careful that you don't write all your notes on the first page. Once that page has been flipped, they will no longer be available to you.

For easy reference, make tabs out of masking tape. These can be fixed to the edge of the charts, and numbered if necessary. This allows you to go backward and forward with ease. However, remember to put the tab on the page before the one you want, otherwise you will not find the right chart.

Some people prefer to write their material on the charts beforehand. They then cover the words or drawings with strips of paper or cardboard. The strips are then torn away at the appropriate moment. Such flip charts are sometimes called "stripcharts."

CONCLUSION

The lesson summary is an important part of the instructional process. It serves to focus student and trainee attention on the task. At the same time, it acts as a learning aid. Hearing and seeing are two important channels of communication. Unless more than one of the senses are involved, learning is likely to be impaired.

Although lesson summaries can be presented in a number of ways, chalkboards and flip charts are the most common. Regardless of the media employed, lesson summaries should be clear, brief, and to the point. Legibility is also an important concern. For this reason, the color of the board and the colors used in writing the summary need to be carefully chosen.

Chapter 10
Audiovisual Aids

FOCUS

"What is the role of audiovisual aids in the instructional process?"

KNOWLEDGE OBJECTIVES

After reading and studying this chapter, you will be able to:

1. appreciate the role of audiovisual aids in the instructional process;
2. identify the characteristics of nonprojected, projected, and videotape media, as well as simulations and games;
3. select audiovisual aids on the basis of media characteristics and group size;
4. use audiovisual aids in instruction, so as to achieve the objectives of the lesson.

ATTITUDE OBJECTIVES

After reading this chapter, the author hopes that you will:

1. value the importance of audiovisual aids in the teaching-learning process;
2. incorporate the principles into your teaching, so that they become characteristic of your instructional style.

Audiovisuals are an aid to good instruction; they are not a prop for poor teaching.

Sometimes a simple task becomes extraordinarily difficult. Words get in the way. Showing is often easier than describing. Feeling, tasting, and smelling are certainly easier than telling. Audiovisual aids make such instructional tasks simpler.

Audiovisuals, however, are not an end in themselves. They are a means to an end—possibly an efficient and effective one, but a means all the same. Teachers and instructors use them, because they help realize a lesson's objectives. Merit lies in the assistance they offer, not in the way that they are made.

Audiovisual aids range from chalkboards to film projectors. They also range from simulations to games, from a chemical sample to an eggbeater. What they are is not important. They can be something highly complex or something mundane.

THE ROLE OF AUDIOVISUALS

What is important is *how* they are used and *what* they contribute to the teaching-learning process. They are aids to good teaching. However, like all aids, they can get in the way. They can also be clumsily used.

Characteristics of effective aids

Audiovisuals are most effective when they are:

- Simple and to the point.
- Suitable and relevant to the task.
- Essential and necessary.
- Interesting and challenging.
- Saving in effort and time.

The purpose of aids is to simplify instruction. They should not make the process of teaching and learning more complex. If aids become unmanageable, they should not be used.

192

The role of audiovisuals

Audiovisual aids, or media, are sometimes used without thought given to the role they will play in the instructional process. They are selected on the basis of their availability. The part they will play is of secondary importance.

If aids are to be well used, they must be selected because they have a job to do. As aids in the training and education process, audiovisuals fill a number of roles. They function as:

- *Aids to instruction*
  In this role, media serve to help teachers and instructors manage instruction more efficiently. Audiovisual aids:
  - Assist instructors to communicate more effectively,
    e.g., chalkboard, flip chart, overhead projector transparency, wall chart, working model, etc.
  - Take over the operating role of instruction from teachers and instructors.
    e.g., Computer assisted or managed instruction, simulators, slide-tape presentations, motion pictures, games, etc.

- *Aids to learning*
  In this role, media serve to help trainees and students learn more efficiently. Audiovisual aids:
  - Promote understanding. The old saying "A picture is worth a thousand words" is an application of this role. Media help trainees grasp meaning.
    e.g., pictures, drawings, film, audio-tape, TV, working models, etc.
  - Assist in the transfer of training. Sometimes learning one task assists in the learning of another. The skill "transfers" to job situations.
    e.g., simulators, games, case studies, etc.
  - Assist in assessment. Audiovisual aids can be used in assessing or evaluating mastery performance.
    e.g., simulators, videotapes, etc.

Whatever their role, aids serve both instructors and trainees, teachers and students. They make a twofold contribution. All too often, however, they are seen as aids to teaching and not as aids to learning.

Using audiovisual aids

Audiovisual aids confer a number of benefits to the teaching-learning process. When they are used sensitively, they attract and hold attention. They supplement verbal information, as well as reduce the amount of verbal information required.

Aids can be interesting to watch, challenging and reinforcing. Above all, they illustrate relationships in a way that is simply not possible with words. However, they must be used properly. As so often happens, unless they are well managed, they reduce rather than increase efficiency.

Using audiovisual aids is a three-stage process. Although all three are obvious, stages one and three are often ignored. The three stages are:

- *Setting up and rehearsing beforehand.*
  This should be done, preferably, before the class arrives. Make certain the screen is large enough, and that there is a long enough extension cord. Is there a spare lamp? How do you switch the aid on and off? Set up the projector and thread the film. As far as possible, insure that the aids do not dominate the room until you are ready to use them. Try to keep them out of the line of sight of the class.

- *Using the audiovisuals as an aid.*
  Once you are ready to use an aid, bring it into your instruction as naturally as possible. Avoid behaving like a conjurer. Manage them; don't let them manage you.

- *Disposing of the aid once it has served your purpose.*
  When you have finished using an aid, get rid of it. Clean the chalkboard, flip over the flip chart, switch off the projector or TV. It is important to keep aids from becoming a distraction.

Setting up, using, and disposing are three keys to the effective management of media in instructional settings.

Visibles and visuals

Audio aids are often better designed than visual ones. Many so-called visual aids are not visual aids at all. They are *visible* ones. Writing words on a flip chart, or projecting them onto a screen, may not add much to the occasion.

Words are not visuals. They do not go beyond what is being said, unless they are set out carefully. Think how often you have suffered through one slide or transparency after another illustrating nothing but sentence after sentence, paragraph after paragraph. Words, words, words.

It is not possible to erase all words from visuals. However, they should be used as if they were rationed. Visuals should not be wordy. Instead, they should be:

- Necessary
- Concise
- Striking

Space is not necessarily there to be filled, from edge to edge, but to be managed. Impact is all important. Detail should be distributed in handouts.

An example of a visible and visual is illustrated in Figure 10:1. The visual goes beyond words and dramatically defines the three concepts in a visual way. Trainees who might have problems with words like "opaque," "translucent," and "transparent" have vocabulary difficulties reduced. Indeed, a good visual reduces the differences between learners rather than increases them.

FIGURE 10:1. **Visuals not visibles.**

Materials can be:

1. Opaque
   i.e. impervious to light
2. Translucent
   i.e. permit partial passage
   of diffused light.
3. Transparent
   i.e. permit the passage
   of diffused light.

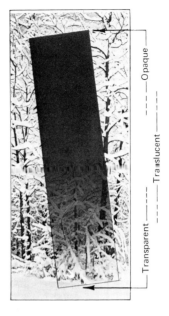

An example of a visible   An example of a visual

(Right hand diagram reproduced from Minor, E & Frye, HR (1977). *Techniques for producing visual instructional media.* New York: McGraw-Hill, 2nd edition)

Unless there is a good reason for using more complex aids, boards should meet most everyday instructional needs. In using them, the important things to bear in mind are to keep the:

- Lettering bold and legible.
- Diagrams bold and expressive.
- Boards uncluttered.

The distinction that has been drawn between visibles and visuals can also be drawn between audio aids and audible aids. The fact that something is audible is not enough. There is another dimension to sound, as any radio buff will tell you.

Sound, carefully used, frees the imagination. An instructor's voice, accompanied by appropriate body language, is one of the most effective of all audiovisual aids. That is why it is so commonly used in the instructional process. The voice is the principal medium of an effective instructor.

NONPROJECTED MEDIA

Boards, of various types, are characteristic of most instructional settings. Typically, they consist of:

- Chalkboards.
- Flip charts.
- Flannel, and hook and loop boards.
- Magnetic boards.
- Plastigraph boards.

All are simple to use and inexpensive. A minimum of skill is required, and little preparation is involved.

A few strong lines or symbols, married to one or two key words, are preferable to complex and wordy displays. Always keep the objectives of the lesson in mind. See Figure 10:2, which shows three examples of the same material. One example is a "visible," the other two "visuals."

FIGURE 10:2.   Three examples of a visual aid.

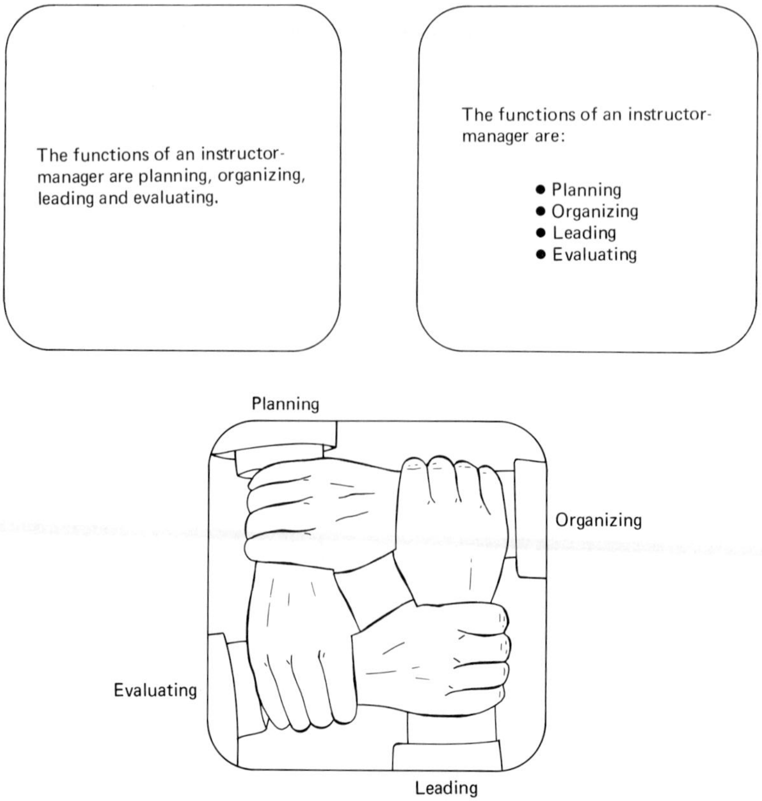

Chalkboards and flip charts are described in some detail in Chapter Nine. Both are essential to good instruction. They allow for a degree of spontaneity that is simply not possible with other aids.

Flannel, hook and loop boards, magnetic boards, and plastigraph boards are different in construction but serve a similar purpose. They are used when an instructor or teacher wishes to build up something in front of the trainees. Starting off with a blank surface, an object is built up step by step as the lesson proceeds. See Figure 10:3.

The construction material used can include colored paper, cardboard, or plastic sheets cut to shape. Photographs can also be included. Chalk, crayon, felt-tipped pens, depending upon the surfaces involved, can also be used. The four boards differ from one another in the way that the material adher~s to the surface.

Flannel and hook and loop boards

Flannel boards are an old form of display. Inexpensive flannel or felt material is tightly stretched across a wooden or metal frame. Cutouts made of cardboard or paper are then backed with sandpaper or felt. Each of these will adhere to the surface when pressure is applied.

FIGURE 10:3.   Building up a visual in five stages.

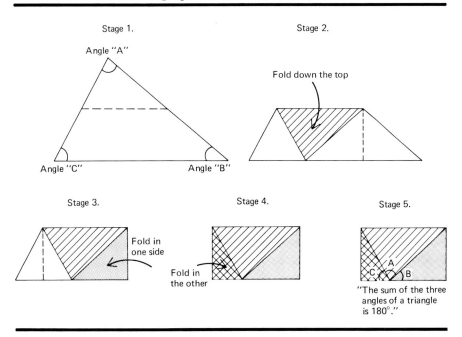

Special flocked paper can also be used for the cutouts. Its pressure-sensitive back saves on sandpaper or flannel backing. As an alternative to flannel or felt, a nylon material made of Velcro® can be used. A velvet-like material, covered with small loops, is used to surface the board. Objects are then backed with a special tape, covered with small hooks.

Since a hook and loop board will support heavy objects, it is possible to make three-dimensional displays. A pot of paint, an electronic component, a manual, etc., can be used as part of the display.

In the absence of flannel or hook and loop boards, instructors can use a simple alternative. A wool blanket stretched across a chalkboard will serve much the same purpose.

Magnetic boards

Magnetic boards consist of a thin sheet of metal, painted the same color as a chalkboard. Small cutout shapes, backed with tiny magnets, can then be used to build a display. Sheets and strips of plastic magnetic material are available. This can also be cut to a desired shape.

Magnetic boards are particularly useful to demonstrate movement. For instance, a map outline can be drawn with chalk. Traffic movement can be illustrated by moving cardboard cutouts of cars across the board surface.

In an emergency, the back of a steel cupboard can be used. It may not be as elegant, but it is certainly larger than most of the boards that are commercially available.

Plastigraph boards

Plastigraph boards are surfaced with a thin sheet of plastic, usually gray. Cutouts can be made from other sheets, which are available in a wide range of colors. The cutouts adhere to the plastic board, once air has been excluded by the pressure of the fingers.

A plastigraph board is useful for showing displays like a profit and loss statement. As with all boards, pie charts, graphs, line graphs, diagrams, etc., can be dramatically employed. The build-up property is the chief advantage of such instructional aids.

PROJECTED MEDIA

Projected media have long been used in instructional situations. Some involve static pictures, others moving pictures. The projector, of course, is less important than the transparency, slide, or film that is being projected. If these are poorly designed and produced, the aid will fail.

The most common types of projectors are:

- Overhead projectors.
- Slide projectors.
- Filmstrip projectors.
- Opaque projectors.
- Film projectors.

In many instances screening is public, so that the whole class can see. Increasingly, however, individual viewing facilities are being used for independent study.

Slide-tape presentations are also used in training. They use a special projector, in which slides and audiotape are synchronized. A trainee, working alone, learns by watching and listening to the instruction. Technical manuals, handouts, and notebooks can be used in conjunction with the audiovisual presentation.

Overhead projector

The overhead projector has become, with the chalkboard and the flip chart, a standard instructional aid. It is easy to maintain and simple to use. The projected image is bright enough to be viewed in a lighted room. Accordingly, no blackout is necessary. A general dimming of the lights, however, helps to sharpen the image.

The other major advantages of the projector are that the instructor operates the machine from the front of the room while facing the trainees or students. The instructor also has to keep the projector in focus.

Teaching with an overhead projector is a straightforward matter. The main points to watch for are:

- Unless you are lecturing, sit rather than stand while using the projector. This allows trainees to concentrate on the visuals.
- Use a pointer, such as a pencil or cocktail stick, to direct attention to detail. Check, however, that your hand does not cast a shadow on the screen.
- Block off unnecessary detail with a piece of paper or card. The transparency can then be revealed by "stripping" the card away.
- Add details to transparencies while you are teaching by using:
  - Felt-tipped pens or crayons during projection. However, in order to protect the transparencies from damage, cover them with a clear plastic sheet.
  - Overlays during projection. These consist of a number of acetate sheets laid one on top of the other. They allow you to build up the image, with more and more detail.
- Turn off the projector when you change transparencies, and when you have finished with it. This avoids glare. It also insures that the class is not left hanging, waiting for the next transparency.

Remember that trainees and students should use an overhead projector when they make presentations. For this reason, they too need to bear these points in mind.

Transparencies for the projector can be professionally produced. However, they are very easy to make. They can be made by hand, by drawing on acetate sheets with felt-tipped pens. Alternatively, most duplicating machines and office copiers will produce them. Some micro-computers with graphic capabilities, like the Hewlett-Packard, will even produce them for you, after you have designed them on a cathode-ray tube!

The same warnings apply as to other visuals. Don't overload the transparencies. Keep them simple. One of the worst transparencies you can make consists of a black and white printed or typewritten page reproduced from a manual. You certainly don't have a visual. You may not even have a visible.

Slide projector

Slide projectors are being used more and more, sometimes with multiple screens. In some training and educational situations, they have been successful in competing with overhead projectors. As a result, slide projectors are again becoming increasingly important in the classroom. Guard against slides that are badly positioned. They will then appear upside down, the wrong way round, or will jam the projector mechanism.

Unless care is taken, slide projectors are great destroyers of instruction. With proper preparation and planning, they are aids to effective instruction. They are flexible. They bring reality into a room cheaply and conveniently. The important thing is to go through the slides one by one. Make certain that they are in the right order, with the right side up.

When using slide projectors as an aid to teaching, be watchful. The main points to look out for are:

- Plan beforehand. Make certain the projector works and the slides are ready to project.
- Organize a full-dress rehearsal beforehand. It is an essential piece of insurance.
- Choose as few slides as possible. Then look at them again, and reduce the number by half. Choose the best view of a piece of equipment; don't show four views from different angles. It is boring, and wastes time.
- Avoid slides that are too verbal, too comprehensive, too complex, too crowded, and too colorless. Tony Jay regards these as the five deadly sins.
- Don't hold the slides too long, and do explain them. Once a slide has been used, move to the next. If you don't need to explain it, why are you using it?

Paying attention to these five points will insure that the aid is used effectively.

Filmstrip projector

The filmstrip projector is a most convenient aid. With slides in the form of a filmstrip, little is likely to go wrong, once the filmstrip has been loaded. It can be used in large group situations as well as for small group and independent study. Its flexibility is a great advantage.

Today, filmstrips are prepared with both visual and audio elements. For a long time, only a visual 35mm format was available, containing images in color or black and white. Nowadays, 35mm and 110 cartridge filmstrips with both audio and visual elements are obtainable. In more sophisticated versions, the film carries a binary code that keeps sound in synchronization. Once the cartridge is inserted in the machine, training begins.

Filmstrips are easy to use, and are completely portable. Although they lack motion, they enable instructors to concentrate on essentials. For this reason, they are increasingly used in both group and individual instruction.

Opaque projector

Opaque projectors are much less used than in the past. Better designed models, however, have resulted in a new interest in them. For the most part, they have been cumbersome and have yielded a poor image even in the darkest of rooms. For this reason, they have been used mainly in the design and preparation of other visuals.

The opaque projector projects nontransparent materials. A book, picture, or even an object can be placed in the machine, and an image projected onto paper or a chalkboard. The image can then be traced, to form the basis of a home-made visual. For instructors who lack graphic skills, an opaque projector is a boon.

Film projector

Motion pictures (whether 8mm, 16mm, or 35mm) are a rich resource for education and training. They present action and recreate real or imagined situations. They bring the real world into the workroom. Not only that, they can take the human eye into situations not normally available to it—for instance, into the inside of a jet engine.

Movement is the key property of the medium. However, time-lapse photography, slow motion, stop motion, and animation are also available. In addition, there are a host of special techniques like micro-photography, X-ray photography, and tele-photography. These add dimensions which are difficult to obtain in any other medium except television.

Most people have become so used to watching films for entertainment that they do not realize that in instruction the films should be used differently.

It is not a matter of sitting down, dimming the lights, and watching a movie. Instructional films need to be managed.

When a film is going to be used for instructional purposes, a number of things need to be done. The instructor needs to:

- *Prepare the trainees for watching the film*
  In order to do this:
  - Introduce the topic, and present the key terms. These should be recorded on the flip chart or chalkboard.
  - Identify a problem, and explain its relevancy to the topic.
  - Develop a list of questions to be answered from the information in the film. Record these on the flip chart or chalkboard. They will act as a guide to viewing.

After the film has been seen, follow-up activities should begin.

- *Organize follow-up activities for the trainees*
  This usually consists of:
  - Discussing the film in groups or small group settings. Each group can be asked to offer a solution to the problem.
  - Possibly showing all or part of the film again, to clear up any misunderstandings.
  - Practicing the skills demonstrated, obtaining further information, or obtaining contrary points of view.

An instructional film has to be exploited. Watching is not enough. Students and trainees need to be briefed and debriefed, if learning is to be effective.

Super-8 film projectors

An increasingly popular alternative to the conventional 16mm film projector is the Super-8 cassette film projector. It is a self-contained unit, with synchronized sound. Since it is readily portable, it can easily be moved from one location to another.

The projector comes with its own $8 \times 10''$ (203×254mm) or $10 \times 13''$ (254×335mm) rear projector screen for individual or small group viewing. A flick of a switch changes the projector to front projection. A larger group can then watch the presentation. The projector uses front-loaded cassettes, which contain a continuous loop of super-8mm film.

The projector system eliminates threading, rewinding, and rethreading. Each film can be shown nonstop, or with an automatic stop at the end of the film. Cartridges typically come in two sizes for either 12-minute or 23-minute showings.

The Super-8 film projector is used in a number of ways in instructional situations. It is good for:

- Demonstrating a skill like carving meat or dealing with sales objections.
- Teaching single concepts like sales resistance or chemical reactions.
- Presenting a body of factual information such as legal requirements.

The projector is used both for independent study and for small group work. It is a versatile and flexible form of media.

AUDIO MEDIA

Audio materials have grown in importance over the last few years. An enormous number of commercially made materials are now readily available. They include not only musical, literary, and documentary materials, but also materials for foreign language instruction and effective listening. Dramatized case studies are available, as well as courses for independent study.

The development of compressed speech allows rapid listening. Compressed speech is recorded at a normal rate of delivery. It is played back at faster speeds, without noticeably affecting pitch. The technique enables trainees to work through and review materials at speeds of up to 400 words per minute. In this way, training time can be reduced by 15–35 percent, with related economies in training costs.

The availability of inexpensive tape recorders has also had its impact. Instructors and teachers can record speech, engine noises, and other sounds for use in a lesson. Whole modules can be recorded on a cassette for "instant learning." However, trainees need to be prepared for listening. They must know what to listen for, and should be encouraged to talk about what they have heard.

An audiovisual course has recently been developed by a major company for its maintenance personnel. Along with a cassette tape recorder, each maintenance worker is required to study a number of instructional modules. The modules studied depend upon the person's trade and current skill level.

Each module consists of a ring-binder containing instructional materials and worksheets. A small slide set and hand viewer are also included, together with an inexpensive tape recorder and sound cassette.

The tape "walks" the trainees through the ring-binder. It points out important information, tells them when to look at slides in the hand viewer, and gets them to read certain materials. Trainees switch the tape recorder on and off, according to instructions.

In this way, trainees get some of the benefits of classroom instruction. For most of them, independent study is the only type of training possible. The work force is small, and it is not possible to organize formal instruction. Instead, they work on the material whenever there is a lull on the job.

Instructors visit them on the work site, when they are scheduled to do a related maintenance task. They then demonstrate certain skills, as well as assess the maintenance workers for mastery. At the same time, they give remedial instruction on a one-to-one basis.

VIDEOTAPE TELEVISION AS MEDIA

One type of media to be discussed is videotape television. For the professional type of TV production, a great deal of skill and equipment are required. Most instructional situations, however, do not call for sophisticated production. As long as some of the more blatant errors are avoided, videotape is a useful aid to teachers and instructors alike.

Videotape has great flexibility. It is also an intimate medium. If a mistake is made during its production, instructors can erase and start again. Trainees can stop and start the tape at will, without damage to the equipment. Nothing like this is possible with film. Under best conditions, motion film has a life of only some 250 showings. If conditions are bad, film may not survive 60 showings.

Videotape is well nigh indestructible. Material can be taped under poor conditions, with inexpensive portable equipment. It helps instructors to do almost the impossible. A basic system consists of a videotape recorder, camera, and monitor.

A more sophisticated one may include a two-hour video recorder with two-track audio, a portable two-hour video recorder, two studio cameras, switchers, color monitors, microphones, and much more. But the basic system, particularly if it is portable, has much to offer.

Of special significance to instruction is the video disc. This system uses a laser to produce television pictures from a disc or record, lasting sixty minutes each side. The disc's high fidelity audio channels make it particularly useful for communication skills.

Videotape television makes possible *instant* production. Workshop demonstrations can be recorded, as well as laboratory experiments, job skills, case studies. It can help trainees as well as instructors. Tapes can be made of trainees and students acquiring and practicing skill. In this way, they can critique their own performance.

Since all videotape is reusable, the cost involved is minimal. There is no expensive film processing. No waiting. If you don't like what you see, the whole thing can be erased. The flexibility of video is endless. Such flexibility is especially useful when the medium is combined with other instructional tactics.

However, there are a number of things to watch for if the medium is to be properly used. Among the more important points are:

- Beware of talking heads. Tape visuals, not visibles.
- Avoid taping yourself. Point the camera at places, objects, and things. Don't point it at yourself. Few instructors are spellbinders on TV.

- Use the camera to record visual data that cannot easily be collected some other way. Use the flip chart for things flip charts do best, and video for things TV does best.
- Keep it short. Long productions demand professional expertise. A short ten-minute taping can get along despite a host of production faults.

The simpler you keep it, the better. The more sophisticated you try to become, the more your amateurism will show. And, oh yes: avoid taping yourself.

GAMES AND SIMULATIONS AS MEDIA

Active participation is one of the principles of learning. Creating ways for it to occur naturally in the classroom is often difficult. It is especially so for beginning teachers and instructors. Games and simulations, however, are an effective way of involving learners in the instructional process.

Instructional games

Instructional games are now fairly commonplace in education and training. Some involve boards and dice, others simply place participants in a competitive setting. Still more sophisticated ones depend upon computers.

War games have long been a part of military training. Other games like Wff'n Proof, developed by Layman E. Allen, have become classic. Students learn logic and mathematical concepts by using dice to form equations. Games in management, social studies, safety training, counselling, supervision, and finance are also available.

A full listing will be found in David Zuckerman and Robert Horn's *Guide to Simulations and Games in Education and Business*. The directory is regularly brought up to date. It is very comprehensive.

Most games are highly interactive. They provide opportunities for low-cost, intensive trainee participation. Trainees learn to analyze problems and manage real life situations. They make decisions, meet deadlines, control projects, and experience the consequences of their actions. Since games generally have a built-in scoring method, they can also be used for assessment purposes.

One such game is *Control*. It sets out to teach participants how to plan their time, manage projects, and develop subordinates. Another is *Reinforcement*. In this game, a participant assumes the role of supervisor of an audiovisual production department.

As problems occur, the supervisor, together with a staff of five, deal with them. They use the techniques of reward or reinforcement. The game is realistic and flexible and can be used in a variety of situations. The aim of the game is to so manage each situation that undesirable behavior in subordinates is extinguished.

As with all audiovisual aids, careful briefing and debriefing are essential. If trainees and students are to gain the maximum benefit from the learning situation, they must be adequately prepared for the experience beforehand. So it is with debriefing. Once the game is complete, time should be found to discuss what has been learned. Only in this way will the skills acquired transfer to the job situation.

Simulations

In a technical sense, games are also simulations. They simulate the real world. Nevertheless, the term "simulation" has taken on a more specific meaning. Games take place in instructional settings such as a classroom. Simulations take place in job settings—or at least theatrical versions of them.

The most famous of all simulators are those that are used for pilot training. However, simulators are also used to teach office skills, hospital and emergency room procedures, and a whole host of conditions in factories. Regardless of the application, the general idea is the same.

For training pilots, a simulator looks exactly like the cockpit of an aircraft. Every dial, gauge, button, switch, light, and control are the same as in, say, a Boeing 727. The controls and instruments, however, are connected to a computer. As a result, the aircraft performs, in a simulated way, exactly as it would in the air or on the ground.

During training an instructor varies the weight of the aircraft, its center of gravity, and its fuel supply. The aircraft "flies" in day or night, in clear weather or the worst storm imaginable. The instructor controls for outside temperature, wind velocity, and direction. Mist, fog, and runway conditions (ice, dry, wet) are also varied.

Abnormalities in the working of the aircraft are also simulated. In this way, a pilot's reactions are recorded, analyzed, and evaluated. This is done again and again. Pilot and instructor examine the computer print-out and discuss the actions taken. Such simulators are used not only to train newly recruited pilots, but to train pilots who are transferring from one aircraft type to another. They are also used for mandatory proficiency checks that occur every six months.

SELECTING AUDIOVISUAL AIDS

Audiovisual aids are a means to an end, not an end. The sophisticated equipment that is available today is very attractive to the unwary. What matters, however, is not their design, but what they can do for you and your trainees.

Everything, of course, depends upon the:

- Objectives to be realized.
- Lesson plan that has been prepared.

- Trainees and students involved.
- Size of the class or group to be instructed.

Audiovisuals should not be looked on in isolation. They are part of a larger instructional plan. What is attractive by itself may no longer have the same appeal when viewed in the total scheme of things.

Research* indicates that one of the more useful ways of selecting media is to use "media attributes" as the basis for selection. Media attributes is merely the researcher's way of talking about characteristics like:

- Color.
- Sound.
- Motion.
- Visual form.

Also important is the size of the group. The kind of activities the trainees and students will be engaged in is also relevant.

Figures 10:4, 10:5, and 10:6 attempt to include all of these elements. In order to decide what type of media should be selected, instructors and teachers should:

- First, decide on the size of the group.
  e.g., independent study, small group instruction, regular size class or large size group.
- Second, on the type of learning experience required.
  e.g., realistic, verbal, audio, etc.
- Third, the properties of the media desired.
  e.g., still, motion, multi-image, audio, etc.

Once these questions have been answered, reference to the three illustrations will help you make a selection.

It is important to bear in mind, of course, that the diagrams do *not* make the choice for you. They suggest what might work. There will be times when you want to overrule them. Do so. You will have information available to you that the three charts do not have. As with all things, making a selection is a personal decision.

Media selection and copyright

Once appropriate media have been selected, a problem of materials copyright sometimes appears. Care must be taken to follow the intent of the law.

The exact meaning of the 1978 copyright law is still being tested in the courts. Nevertheless, it is certainly unethical and probably a criminal offense to

---

*Readers who are interested in looking at the problem of selection in more detail are referred to Ron Anderson's book, *Selecting and developing media for instruction.* Jerry Kemp's book, *Planning and producing audiovisual materials,* is an excellent "how to" guide.

FIGURE 10:4. Selecting media for independent study.

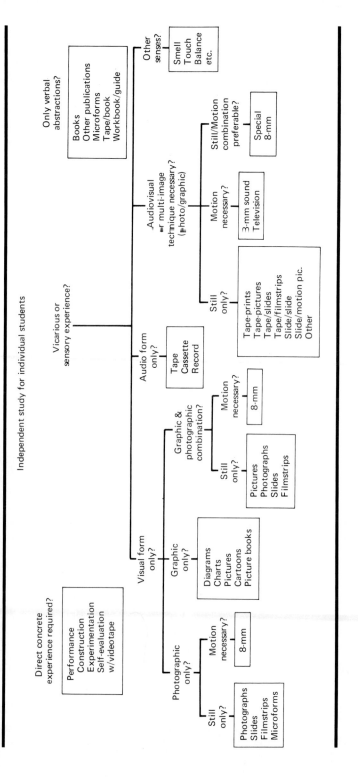

Independent study for individual students

Direct concrete experience required?

Performance
Construction
Experimentation
Self-evaluation
w/videotape

Vicarious or sensory experience?

Only verbal abstractions?

Books
Other publications
Microforms
Tape/book
Workbook/guide

Other senses?

Smell
Touch
Balance
etc.

Visual form only?

Audio form only?

Tape
Cassette
Record

Audiovisual or multi-image technique necessary? (photo/graphic)

Still only?

Tape-prints
Tape-pictures
Tape/slides
Tape/filmstrips
Slide/slide
Slide/motion pic.
Other

Motion necessary?

3-mm sound
Television

Still/Motion combination preferable?

Special
8-mm

Photographic only?

Graphic only?

Diagrams
Charts
Pictures
Cartoons
Picture books

Graphic & photographic combination?

Still only?

Pictures
Photographs
Slides
Filmstrips

Motion necessary?

8-mm

Still only?

Photographs
Slides
Filmstrips
Microforms

Motion necessary?

8-mm

FIGURE 10:5. Selecting media for small group interaction.

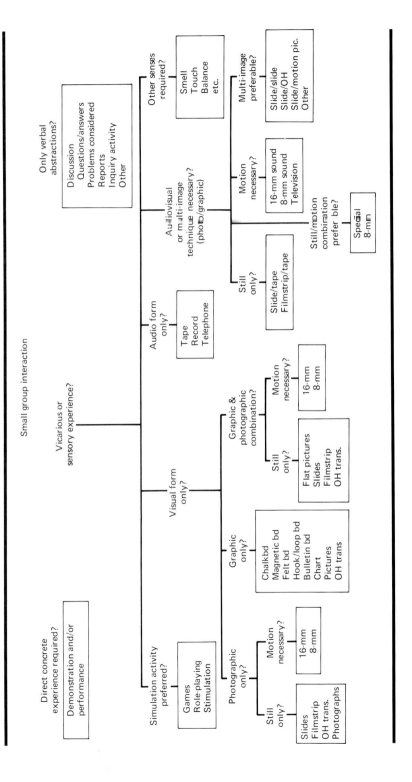

FIGURE 10:6. Selecting media for medium & large groups

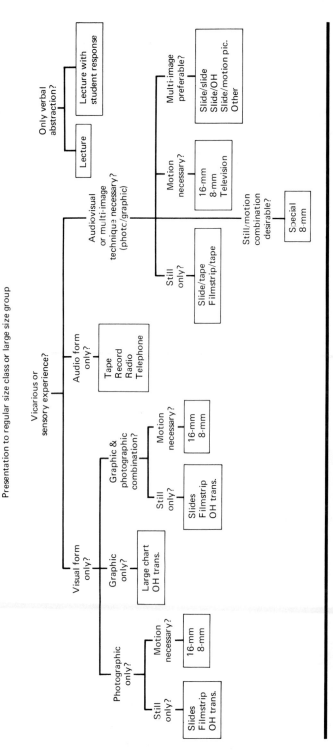

"Media Selection Diagram" p. 49 in PLANNING AND PRODUCING AUDIO-VISUAL MATERIALS (3rd Ed.) by Jerold E. Kemp (Thomas Y. Crowell). Copyright © 1963, 1968, 1975 by Harper & Row, Publishers, Inc. Reprinted by permission of the publisher.

copy materials without the written permission of the copyright holder. Currently being tested in the courts is an interpretation of the fair-use doctrine for instructional use. Such use might include copying materials, without written permission, on a once only spontaneous basis.

Although it may be inconvenient:

- Do *not* make unauthorized photocopies of material in books and magazines and use them as class handouts.
- Do *not* make unauthorized copies of case studies, games, and other training exercises.
- Do *not* duplicate, in whole or in part, videotapes, films, and audio materials.
- Do *not* use preview prints of films for instructional purposes. They are for evaluation purposes only,
- Do *not* use copyrighted music as background for your own materials.

Instead write to the copyright owner and request permission to use the materials. "Ask before you act" is the best rule you can follow.

Once you have obtained written permission, don't forget to include this on the materials you have copied. You should also add full details of their origin. This should include such information as the author, date of copyright, title and publisher or distributor. If it is from a book or magazine, add the page numbers.

CONCLUSION

All instructors and teachers use media of one kind or another. Many use only their voice and body language. Others also use board graphics, projectors, videotape, games, and simulations as media. There is a richness of choice, for media embrace the real world.

Although all instruction is mediated, not all of it is well used. A great deal lack efficiency and effectiveness. Sometimes this happens because media are used for their own ends. More often it is because media are misused, and the wrong selection is made. Variety is important, but so is making the right decision.

All media problems, however, can be simplified. There are really only two critical issues. *Why are media being used?* In other words, can the same effect be achieved without it? *How can media be kept as simple as possible?* All too often there is a temptation to employ media that are unnecessarily complex for the task they are to do. The ultimate advice is to keep audiovisual aids simple and relevant.

Chapter 11

Trainee
Note-taking
and Handouts

FOCUS

"What is the role of note-taking, group handouts, study guides, instruction sheets, and book lists in the instructional process?"

KNOWLEDGE OBJECTIVES

After carefully reading and studying this chapter, you will be able to:

1. recognize the importance of having trainees and students make notes;
2. instruct trainees and students in the skills of effective note-taking;
3. design effective group handouts, study guides, instruction sheets, and book lists.

ATTITUDE OBJECTIVES

After reading this chapter, the author hopes that you will:

1. value the importance of note-taking and group handouts in the teaching-learning process;
2. incorporate the principles into your teaching, so that they become characteristic of your instructional style.

Note-taking and class handouts facilitate learning.

The flip chart, overhead projector, and chalkboard are the everyday media of many instructors and teachers. Trainees and students, though, benefit from another type of media. These are characteristically their own, consisting of:

- Student and trainee notes.
- Class handouts and study guides.
- Instruction sheets.
- Course book lists.

Such materials play an important role in the teaching-learning process. They represent tactics within the overall instructional strategy.

In some cases handouts, study guides, instruction sheets, and book lists will have been developed by the author of the course. There is little, therefore, for an instructor to do, other than distribute the materials. Nevertheless, teachers and instructors may wish to add to them or update them.

Sometimes instructors will want to develop materials of their own. In such circumstances, there are a number of principles to be considered. Sometimes these media can be overdone, and too many materials produced. The important thing is to maintain a balance between the "musts," "shoulds," and "coulds."

TRAINEE NOTE-TAKING

Note-taking is a fairly common activity with some trainees and students. For a number of reasons, it should be encouraged rather than discouraged.

Research into the matter indicates that note-taking has a positive effect upon learning. Furthermore, learners who take notes retain more than those who don't. Note-taking, though, can get out of control. Like most things it needs to be managed.

The role of note-taking

Trainees and students take notes for many reasons. Not all of these are directly concerned with learning. There appear to be two main sets of reasons:

- *Taking notes helps trainees*
  - Maintain attention and interest
  - Organize lesson material
  - Remember lesson material
- *Notes provide trainees with*
  - Evidence of the work they have done
  - Material for review and reference
  - Opportunities for reorganizing material

These reasons are sufficiently important to justify the time spent in taking good notes.

The research evidence

Research shows that taking notes aids learning. Trainees, however, learn more when note-taking is controlled. Instead of taking notes continuously throughout the lesson, it is better if there are breaks for note-taking. These should come at regular intervals during the instruction.

Reviewing notes, after they have been taken, is also worthwhile. It is better if the notes are the trainee's own. They can be other people's, but some of the impact is lost. The quality of the notes has an effect. Reviewing "good" notes is better than reviewing "poor" ones. It is important, therefore, that students and trainees be instructed in effective note-taking skills.

Figure 11:1 lists some additional research findings. The important thing to remember is that instructors influence note-taking in a dramatic way. For instance, humorous examples are more often recorded than non-humorous ones.

FIGURE 11:1.   Some research findings about trainee note-taking.

Trainees and students who:

- Take detailed notes do better than those who take sketchy ones.
- Have a good memory do even better when they take notes. (Having a good memory, therefore, is *not* a reason for not taking notes.)
- Are experienced or trained take better notes than those who are inexperienced or untrained.
- Take notes make most errors in their notes when they summarize poorly designed audiovisual aids.
- Know they will be assessed on the skill immediately take fewer notes than trainees who know they will be assessed in a week or two.

Key points written on a flip chart or chalkboard are more likely to be written down than spoken ones. Using verbal signposts like: "Remember . . . ," "Don't forget . . . ." "A most important principle is . . . ." etc., also assists trainees to record the right things.

Guidelines for better note-taking

Informing trainees and students of the importance of note-taking has a greater impact on note-taking than any other factor. Figure 11:2 summarizes the main principles of effective note-taking. It will be seen that it is essential that instructors

FIGURE 11:2.   Guidelines for effective note-taking.

	Instructor	*Trainees*
During note-taking	<ul><li>Identify key teaching points.</li><li>Organize them into a meaningful framework.</li><li>Fill in the framework with necessary detail.</li><li>Identify key examples and illustrations.</li></ul>	<ul><li>Record key points.</li><li>Organize them into a framework that reflects:<ul><li>The instructor's framework, or</li><li>One meaningful to yourself.</li></ul></li><li>Add necessary detail to the framework. Don't record it as isolated facts.</li><li>Add material from your own experience or readings.</li></ul>
Using notes	<ul><li>Show that you approve of the note-taking.</li><li>Examine trainee notes, so as to get feedback about the effectiveness of your teaching.</li></ul>	<ul><li>Improve your notes.</li><li>Design a framework for your own, as a result of:<ul><li>Further reading or skill.</li><li>Thought and reflection.</li></ul></li><li>Review your notes, highlighting key points.</li></ul>

- Notes should be taken in note-form, and not in continuous sentences and paragraphs.
- Generous amounts of space should be left, so that additional notes can be added at a later date.
- Underlining or highlighting points in color is useful.

Most important of all, notes should be recorded in a notebook or ring-binder. Odd sheets of note paper will be mislaid or lost.

and teachers show interest in note-taking activities. The activity should not be ignored or underrated.

The following points should be borne in mind:

- Notes should be reviewed and added to once they have been made.
- Notes recorded in the vocabulary of trainees are more meaningful than notes in the vocabulary of the instructor.
- Time should be made available for note-taking. This time should never be forfeited.

There are basically two styles of note-taking. Both are illustrated in Figure 11:3. The two styles are:

- Formal layout of words and phrases.
- Key word "mapping," in which key terms are set out in a diagrammatic manner.

Key word mapping is less verbal, speedier, and more visual than the formal layout method. They are, however, a matter of personal preference.

Most people prefer to use paper that has horizontal lines, for ease of writing. However, there is evidence that graph or quad paper, with vertical and horizontal lines, helps trainees to manage space more effectively. The vertical lines help with indenting. They also encourage people to use fewer words and more graphics.

FIGURE 11:3. Two methods of taking notes: formal layout (above) and key word mapping (below).

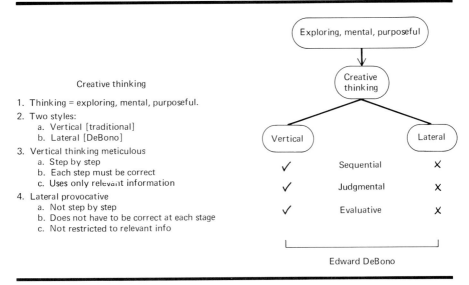

HANDOUTS AND STUDY GUIDES

The trend in a great deal of instruction is to distribute duplicated or printed notes as class handouts. Trainees, it is felt, may not make an accurate record of key points. They may write down information inaccurately. Distributing class handouts, of course, also saves time.

Group handouts

However, while handouts are important, they do not replace trainee notes. Each serves a different function. Most people like to collect handouts during a course; not everyone reads them. They too need to be managed.

Handouts serve to supply trainees and students with:

- Additional information, not readily attainable elsewhere. (Notes take on the role of a supplementary textbook.)
- Up-to-date information that may amend material in technical or operating manuals.
- Procedures or technical details that are too complex to be included in audio-visual aids.
- Material that is too lengthy or complex for trainees to copy into their notes.

In other words, they take on the role of supplementary manuals, visual aids, or amendments to established procedures.

Handouts are normally complete in themselves. However, parts can be left incomplete. Instead of trainees recording notes in a notebook, they can write on the handout. For example, a key diagram can be printed and distributed to the class. As the lesson progresses, trainees and students can label it stage by stage.

Alternatively, a lesson summary can be printed in outline as part of the handout. Trainees add to it as the lesson proceeds. In these circumstances, the handout takes on the characteristics of a worksheet. Instead of starting out with a blank sheet of paper, trainees are given assistance which "shapes" their notes. See Figure 11:4.

Study guides

Handouts are specific aids. They usually refer to particular lessons or learning experiences. Study guides, on the other hand, deal with a whole course. They provide trainees with a map of what is involved.

Most guides contain:

- The aim and objectives of the course.
- A timetable of the sessions.

FIGURE 11:4. Example of an outline handout designed to be completed by trainees as the lesson proceeds.

Warehousing and Bulk Storage

1. *A warehouse exists to:*

   A. _____
   B. _____
   C. _____
   D. _____

2. *Flexible planning is needed to allow for:*

   A. _____
   B, _____
   C. _____

3. *Factors to be taken into account in the siting of a warehouse include:*

   A. _____
   B. _____
   C. _____
   D. _____
   E. _____
   F. _____

4. *The chief storage methods are:*

   A. _____   B. _____
   C. _____   D. _____
   E. _____   F. _____
   G. _____   H. _____

5. *Handling equipment includes:*

   A. _____   B. _____
   C. _____   D. _____
   E. _____

- Details of the topics to be covered.
- Details of field trips, visits, internships, etc.
- Details of work assignments and how they will be assessed.
- Self-test and review questions.
- Book lists and other reference materials.
- Resumés of instructors and guest lecturers.
- Names of trainees and students attending the course.
- Housekeeping information and dress codes.

As far as practical, the guide should be concise and to the point.

Sometimes the guide will include handouts. Instead of being distributed in class, they are enclosed in the guide. This relieves instructors of the chore of collecting them from the office and giving them out in class. Unfortunately, it also reduces their impact. Generally speaking, it is better to give material to trainees when it is needed.

INSTRUCTION SHEETS

Instruction sheets fill two particular needs. They are used to help learners:

- *Follow a procedure*
  e.g., to purge a system
  to recruit new employees within affirmative action guidelines
- *Make decisions or solve problems*
  e.g., to identify a fault
  to decide whether to buy or not buy

FIGURE 11:5.   Example of an instruction sheet setting out the different methods of collecting information for fault or problem identification.

Methods of collecting information for fault or problem identification

1. *Comparative method*
   This consists of two techniques:
   a. *Automatic*
      1. *An alarm*
         e.g., a low level alarm on a vessel
               payment refused on a check
      2. *Shutdown*
         e.g., centrifuge torque
               shutdown
               account closed.
   b. *Manual*
      1. *Random*
         e.g., voltage or flow recorders
               labor turn-over
      2. *Sampling*
         e.g., oil sampling
               productivity
2. *Sequential method*
   This consists of two techniques:
   a. *Random*
      1. *Random check*
         e.g., random check of fuses
               random check of absenteeism
      2. *Experience*
         e.g., gut feeling, intuition
   b. *Systematic*

Rather than set out each step on a flip chart or chalkboard, it is much easier to distribute the job aid as an instruction sheet.

Typically, instruction sheets include the following information:

- A title.
- A statement of purpose.
- A list of equipment, tools, materials, aids, and manuals needed to do the job.
- A step by step procedure to be followed.
- Details of safety precautions that must be observed.
- References to books and technical manuals, where additional material will be found.

Such information should be laid out in an attractive and informative manner. Lists, tables, and diagrams are preferable to continuous prose.

Two examples of an instruction sheet are illustrated in Figures 11:5 and 11:6. The first example details two methods of identifying faults or problems

1. *Physical*
   a. *Visual search*
      e.g., bearing damage, corrosion
         product quality
   b. *Other senses*
      e.g., noise, vibration, smell
         job satisfaction
2. *Operational*
   a. *Split half*
      e.g., piping, electrical circuits
         double entry balances in bookkeeping
   b. *Input to output*
      e.g., seal lubrication system
         training program
   c. *Output to input*
      e.g., compressor train
         inventory check
3. *Reliability*
   a. *Specific reliability*
      e.g., reliability data system
         reliability of a selection procedure
   b. *Relative reliability*
      e.g., comparison of the performance of similar pumps
         comparison of one trainee's performance with the
         performance of the class as a whole

FIGURE 11:6. An example of a decision table for identifying the correct procedures to be followed during abnormal conditions.

Underlying principle:

Standby condition is a function of weather, probable duration of the abnormality, and raw material state.

Variables	Conditions					
Weather						
November to March (cold)	✓	✓	✓	✓		
April to October (warm)	✓	✓			✓	✓
Probable duration of abnormality						
Short standby (up to 1 hour)	✓					
Medium standby (up to 8 hours)		✓				
Long standby (more than 8 hours)			✓	✓	✓	✓
Raw material state						
Can run raw material	✓	✓	✓		✓	
Cannot run raw material	✓	✓		✓		✓
Move to standby condition						
Number 1	*					
Number 2		*	*		*	
Number 3				*		
Number 4						*

in an electrical, mechanical, or human system. The procedures are the ones used to repair such varied systems as aircraft, washing machines, automobiles, electric typewriters, etc.

The second example illustrates an instruction sheet for a different type of task. In this case, a decision is involved. Operators who use the sheet will be able to decide which standby condition should be followed when certain abnormal conditions are experienced. This type of instruction sheet is called a decision table.

Instruction sheets can be used in either an instructional setting or in a job situation. Not only do they "de-skill" the job; they also lay out the framework in which each of the operations is carried out. Relatively inexperienced people, using an information sheet, can perform a job function in a systematic and competent manner.

BOOK LISTS

Most teachers and instructors distribute book lists. Sometimes they are extremely long, so that learners are overwhelmed. At other times, the book lists are so short that there is little choice. Short lists can also mislead people into believing that there is little to be read.

In either case, students and trainees are given little guidance as to what they must read. Some things are important; others are not. Book lists for a course should be put together with some care. Minimally, they should be:

- Long enough to offer choices, yet short enough so that trainees are not overwhelmed.
- Compiled at the level of the learners' reading and skill levels.
- Annotated so that they know what they "must," "should," and "could" read.
- Designed so that they include standard references, as well as more up-to-date materials.
- Periodically revised, so that out of date materials are removed.

Book lists should also include a wide range of titles. Students and trainees need to be provided with a solid as well as a varied selection.

As a general rule, book lists should be distributed to trainees as early in the course as possible. It is also advisable to send a copy of the list to the company librarian, as well as to the local town or county library. Local bookstores, too, appreciate getting advance notice of what books people will be interested in purchasing.

When the list is compiled, make certain that the information is complete and up-to-date. Every reference should include: author, title, publisher, edition, and pages to be studied. If possible, include the library call number. It will save a great deal of time.

Many people place symbols alongside the books indicating whether the reference is:

- "Essential introductory material."
- "Elaboration of material given in class."
- "Useful reference book or manual."
- "Controversial."
- "Consider buying," etc.

In this way, learners get guidance. They know what they have to read. They can branch out, so as to follow their own interests without losing touch with the theme of the course.

Once the book list has been put together, some thought should be given to the provision of the materials. Obviously, every title should be available in the library. But in what quantities? It might be best to restrict the period of loan for some of the more essential and popular titles.

CONCLUSION

Note-taking is an important aid to learning. Trainees and students who take notes generally learn more efficiently than those who do not. However, note-taking should be controlled. Periods of note-taking should be set aside during a lesson. It is not wise to allow trainees to take notes continuously during the instruction.

Handouts, study guides, instruction sheets, and book lists also have an important role. Sometimes they are taken so much for granted that their importance is underrated. None of them should be thought of as a replacement for note-taking. Each has its own particular role and function.

Chapter 12
Assessment Techniques

FOCUS

"How can learning be assessed?"

KNOWLEDGE OBJECTIVES

After reading and studying this chapter, you will be able to:

1. recognize the role of assessment in the teaching-learning process;
2. identify four sources of information for assessment purposes;
3. take steps to insure that assessment is carried out in an ethical and responsible manner;
4. use both norm-referenced and criterion-referenced assessments, depending upon the objectives of the situation;
5. Use standardized performance check lists, critical incident methods, and objective style tests as assessment procedures.

ATTITUDE OBJECTIVES

After reading this chapter, the author hopes that you will:

1. value the importance of assessment in the teaching-learning process;
2. incorporate the principles into your teaching, so that they become characteristic of your instructional style.

Nothing encourages a learner so much as an instructor's eye.

A great deal of time and effort are invested in the design, development, and teaching of an educational or training program. However, the responsibility of course designers and instructors does not end there. Designers have a further responsibility. They must evaluate the success of the program and take whatever corrective action is necessary.

Teachers and instructors, similarly, have a responsibility to monitor a learner's progress toward mastery. If necessary, they must take remedial action. It is important to deal with learning problems as they occur, and not leave them until it is too late.

The purpose of instruction is to facilitate learning, and to make it a satisfying experience. For these reasons, some type of assessment is essential. Decisions that have been made in the course of teaching can then be reevaluated and changes implemented.

THE NATURE OF ASSESSMENT

The word "assessment" is used in a number of different ways. Some people associate it with formal examinations. Others associate it with judgments about a person's intelligence, ability, or aptitude. Yet both meanings are specialized uses of the word.

Assessment is concerned with people. Evaluation, on the other hand, is concerned with programs and courses. Both involve measurement in one form or another. However, the end products are different. Evaluation is a post mortem. It is a terminal activity.

Assessment is not terminal; it is ongoing. It is concerned with the progress that people are making toward mastery. Are the learning objectives being realized? If not, why not? How can problems be rectified before they become serious? Knowledge, skill, and attitudes are involved.

Assessment is concerned with keeping people on target. It is a continuous process. It is not something that should be left to the end of a course or program. Then it is probably too late to do much about it. Instead of being a post mortem, assessment involves the continuous monitoring of a person's "health" as a learner.

The purposes of assessment

Assessment involves more than one goal. All are interrelated in one way or another. Assessment helps *both* learners and instructors to:

226

- Monitor, on a continuous basis, the progress that learners are making toward mastery.
- Identify strengths and weaknesses, so that help can be given in a timely manner.
- Identify and reward special ability and efforts beyond a mastery level.
- Determine when mastery has been achieved.

Assessment also serves a supplementary purpose. It yields information that can be used to make predictions about the future performance of trainees. Assessment information is also useful to course designers. They can use such information when making changes in the training program.

Knowledge of results

Knowledge of results is an important principle of learning. Assessment is the primary means by which such information can be fed back to trainees and students. For it to be effective, however, feedback of information to learners should be:

- Specific rather than general.
- Motivating rather than destructive.
- Useful rather than judgmental.

It is also beneficial if some of the feedback can be obtained as a result of the trainee's own efforts. The efforts of instructors and teachers should not be the only source of information.

For example, trainees would not find it particularly useful to be told that they had failed on a case study dealing with product planning. A more useful and specific type of feedback would be to tell them, while the exercise was underway, that they needed to be: better prepared, start the discussions on time, and present rationales for their decisions.

Under such circumstances, assessment, knowledge of results, and feedback are different facets of the same process. Feedback is immediate, specific, constructive, and helpful.

INFORMATION FOR ASSESSMENT

The sources of information for assessment purposes are limited only by the imagination of the people involved. Generally speaking, useful information can be obtained from four sources. Since a complete picture is better than a partial one, it is best to obtain data from as many directions as possible.

The chief sources of information for assessment are:

- Mastery learning.
- Job performance.

- Organizational effectiveness.
- Learner and supervisor reactions.

Sometimes information from one source will be more readily available than another. The important thing, however, is still to try to collect as wide a range of information as possible.

Information about a test score, for instance, may be incomplete. Knowing that a trainee has scored 70 in a test is only part of the picture. The trainee's job performance may be less than satisfactory. Furthermore, the supervisor may feel that the trainee is still not convinced of the necessity of following laid down procedures.

Information about mastery

Objectives form a basis for making an assessment of what trainees and students have learned. The goal, by and large, is for them to achieve at least 90 percent of the objectives. However, if only a few people in a training program learn this much, a few do quite badly, and the majority come somewhere in the middle, there is reason for alarm. Learning, not failure, is what instuction is all about.

One common way of measuring learning is to use a test or examination. It can be written or oral, knowledge- or skill-based. Sometimes, such a test is given before instruction, and again after instruction is complete. The difference between the two scores is then taken as measure of what trainees learned.

For example, suppose a trainee scored 15 percent in the pre-test at the beginning of training, and 95 percent in the post-test at the conclusion of training. The difference between the two test scores would indicate a gain in learning of 80 percent.

Such measures, however, are indirect. They may not reflect actual learning. For instance, rather than poor learning, low test scores may indicate that a learner was:

- Tired, anxious, or lacking in attention.
- Feeling ill or upset.
- Unable to understand the instructions given.
- Lacking in practice, if a skill of hand, eye, or limb was involved.
- Experiencing a loss of retention, if verbal material was involved, and there was a long delay before the test was taken.

In these circumstances, poor test performance will be an inconclusive reflection of what the learner can do.

Similarly, good test scores may exaggerate skill or knowledge. The trainee may have been lucky. Perhaps the learner was asked only what was known. The questions asked may have been correctly predicted. Alternatively, the test may have been badly designed, so that it was possible to guess at many of the answers.

Despite all these problems, the measurement of learning does have a place in assessment. As long as care is taken in the design of tests and examinations, valuable information can be obtained. Such tests, furthermore, should not be left to the end of the course. They should be used to indicate the progress of the learners, as well as their performance at the end of instruction.

Job performance

One of the more effective ways of measuring people's performance is to look at the way they behave in a work situation. Sometimes this is done on the job site; sometimes under simulated conditions. The important thing about this type of measurement is that it is concerned with real world matters.

Trainees and students who know they are being assessed behave somewhat differently. For this reason, they may use correct safety procedures when they are watched but ignore them at other times. Measurements of job performance, therefore, need to be carried out as unobtrusively as possible.

Unobtrusive measurement occurs when people do not realize that their performance is being observed. For example, an unobtrusive measure of a trainee's ability might be obtained by sampling, on a random basis, work that had been done the previous day. Examples of unobtrusive measures include: lost production, mean time to repair, availability records, waste materials, damage to equipment, increase in overtime, declining sales, etc.

Some people may do well under instruction but badly when put into a job situation. Their knowledge, skill, and attitudes do not *transfer* from the artificial environment of training to the real world of work. Sometimes, the responsibility of the job is too demanding. At other times, they need to be systematically "weaned" to the new situation.

Despite the difficulties that learners experience, measures of job performance are critical. Trainees and students are being prepared for the world of work, not for the world of learning. For this reason, it is essential that they ultimately be assessed in the job environment.

The work environment is also a source of preinstructional and postinstructional information. For instance, supervisors can be asked:

- *Preinstructional questions like*
  - What could the trainees do before they came to me?
  - What couldn't they do?
  - What particular difficulties did they have?
  - What do they need to learn?
- *Postinstructional questions like*
  - What have they learned?
  - What can they do now, that they couldn't do before?
  - Have you noticed any differences in their behavior?
  - How have they improved?
  - What do they still need to learn?

When the two classes of information are compared, a sense of what the trainees have learned can be gained.

Organizational effectiveness

Important information can also be obtained by looking at learning from the perspective of the organization or institution. Training occurs because there is a problem. Errors in job performance are either being made or are likely to be made unless some action is taken.

The question that needs to be asked is "Okay, they've learned, but has the problem gone away?" This is what Michalak and Yager call the *so what* question. The question is another way of asking "What are the results of learning?" If people have learned, there should be some payoff to the organization.

For example, suppose an educational program was concerned with teaching listening and concentrating skills to middle managers. Although the trainees successfully completed a post-test at the conclusion of instruction, a company may find that listening did not appear to improve. In such circumstances, it is reasonable to conclude that the organization has not benefited from its investment. There is no apparent payoff.

The answers to eight questions, first suggested by L.G. Lindahl, can be used to measure the benefits of learning to an organization. The questions are:

- How has the quality of work improved?
- How many people have been able to reach job standards?
- What is the time required to do a specific job?
- What damage is now being done to material or equipment?
- What is the absenteeism record?
- What is the labor turnover?
- What are the running costs?
- What is the level of job satisfaction?

Interestingly enough, it will be noticed that most of these questions involve unobtrusive measures.

The contribution of learning to increased organizational effectiveness is an important one. If it is felt that instruction has not made a meaningful contribution, management commitment to training and education programs will be quickly eroded. Success comes from *meeting* a need, and then *demonstrating* that it has been met.

Learner and supervisor reactions

Much of the information that is collected about mastery, job performance, and increased organizational effectiveness is "hard" data. This means that it is concrete and objective. It is, to a large extent, trustworthy.

Information, on the other hand, that is obtained from learners and supervisors about their reactions is largely "soft" data. It is subjective and somewhat untrustworthy. This is exactly the problem with any opinion poll. Unless care is taken with the collection and interpretation of the data, the information will be misleading.

Nevertheless, such information has a role. If interviews and questionnaires are carefully used, valid data is obtained. Trainees can be asked what they learned and what they enjoyed about the instruction. Supervisors, on the other hand, can be asked whether it was worthwhile and relevant.

Information can be collected about learners' reactions to:

- Content of the instruction.
- Instructional methods employed.
- Worth of the objectives.
- Efficiency of the administration.
- Comfort of the instructional environment.

Continuous assessment, it will be remembered, is more useful than assessment carried out only at the end of the course. For this reason, reactions should be collected at frequent intervals. Then, there is still time to do something about them.

Some of the more interesting reactions are collected two or three months after a course has finished. It is then useful to ask former trainees "How useful has the learning been?" "What have you found to be of particular value in the job situation?" "What ought to have been included, but wasn't?" "How could skill levels be improved?"

ETHICAL CONCERNS ABOUT ASSESSMENT

Assessment involves making decisions about people. It is essential, therefore, that any information used be the best that can be obtained. Furthermore, the information must be obtained in an ethical manner. Trainees and students must not be embarrassed or frightened. Their interests must be protected.

In order to protect the rights of learners, certain steps should be taken by instructors and teachers. It is important for them to bear in mind that learners have certain rights:

- *Right to privacy*
  Trainees have a right to keep certain information private. They should only be asked for essential information. Don't publicize the results of an assessment. Don't use other trainees to assess someone. Don't ask publicly who did well and who did badly. Don't ask who got something right and who got something wrong.

- *Right to confidentiality*
  Trainees have a right to expect that information will be kept confidential. Keep assessment information in a secure place. Be careful about giving the information to other people.

- *Right to expect responsible assessment*
  Trainees have a right to expect that instructors and teachers will behave in a responsible manner. Learners should not be "hurt" as a result of participating in an assessment procedure. It is also essential that assessment honestly reflect a person's mastery of the task or job.

Ethical considerations dictate that assessments be reliable and valid indicators of a learner's achievement.

Reliability

Assessment should be reliable. This means that the information on which the assessment is based should be trustworthy. Data obtained from a casual conversation with a trainee, for instance, is unlikely to be reliable. Information gathered from a well prepared interview, and a planned meeting with a supervisor, is likely to be more accurate.

Since it would be irresponsible to use unreliable information, teachers and instructors are obligated to take whatever steps are necessary to insure that assessment is reliable. It is important to remove all error. The results should be consistent and trustworthy.

If an assessment procedure is completely reliable, certain things can be expected. For instance, all trainees who gain mastery will "pass"; all trainees who do not gain mastery will "fail." Such perfection, however, is probably unreasonable. However, matters should be so arranged that as few mistakes as possible are made.

There are, in fact, three specific things that can be done to determine whether an assessment is reliable. They are:

- Repeat the assessment procedure at least twice with some of the same trainees and students.
- Design two parallel versions of the same assessment procedure. This saves having to give the procedure twice.
- Compare the results from one half of the procedure with the results from the other half.

If the assessment procedures are clearly written, and if there are specific instructions for their administration, reliability will be increased. There should also be a standard scoring guide, to insure that tasks are scored in the same way for all trainees.

If some people are assessed twice on the same task, and achieve similar scores, the procedure is probably a reliable one. Sometimes it is possible to design two versions of the same mastery test. Performance on one version can then be compared with performance on the other. If the two sets of results are similar, the procedure is reliable.

A variation of these two procedures is to compare the results from two halves of the same test. For instance, odd number tasks could form one set, and even ones the other. If trainees performed similarly on both halves of the assessment procedure, then the method is trustworthy.

Validity

Validity is the heart of assessment. Responsible procedures must be valid. It is essential that a procedure measure what it sets out to measure, and nothing else. For example, if a performance test measures someone's ability in inter-personal skills, then the test is valid. If it only measures their ability to talk about the skills, and not to practice them, the test is invalid as far as the job is concerned.

This is one of the reasons for doubting the usefulness, on a large scale, of pen and paper tests and examinations. They tend to be academic and can have little relevance to most work situations. If some kind of certification is involved, then pen and paper tests will be a valid way of gathering information.

Instructors and teachers can do three things to assure that their assessments are valid. All of them involve job-related information. The three steps are:

- Examine the assessment procedure, and decide whether it looks acceptable. Remember, inspection is a valid way of making judgments. Houses, diamonds, and equipment, for instance, are all assessed on the basis of some type of inspection.
- Ask supervisors to look at the assessment procedure and determine whether it is a complete and accurate measure of job mastery. Any information from job analysis and task analysis is useful at this stage.
- Find some people who are already doing the job successfully. See how they do on the assessment procedure. If they fail, something is wrong!

A valid assessment procedure should still be reviewed over the years. Jobs and methods change.

If procedures are no longer useful predictors of human performance, their validity is called into doubt. For example, suppose an assessment procedure measures a person's ability to interview prospective employees. Any evidence that people who have successfully completed the procedure are not able to do the task to a supervisor's satisfaction calls into doubt the validity of the test.

Reliability and validity are different things. A procedure can be reliable but invalid. Similarly, it can be valid but unreliable. Responsible assessment mandates that it be both valid and reliable. Otherwise, it should not be used.

Some legal concerns

Some instructors are worried by the idea of using tests in formal assessment procedures. They feel that tests may be illegal. Testing, by and large, is not only legal; it is specifically authorized by statute.

The important thing about any testing procedure is that it must *not* be designed, intended, or used to discriminate. Accordingly, the following points should be borne in mind:

- The language used in an assessment procedure should be familiar to the trainees and students taking the test. It should be cast at their level.
- Tests should be directly related to the requirements of the job or task. Job analysis and task analysis are necessary sources of information for the contents of an assessment procedure
- Assessment should *not* result in a disproportionate number of one group of people being favored at the expense of another.
- Assessment procedures should be both reliable and valid.

In other words, ethical and responsible assessment is essential. If assessment procedures are carefully designed and responsibly used, there is no cause for concern. Validity is essential.

NORM-REFERENCED AND CRITERION-REFERENCED ASSESSMENT

The objectives of assessment influence the techniques that are used and the kinds of decisions that can be made. For this reason, it is important to distinguish between two different schemes. These are referred to by the terms *norm-referenced assessment* and *criterion-referenced assessment*. For teachers and instructors there is no more important distinction. Two quite different values are represented.

Norm-referenced assessment

Most traditional pen and paper examinations are norm-referenced. When an instructor says that Smith was the best trainee, and Jones the worst, a norm-referenced statement is being made. One person's performance is being compared with another. In order for someone to do well, someone has to do badly.

Norm-referenced assessment is used when there is a need to:

- *Make predictions about a person's future performance*
  This would occur if assessment was being used for making decisions about:
  - Selection.
  - Promotion.

- Further training.
- Salary increases.
- Performance reports.
- Measures of productivity.

- *Measure mastery against some known standard*
  This would occur if assessment was being used for deciding:
  - How much people have learned.
  - How much people can do.
  - How much better (or worse) one person is compared to another.

In all cases, people are being compared. What one ends up with is a list of people arranged in a rank order. Someone is first, someone second . . . someone last.

Criterion-referenced assessment

Criterion-referenced assessment is not interested in making distinctions between people. Instead of comparing one person against another person, people are compared against a standard. It is nothing more than a measure of mastery learning. The question asked is "Has this person reached mastery?"
    Criterion-referenced assessment is used when there is a need to:

- *Monitor learner performance*
  This would occur if assessment was being used to:
  - Motivate and encourage learners.
  - Provide learners with feedback of the progress they are making toward mastery.
- *Determine whether mastery has been achieved*
  This would occur if assessment was being used to make decisions about:
  - Mastery.
  - Attitudes.

The idea of judging a person on a standard of performance has great appeal. It is the basis of the 90/90/90 criterion discussed in Chapter One, in the context of mastery learning.

Norm- and criterion-referenced distributions

Training, for the most part, is oriented toward the present. The basic question is "Have learners acquired mastery?" For this reason, criterion-referenced assessment is more important than a norm-referenced one.
    Education, on the other hand, is interested primarily in the future. It is concerned with the acquisition of skills for life rather than for an immediate job role. Thus, the basic question is "Are learners acquiring the skills for long-term

job and personal growth?'' For this reason, norm-referenced rather than crite-rion-referenced assessment is a matter of some importance.

The essential difference between the two assessment schemes is illustrated in Figure 12:1. In the norm-referenced assessment, learners are rated as "bad," "poor," "satisfactory," "good," and "excellent." The number of people in each class, however, is restricted. Differences in individual ability can be seen at a glance.

In the case of criterion-referenced assessment, however, over 90 percent of the learners have "passed." In other words, they have realized the objectives and achieved mastery of the task or job. Some of these people might be ex-cellent, but we have no information. We only know whether they obtained mastery.

FIGURE 12:1. Norm- and criterion-referenced assessment.

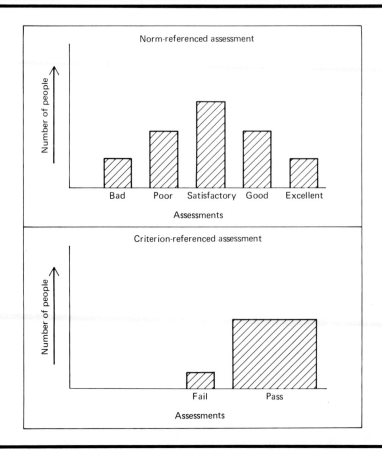

SOME ASSESSMENT PROCEDURES

When thinking of the do's and don'ts of assessment, instructors and teachers need to give particular attention to the details of three procedures. They are:

- Standardized performance checklists.
- Critical incident methods.
- Objective style tests.

These procedures are of special importance when collecting information on mastery learning and job performance.

However, regardless of the procedure employed, a number of general comments need to be made. These comments apply to these procedures, as well as to all assessment procedures in general.

General comments

The importance of behaving in a responsible manner has already been stressed. There are a number of things instructors and teachers must do when they are ready to start collecting information for assessment purposes.

While some of the information can be collected in an unobtrusive manner, it should not be collected in an underhanded manner. For this reason, instructors should:

- Inform learners when information is going to be collected for assessment purposes.
- Inform learners how assessment will be carried out, and how information will be weighted. Some information will be worth more than other information.
- Base all assessment on the objectives that have been identified for the task or job.
- Decide whether criterion-referenced or norm-referenced assessment is appropriate.
- Carry out assessment in a relaxed rather than a high-pressure manner.
- Inform learners of the results of assessment as soon as possible after the procedure is completed. They should also be debriefed, and the results explained.

Once assessment is complete, an action plan for improvement should be written, in consultation with every trainee and student. Otherwise an opportunity is lost.

Standardized performance checklist

Checklists are used in two types of assessment:

- When the task to be assessed involves a sequence of operations. For example, the job involves assembling a component or completing a statistical report.
- When the task to be assessed involves a systematic analysis of a problem situation. For example, the job involves analyzing machine breakdowns or sales data.

In both circumstances, a checklist sets out the steps that must be followed.

In order to carry out assessment, the checklist is obtained by observing a trained person doing the job. It is wise to get a supervisor to make certain that the list accurately shows what should be done. Once the list has been designed, it can be used for both instructional and assessment purposes.

An example of a checklist is illustrated in Figure 12:2. As a trainee completes each step in the procedure, an instructor checks off the operation. In the example shown, it will be seen that the trainee forgot the critical step of holding the rotary joint when the support was removed.

When the assessment is complete, trainees are usually given a copy of the completed list. They can see where they went wrong, and what they need to do to reach mastery. Feedback, under such circumstances, is immediate and to the point.

FIGURE 12:2. Part of a standardized performance checklist to be used in assessment of a disassembly skill.

Disassembly of Elevation Drive Unit	Yes	No
1. Remove two co-axial connector nuts.	✔	
2. Remove six retaining screws.	✔	
3. Depress two co-axial connectors into end plate.	✔	
4. Remove end plate.	✔	
5. Remove six flathead screws.	✔	
6. Remove closure seal.	✔	
7. Remove V-seal.	✔	
8. Remove four screws and screw guard.	✔	
9. Disconnect two co-axial connectors.	✔	
10. Remove six screws and six washers.	✔	
11. Remove (1) rotary joint support, and hold (2) rotary joint with one hand.	✔(1)	✔(2)
12. Disconnect two co-axial connectors.	✔	
13. Remove rotary joint.	✔	
14. Remove two co-axials.	✔	

Critical incident method

The critical incident method is a short form of the previous method. It involves collecting on-the-job behaviors that supervisors consider to be critical. They might be either "good" or "bad." They are then arranged in the form of a checklist.

One great advantage of the critical incident method is that it can be used for a wide range of tasks. They do not have to be procedural in nature, nor do they have to involve problem-solving skills. An example of the rating sheet for the job of a salesperson is shown in Figure 12:3.

The method is a simple one. It is a very rapid way of assessing learning in either a simulated or real job situation. Since only critical incidents are involved, it focuses on essentials. No attempt is made to include every step or operation.

Objective style tests

Although pen and paper tests are not as relevant to training as they are to education, some thought needs to be given to them. When they are appropriate, they have advantages over essay type examinations and papers.

The main advantages of objective style tests and examinations are:

- They are easy and quick to grade.
- They can be graded by nonspecialists.
- They are good at assessing a learner's ability to recognize and recall information.
- They are more reliable than essay type tests.
- They are excellent for sampling a whole syllabus in a short amount of time.

FIGURE 12:3. Part of a critical incident checklist for the job of a salesperson.

Critical incidents in selling	Yes	No
1. Calls on customer immediately after complaint.	✔	
2. Discusses complaint.	✔	
3. Resolves complaint to customer's and company's satisfaction.	✔	
4. Lays out sales plan a month ahead.		✔
5. Plans each day's activities in advance.	✔	
6. Gathers sales information from wide range of sources.		✔
7. Calls on customers regularly.	✔	
8. Follows up on visits.		✔
9. Is truthful in dealing with customers.	✔	

FIGURE 12:4.   Examples of a range of objective questions.

True-false questions

State whether the following items are true or false, by circling the appropriate word.

Aluminum cannot be welded.   True / False
Resistance is measured in Ohms.   True / False

Multiple-choice questions

Indicate the best answer by circling the number.

The most important property of an objective test is:
1. Ease of marking.
2. Accuracy of scoring.
3. Its reliability.
4. Its validity.
5. Complete sampling of the syllabus.

Matching item questions

For each item, write a number to indicate that the statement applies to:
1. Norm-referenced assessment.
2. Criterion-referenced assessment.
3. Both norm and criterion-referenced assessment.
4. Neither norm nor criterion-referenced assessment.

_____ Assessment is mastery-based.
_____ Some people must fail; otherwise assessment is too easy.
_____ Assessment is useful for making predictions.

Rank-order questions

Rank order the following principles in order of importance, using "1" to indicate most important, "2" second, "3" third, and "4" least important.

The four responsibilities of an instructor-manager are:
Leading
Planning
Controlling
Organizing

Completion questions

Complete the following sentences as carefully as you can:
1. The four characteristics of communication are:

    _____   _____

    _____   _____

2. Giving feedback means _____ .
3. Feedback should be _____ to be effective.

Unfortunately, with the advantages go a number of disadvantages. The most important of them is the question of validity.

Multiple-choice tests are useful to assess knowledge-based learning. They have little role in assessing skills and attitudes. The only way to assess someone's skill at driving a car is to go out with that person on the road. There is a world of difference between their performance on paper and their performance behind the wheel of an automobile.

Examples of objective style questions are shown in Figure 12:4. Such examinations, of course, can be carried out under closed or open book arrangements. In the open book situation, learners can refer to any reference materials or job aids that are appropriate.

While an examination or test is in progress, instructors should:

- Move around the room. Make sure that learners are following directions. Answer any questions about the procedure.
- Avoid smiling or frowning. Body language gives trainees an advantage when they are puzzling over a question.
- Head off cheating. If it happens, deal with it firmly but unemotionally. Review the purposes of assessment, and discuss the problem as a problem and not as a crime.
- Call out time at half-time, three quarters, and a few minutes before the end.
- Encourage people who finish early to check their work. No marks are given for leaving the room early.

The important thing is to be encouraging. There is no point in creating a threatening environment. Be fair, but be sympathetic as well.

CONCLUSION

Assessment is an emotional term, but it does not have to be an anxiety-provoking experience. Trainees and students need to see the process in a positive light. It is a contradiction to learn without knowing how you are doing.

Assessment serves many purposes. One of the most important is to determine whether mastery has been gained. Another is to identify learning problems, so that remedial action can be taken. In either case, the procedure depends upon the objectives that have been set. Without clear objectives, it is not possible to devise a responsible assessment procedure.

Part Three

Instructional Concerns

*Concerns vanish
with understanding.*

Instructional strategies and tactics deal with the "why" and "how" of instruction. However, there are still a number of related issues which are unresolved by such a synthesis. These are the concerns that instructors and teachers have about direct training that are outside these two dimensions.

These concerns are both troublesome and anxiety-provoking. They involve issues for which there are no clearcut solutions. Often there is no really good way of going. Furthermore, to confound the problem even more, the concerns are usually ones about which people have quite strong opinions.

Such concerns are many. Among the more troublesome of them are the following topics, which form the content of Part Three:

- Acquiring knowledge, skill, and attitudes
- Harnessing trainee motivation
- Individual differences
- Discussion techniques
- Managing time and paper
- Out of class assignments
- Personality of the instructor

By appreciating the nature of these problems, it is possible to deal with them in a constructive and positive fashion.

These concerns do not in any way eliminate the potential of instructional strategies and tactics. They do, however, limit and change them, since they make it difficult to distinguish between cause and effect.

While the concerns can be separated from the techniques of instruction, they cannot be separated from the objectives of it. In effect, they inhibit both the efficiency and the effectiveness of the instructional-learning process. In understanding them, however, instructors and teachers gain power over them.

Chapter 13

Acquiring Knowledge, Skill, and Attitudes

FOCUS

"How are knowledge, skill, and attitudes acquired?"

KNOWLEDGE OBJECTIVES

After reading and studying this chapter, you will be able to:

1. apply the principles of learning to the instructional process;
2. design instructional situations conducive to the acquisition of knowledge;
3. design instructional situations conducive to the acquisition of skill;
4. design instructional situations conducive to the acquisition of appropriate attitudes.

ATTITUDE OBJECTIVES

After reading this chapter, the author hopes that you will:

1. value the stages in knowledge, skill, and attitude acquisition;
2. incorporate the principles into your teaching, so that they become characteristic of your instructional style.

Skill transforms human performance into mastery.

The ultimate objective of instruction is the achievement of mastery. Relatively inexperienced and naive trainees and students are raised to a level of adequacy in a task or role. Adequacy, in such a context, is normally referred to as the *Experienced Worker Standard* or EWS.

The standard is defined in a number of ways. Mostly, however, it is measured in terms of output or services over time. These are calculated in terms of number, weight, volume, or area. Quality, mistakes, wasteage, and similar factors are often added to the calculation.

The standard is obtained from work study or job analysis. It is agreed on by managers, supervisors, and union representatives. The standard can also be recognized intuitively on the basis of experience and knowledge. Most people, for example, have a good idea of whether someone is adequate or not in a role or job.

It is important that instructors and learners recognize adequate performance. The purpose of instruction is to help people prepare themselves for the world of work and leisure. Instruction is credible as long as trainees and students reach an EWS standard.

Training and education, in other words, must be tied to standards. Some of the standards will come from instruction. Others come from outside. Training objectives are one thing, learning objectives are another. Standards for learning must be derived from what is required for adequate performance.

THE PRINCIPLES OF LEARNING

In order for someone to move from a level of inadequacy to a level of adequacy, learning must take place. The word "learning" is an everyday term, yet it is difficult to define. Most dictionary definitions focus on the process, rather than the product of learning. They talk about gaining knowledge as a result of instruction.

A definition of learning

A more useful definition, at least from the point of view of the teaching-learning process, is to think of learning as a product. Learning refers to: *a change in behavior that can be observed and measured.* If learning cannot be seen, and cannot be assessed, instruction is difficult.

246

Unless learning involves change, it would be difficult to identify an instructional need. Also, it would be almost impossible to monitor the progress of learning. Finally, it would be next to impossible to determine when learning had taken place and adequacy was achieved. Defining learning as a change in behavior makes instruction easier.

Such a definition casts instructors and teachers in the role of a "change agent." Instructors, in other words, have a responsibility for initiating, assisting, reinforcing, and assessing change. The managing role of an instructor is more important than the operating one. Management implies goals will be achieved.

Some teachers and instructors feel negative about a definition of learning that includes the word "behavior." They regard the word as narrow and mechanistic. They associate it with B.F. Skinner and "behaviorism."

However, everyone is interested in human behavior. What distinguishes behaviorists from nonbehaviorists is one word. Behaviorists argue that learning *is* a change in behavior. Nonbehaviorists prefer to say that "learning refers to" or "learning results from" a change in behavior.

Learning and performance

Learning and performance are not the same thing. There is a difference between the two behaviors. The difference involves a key factor in instruction and teaching. In effect:

- *Learning* involves the acquisition of knowledge, skills, and attitudes associated with job mastery.
- *Performance* involves using the knowledge, skills, and attitudes to demonstrate that mastery has been realized at an EWS level.

Learning gives a person potential. Performance indicates that the potential has been realized.

Many things are learned that are not immediately put into effect. For instance, people may learn a great deal from watching a film on safety. They will learn about the different kinds of safety clothing and the procedures that should be followed when working on a particular job.

None of this learning, however, guarantees that they will *wear* the clothing and *follow* the procedures when they carry out the task. Performance on the job has still to be demonstrated. To a large extent, it will depend upon the values, attitudes, and opinions that people have acquired during instruction. If safety is not attractive, they will ignore it.

Two ways of knowing

Although learning is often spoken of as a single thing, there are two dimensions of knowing:

- *Explicit dimension*
  This dimension involves clarity. It values good communication. Its objective is to make everything crystal clear. Understanding is the ultimate objective.

- *Tacit dimension*
  This dimension involves something beyond words. We know more than we can tell or put into words. Its objective is concerned with feelings, with personal knowledge.

The explicit dimension is important in learning, while the tacit one is important in performance.

Skill involves tacit knowing. It is difficult, for example, for someone to describe when to change gear in a nonautomatic car. It is even more difficult to explain how you know that you have just made a good shot in golf. How can you tell? You just know. Words cannot describe your knowledge.

Skill resides in an inner feeling. Clarity and explicitness are obviously important in instruction. But they are not enough. Somehow the tacit dimension must be put to work. Media, especially film and television, is helpful. Role playing, simulations, apprenticeships, practicums, internships, and well conceived demonstrations help. Practice and experience are essential. So are continuous assessment and feedback.

FIGURE 13:1. Some principles of learning useful to instructors and learners.

Learning from the point of view of the learner

- Learning is a natural process. It is not something that is only done in a formal instructional setting.
- People are different. Provision has to be made for differences in ability, aptitude, and experience.
- Anxiety is essential for learning. However, anxiety must be managed. Too much anxiety is as bad as too little.
- The atmosphere of the instructional group affects learning. People learn best in a warm, participative environment.
- People who see a learning task as relevant and worthwhile learn better than people who see it as irrelevant.

Learning from the point of view of behavior

- Learners should be active. People learn better when they are active rather than passive.
- Learning involves practice and rehearsal. Overlearning, obtained from repetition, is essential for performance.

Principles of learning

Although learning involves many tactics and strategies, there are a number of general principles that can act as guidelines in lesson preparation and implementation. The principles are summarized in figure 13:1.

The most critical points for instructors and teachers to implement are:

- Learners must be active rather than passive.
- Frequency and recency are important. The more something is done, and the more recent the performance, the better the learning.
- Learning is purposeful; it is not a reflex. There is a conscious purpose, and this motivation needs to be recognized.
- Reinforcement and feedback are essential. If people are not rewarded they will not learn. If they don't get feedback, their learning will not improve. They will fall into bad habits.
- Learning should be pleasant and enjoyable. Unpleasant situations are avoided.

Learning can be right, and it can be wrong. People learn bad habits as easily as good ones.

Fatigue

Fatigue occurs when physical and mental energy is expended at a faster rate than recovery. Many factors contribute to it. Among them are length of work

---

- Learning must be reinforced. Rewards are better than punishment. They can come from the learner or the instructor. They can come from the instructional group or the situation itself.
- Learning should be generalized. If the task is to be carried out in a wide range of settings, practice and rehearsal should be carried out in a variety of contexts. In this way, learning will be generalized from the one situation to the other.
- Learning should be shaped. It is foolish to expect perfect performance the first time. Learning is a matter of successive approximations towards mastery.

Learning from the point of view of understanding

- Learning is purposeful. Objectives are an important part of the process.
- People learn in different ways, according to their learning style. Some like to be told, some shown. Some like to work in groups, some by themselves.
- Learning that is understood is less likely to be forgotten. Meaning is important.
- Well organized tasks are easier to learn than poorly organized ones.
- Knowledge of results, called feedback, is essential to learning.

period, speed of work, extent that muscles are involved, tensions around the task, and boredom. Environmental factors like noise, heat, cold, and humidity also contribute.

Fatigue shows itself in learning tasks in a number of ways. They include:

- Reduced concentration and vigilance.
- Reduced attention and interest.
- Reduced speed and smoothness of movement.
- Reduced reaction speed and coordination.
- Physical discomfort and tiredness.
- Reduced resistance to stress and anxiety.

These show themselves in a lowering of motivation toward further involvement in the learning task.

From the point of view of physical and mental activity, instructors and teachers should allocate:

- The most exacting work in the morning.
- The more interesting work during the afternoon.
- Arduous mental activities to daytime. The evening should be avoided for such activities.

Figure 13:2 illustrates a fatigue curve for an instructional day. The only break is at lunchtime.

It will be noticed that the most productive times are the early morning and afternoon. Late morning and late afternoon, as a general rule, should be avoided, as far as sustained mental activity is concerned.

Fatigue, however, can be dramatically reduced in three ways. Instructors and teachers can introduce into the lesson:

- *A change of pace*
  take the pressure off, let the learners proceed at a more leisurely pace for a time.

FIGURE 13:2. Fatigue during an instructional day.

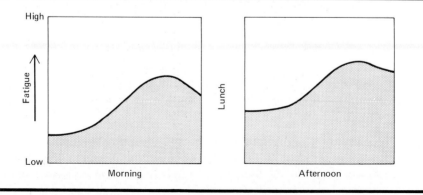

- *A change of activity*
  change from a demonstration to a discussion.

- *A work break*
  a moment to stretch, talk, and walk around; a coffee break or just ten minutes free time.

Introducing a change of pace or activity or giving learners a short break will delay the onset of fatigue. It will increase the efficiency and effectiveness of the learning-teaching process. It is better to have four half-hour sessions, with a change or break between each, than to have one continuous two-hour block.

Domains of learning

Although learning is unitary, it is usual to divide it into three parts, called "domains." The three domains are:

- Knowledge domain
- Skills domain
- Attitude domain

Dividing learning in this way is artificial and a matter of convenience.

There is a skills and attitude component to knowledge, just as much as there is a knowledge and skills component to attitudes. They are facets of the same thing. However, the acquisition of skills and attitudes presents a number of particular difficulties.

Figure 13:3 illustrates something of the relationship between the three domains. Each domain supports the other. Good instruction demands that adequate attention be given to all three. In some situations, one domain will be more important; in other situations the others may become dominant.

THE ACQUISITION OF KNOWLEDGE

Knowledge is fundamental to skill and attitude. Skill and attitudes that are firmly based on knowledge are strong and long-lasting. In the past, most people earned their livelihood as a result of the skills they possessed. Today, because of rapidly changing technologies, the knowledge worker is preeminent. The day of the manual worker has largely passed.

The human memory

The word "memory" is rather old-fashioned. When we talk about someone having a good memory, we are really talking about their ability to *remember*. We are commenting on their ability to retain, recall, and recognize knowledge or skill. It is the opposite of forgetting.

FIGURE 13:3. The three domains of learning.

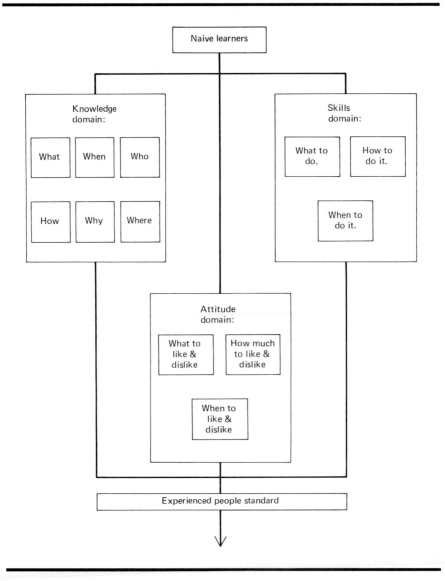

Forgetting is not all bad. It would be foolish for learners to try to remember everything. Some information is more important. Some experiences are pleasant. A great deal of what we hear and see is trivial and unimportant. What is important is to be able to sort out the forest from the trees. This is where an instructor plays an essential role. Learners need guidance and encouragement.

The human brain

The part of the brain involved in learning contains about ten to twelve billion cells. Only about 15 percent of the capacity of those cells is ever realized, even by the ablest of people. As a result, there is no known limit to learning.

The problem with forgetting does not involve the capacity of the brain. Age, also, is not a factor. Some brain cells die every day and are not replaced. The number, however, is too small to affect learning. Most of the learning problems that occur with older people are the result of sickness, poor motivation, and physiological change.

Rather than declining with age, there is evidence that human abilities grow with use. Just as unused muscles waste away, so brain cells fail to develop. As the brain matures, a near white fatty substance called "myelin" develops around the cell fibers. The development of this essential substance is assisted by intensive learning.

Practice makes perfect. It also helps the brain mature. In this way, further learning is possible. Fatigue, of course, can occur, but it does not arise in the brain. There is no such thing as "mental fatigue." It is a misnomer. Long periods of mental effort do the brain no harm.

It is the body, not the brain, that becomes tired. What is taken for mental tiredness is likely to be the product of:

- Boredom and lack of interest.
- Loss of concentration.
- Muscular fatigue in the eyes, neck, shoulders, and back.

The resulting discomfort can become so distracting that further concentration is impossible.

Types of memory

Most people talk about the memory as a storehouse. However, it involves nothing more than an electro-chemical change. This takes place in the nerve cells of the body's central nervous system, as well as in the brain's nerve fibers. In other words, every time something is learned a physical change takes place in the nerve cells and fibers.

From the point of view of the teaching-learning process, it is useful to distinguish among three types of memory. They are:

- *Surface memory*
  Everyone is surrounded by things that compete for attention. Some of the stimuli are weak, some strong. Some are relevant, and some are irrelevant.

  The surface memory retains information for about ten to fifteen seconds. Unless it is transferred to the short-term memory, it will be forgotten.

  The surface memory enables us to repeat a piece of information immediately after it is heard. Half a minute later it can be forgotten.

- *Short-term memory*

  Selected items from the surface memory are transferred to the short-term one. They are stored there one or two days.

  The short-term memory enables us to remember something today, but not next week. Facts are important to the short-term memory. Meaning is important to the long-term memory.

- *Long-term memory*

  A minority of the information in the short-term memory is transferred to the long-term one. Storage capacity is almost unlimited. Information can be held indefinitely.

  Everything we know that is older than about two days is stored in the long term memory. All experiences that we have had, everything we believe in.

  In order to get things out of the long-term memory, effort is needed. Forgetting does not involve a loss, but a problem of access.

Instructors and teachers have a dual responsibility. They must help learners attend (surface memory), and then help learners transfer key points through the short-term to the long-term memory.

Work by Ernst Ludwig suggests that if an instructor presents a large number of teaching points during a thirty-minute lesson, only about twenty will pass into the short-term memory. Of the twenty, only six to seven will then pass into the long-term memory.

If the same material is re-presented two to four weeks later, better results will be achieved. In fact, the number of points stored in the long-term memory can be doubled. Ludwig's work also indicates that it is important to keep the surface memory occupied. Unless it is fully stimulated, learners will let their thoughts wander away from the lesson.

The moral is clear. Instructors and teachers should take steps to:

- Keep the surface memory stimulated and occupied. It is not enough to gain a learner's attention; steps must be taken to keep it.
- Make sure that the key teaching points pass from the short- to the long-term memory. If only a few points are likely to get there, it is essential that the process is not left to chance.
- Assist in the transfer from superficial to short-term and on to long-term. This can be achieved by repetition, emphasizing key points, and using a variety of instructional tactics.

There is a limit on what can be transferred from one memory to another.

Photographic memories

Some people have what is called a "photographic memory." Technically, it is called *eidetic imagery*. Long after they have looked at a picture or a page of a book, these people are able to imagine and describe what is there. In fact, they are able to inspect the picture or book and extract new information. Some people can do the same thing with lesson summaries.

Eidetic imagery is more common in children than in adults. It is also more common in individuals with brain damage. This suggests that the ability involves an abnormal functioning of the brain. People who possess the skill, however, may be perfectly normal, functioning people.

About 10 percent of children have photographic memories, with a peak around puberty. Only about 2 percent of adults possess the ability. Learning would be a great deal simpler if all trainees and students possessed the skill. However, too few people have it for it to make much difference to instruction.

Availability and accessibility

It is not possible to remember material that has not been learned. Once instruction has taken place, mastery becomes a matter of:

- *Availability*
  Knowledge and skill must be stored in the brain or nervous system. If they are not stored, they are not available for use.

- *Accessibility*
  Once something is available, there can be a problem of gaining access to it. Everyone knows the problem of having something on the tip of your tongue. Somehow you just cannot bring it to mind.

The distinction is an important one.

It suggests that first an instructor or teacher must take steps to be sure that information is available. Once it is available for use, steps must be taken to make certain that it is accessible. Neither availability nor accessibility should be taken for granted. Practice, consolidation, review, and feedback are essential.

Tactics for remembering

Instructors and teachers can help learners remember. In order to do this, a plan for availability and accessibility must be prepared. Assessment procedures must mesh into the plan. It is unreasonable to test learners in a way that makes availability and accessibility difficult.

Suppose trainees learn to use a hand calculator. It would be unfair to ask them to describe how they would use it. A different skill is involved. Ability with words is not the same as ability with the calculator.

Figure 13:4 outlines tactics for remembering. The important points for instructors and teachers to bear in mind are few in number. They include:

- Material must be meaningful to the learner. Nonsense or meaningless material is difficult to remember.
- Order and pattern are essential. Material that is organized, so that a pattern

FIGURE 13:4. Tactics for making things easier to remember.

Remembering is improved when instructors take steps to emphasize:

- *Order, sequence or place*

  Procedures, principles, components and classifications depend upon order, sequence, or place. Memory devices like rhymes, mnemonics, sentences, and stories help people remember.

- *Key points*

  Only a limited number of items can be transferred from one memory to the other, at any one time. Material, therefore, should be reduced to "must knows." Point out the essential from the trivial.

- *Pattern or organization*

  Material that is organized into patterns is helpful. Diagrams, charts, tables, or other graphics help people remember.

- *Meaning*

  Material that is meaningful is better remembered than material that has little meaning. Try and make topics worthwhile and relevant to the learners. Stress importance.

- *Relationships in time and space*

  Material that is presented so that relationships are obvious is better remembered. Try and "key" material into what the learners already know. Stress how one thing is related to another thing.

---

or plan appears, is easier to learn. Material that is disorganized is difficult to learn and remember.

- Material that is relevant and worthwhile is more easily learned and recalled. Material that appears worthless or irrelevant is difficult to master.
- Material that is presented in a vivid, imaginative, and exaggerated way is easy to remember.
- Material that is reviewed and consolidated is more easily remembered than material that is presented only once.

The tactics are hardly new. Nevertheless, they are effective and efficient.

Recall varies over time. Under normal circumstances, learners will best remember material that has been:

- Presented at the beginning of a lesson.
- Presented at the end of a lesson.
- Reinforced by repetition, feedback, understanding, rhymes, mnemonics, and other memory devices.

They are likely to remember less of the things in the middle section of the lesson.

If recall is to be kept at a reasonable level throughout the whole of the lesson, a simple tactic is required. After about twenty minutes, arrange for a brief break or change of activity. Anything shorter than twenty minutes interferes with the flow and organization of the material. Anything significantly longer than twenty minutes results in a continuing decline in the amount of material that will be recalled.

One further point remains. What happens after the lesson ends? Two things occur that are of interest to both learners and instructors:

- *Learners remember more things immediately after a lesson than during it*
  Recall actually rises to a peak about ten minutes after the lesson ends. This is because learners sort things out. They get things into focus. It takes only a few minutes, and everything drops into place.

- *A decline then takes place immediately*
  The rate of forgetting is discouraging. It is very steep. After about twenty-four hours something like 80 percent has been forgotten.

Figure 13:5 shows the sort of thing that can happen.

The situation, however, can be saved. Frequent reviews help to keep the level of material remembered at a high level. The reviews need not be lengthy ones. A few intensive minutes of revision are better than a half-hearted thirty minutes.

The first review should take place as soon as possible. Additional reviews can be carried out after increasingly longer periods. They can be the next day, the next week, the next month, after six months, etc.

This simple tactic will yield a substantial dividend. The effort that has gone into teaching and learning will not be lost. Spaced review protects learning. The

FIGURE 13:5. Idealized diagram illustrating the advantages of spaced review to keep recall high.

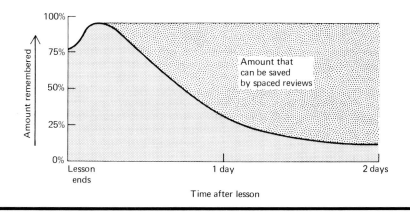

tactic, of course, is also the main justification for lesson summaries and note-taking. Unless students and trainees have something to review, forgetting will take place.

THE ACQUISITION OF SKILL

Earlier in this chapter, a distinction was drawn between learning and perform-ance. There are two types of performance:

- *Unskilled performance*
  This is characterized by a lack of consistency. Performance is irregular. There is no smoothness or skill involved.

  Example: A person can play golf, but performance is irregular.

- *Skilled performance*
  This is characterized by consistency. Performance is regular. There is smoothness and coordination.

  Example: A person plays golf consistently well.

Although most people associate skill with motor tasks as in golf, flying an aircraft, or icing a cake, skill is also involved in intellectual tasks. Some people are skilled with words. Others are skilled with numbers. Still others are skilled at problem-solving and trouble-shooting.

The nature of skilled performance

Skill is an *organized* physical and mental activity. Sometimes only mental ac-tivity is involved; more usually both mental and physical activities are entailed. The important thing, however, is organization. There is a plan to skill. A har-mony and rhythm.

Skilled people are easily recognizable. They are:

- Adaptable and flexible.
- Characterized by a clear sense of purpose.
- People who have speed, accuracy, and style.
- Consistent in the results they achieve.
- Coordinated, smooth, and rhythmic in their actions.

Skill involves practiced ability. It is not something that has been acquired by chance. Skill is the result of training, sustained effort, and practice.

The acquisition of skill

Practice is all-important. So are knowledge and feedback. A skilled person performs more accurately, and at greater speed, than an inexperienced one.

Skill also depends upon an ability to react quickly and accurately to an emerging situation. Ability to anticipate is essential.

Developing such abilities requires a great deal of effort and time. An attitude of mind is also involved. The development of skilled performance goes through three stages. Each stage entails a different set of responses from instructors and learners.

The stages in the acquisition of skilled performance, as suggested by P.M. Fitts, are:

- *The knowledge phase*
  This involves talking about the skill and gaining background information. Instructors give learners information about:
  - What to expect.
  - What to look out for and avoid.
  - The procedures to be followed.
  - What needs to be known.
  - What precautions to take.
  - What standards have to be reached.
    Particular attention should be given to analyzing error. The knowledge phase is short in duration.

- *The acquisition phase*
  This involves acquiring correct patterns of behavior. As they are acquired, they should be "fixed" by practice. Errors should gradually be eliminated. Instructors arrange for learners to have:
  - A demonstration of the skill.
  - Opportunity to imitate the skill.
  - Practice of the skill under real or simulated conditions.
  - Knowledge of results.
  - Guidance and personal assistance.
    This phase may last from a few weeks to many months. In the case of a pilot it would last from the first solo flight to perhaps a hundred hours after a license has been acquired.

- *The automatic phase*
  This involves the gradual acquisition of speed and accuracy. As the skill becomes more and more automatic, resistance to stress increases. Resistance to interference from other activities also occurs, so that concentration grows. Instructors arrange for learners to:
  - Overlearn the skill.
  - Acquire rhythm and coordination.
  - Learn how to resist stress and interference.
  - Gradually increase speed and accuracy.
  - Achieve the Experienced Worker Standard.
    Rhythm is all important.

Each of the phases may overlap to a certain extent. The transitions, too, may also be gentle, rather than sudden and abrupt.

Students and trainees make different progress. Much depends upon their ability, motivation, temperament, and industriousness. A sensitive and observant instructor can do a great deal to help.

The nature of practice

Practice, as we have seen, is essential. Without it skilled performance cannot be obtained. However, practice, to be effective, needs to be managed in a particular way. Instructors and learners have to choose between:

- *Massed practice*
  This involves large blocks of time in which learners practice and rehearse skill without breaks.

- *Distributed practice*
  This involves shorter periods of time for practice and rehearsal. Short breaks should occur every ten minutes.

Massed practice is more efficient. Distributed practice is more effective.

Abundant evidence exists that distributed practice is superior to massed practice. Performance efficiency may rise from 18 to 45 percent, if a rest period of five to twenty minutes is given after every eight minutes of practice. Physical skills can be "practiced" mentally, with good results.

There are, in addition to practice, two mainstays of skill acquisition. They are feedback and guidance. Feedback involves knowledge of results. Guidance entails everything from telling someone what to do, to showing them and encouraging them. Guidance can be given directly, or by means of media like television, slide-tape presentations, and job aids.

Feedback

The importance of feedback has long been recognized in the acquisition of motor skills. However, only since the early 1960's has its role in learning intellectual tasks and attitudes been commonly appreciated. Today, feedback is an essential part of instructional technique.

Feedback is referred to by a variety of names. Some people use the term "knowledge of results," others "information feedback." Probably the most common alternative is "reinforcement." Although "feedback" has engineering associations, it is the term most used by instructors and teachers.

There are a number of different types of feedback. All of them are used in teaching and learning, as well as in job situations. Feedback can come from:

- *Inside the task or job*
  This is called intrinsic feedback. It is inherent in the task. It is obtained through the senses and is immediate.

Examples: the information obtained from the smell of burning lubricant on a lathe

inability to balance an account

- *Outside the task or job*
  This is called extrinsic feedback. It does not originate in the task. Sometimes it is immediate; often it is delayed.

  Examples: the information that is obtained from regular performance appraisals

  quarterly sales figures and bonuses

In instructional settings, it is important that learners be taught how to identify and use intrinsic feedback. It is also important that extrinsic feedback be given as quickly as possible.

Learners require more extrinsic feedback than people who have gained mastery. Extrinsic feedback is required to:

- *Learn knowledge, skill, or attitudes*
  This type of feedback is no longer necessary once mastery has been achieved.

  Example: the information an instructor gives a trainee by saying "That's right, you are doing great."

- *Maintain mastery once it has been achieved*
  This type of feedback is essential in every job situation. Some people, however, don't receive it. They have no idea how they are doing. When they are criticized, or fail to get a promotion, it comes as a big surprise.

  This type of feedback is also important in teaching. If people don't receive it, they forget or slip into bad habits. For this reason, using extrinsic feedback to maintain mastery is an important part of the instructional process.

  Example: "You are not dealing with customer objections as well as you did last month. Remember . . ."

During instruction, people must learn to acquire mastery. However, they must learn it in such a way that removing extrinsic feedback has liitle effect on their performance.

Learners, in other words, must be prepared for the real world. Extrinsic feedback, during training and education, should be withdrawn in a planned and organized manner. Trainees must be weaned from the prompts and cues they receive from instructors.

Trainees and students have to learn how to stand on their own feet. They have to learn how to *obtain* and *use* extrinsic feedback themselves. It is essential that they be prepared; otherwise performance will deteriorate when they leave training.

Skilled performance is characterized by an ability to anticipate the requirements of a task or situation. This reduces the probability of error. It also reduces the time necessary to complete a task. Investigations indicate that anticipation is nothing more than an ability to obtain and use intrinsic and extrinsic feedback to personal advantage.

There are, of course, many sources of feedback available to people in instructional and job situations. They include feedback from:

- Progress that has been made toward the realization of objectives and goals. Examples include: learning objectives, management by objectives, sales quotas, targets for productivity, speed, reaction time, time to complete a task, reduction in errors, etc.
- Information obtained from instructors and supervisors. This includes verbal and body language. Examples are performance assessment, grading of work assignments, counseling, guidance, interviews, etc.
- Information obtained from other trainees, colleagues, and work people. Examples include: comparison of own performance with that of others, suggestions for improvement, information about what has to be done and what the standards are, etc. This source is particularly important in the acquisition of attitudes, due to the power of group processes.
- Information that is obtained from the task itself. A great deal of information is available. Examples include: readings on instruments, information obtained from the senses, intuition, and feelings about a situation, etc.

Feedback is always present. People have to learn how to recognize *and* use it.

Research offers a number of guidelines to instructors and learners:

- Feedback is essential to the acquisition of intellectual and motor skills. It is also essential for attitudes.
- Feedback should not be too detailed. It should be specific, factual, and to the point.
- Feedback should not be delayed. This does *not* mean that it has to be immediate. It does mean that feedback should be given before the same action occurs again.
- Avoid giving learners feedback while they are performing the task. It interferes with concentration, and takes away a sense of achievement.
- Learners must be taught to observe and use feedback that is intrinsic in the task or situation. This will help insure that they maintain mastery once instruction is complete.

Feedback is of increasing importance as progress is made toward mastery. In the early stages, guidance from instructors and teachers is more critical.

Guidance

Feedback is one way that learners obtain information. An alternative involves the age-old process of guidance, which also reduces stress and anxiety. Guidance lies at the heart of the instructional process. It identifies a key role for teachers and instructors.

Guidance represents individualized instruction. It is normally given on a one-to-one basis, in which instructor and learner discuss a task together. An attempt should be made to be encouraging and to reduce anxiety. At the same time, specific information is given about the task.

Although guidance has a role in all stages of learning, it is particularly important when learning is just beginning. Research indicates that guidance is more effective than extrinsic feedback in three situations:

- Guidance reduces the chances of error in the early stages of learning.
- It makes certain that learners perform correctly from the start.
- It insures that learners attend to important things and ignore trivial ones.

Guidance at the beginning increases the probability that mastery will be gained smoothly and quickly.

Guidance, however, does have one drawback. Learners can depend upon it to an unhealthy degree. Instead of becoming independent as they progress toward mastery, they may become dependent. This is as true of attitudes and values as it is of intellectual and motor skills. Too much guidance is unhealthy.

A solution is to mix guidance with extrinsic feedback. In the initial stages of learning, encourage *and* guide learners. As progress begins to be made, reduce guidance and introduce extrinsic feedback. Toward the final stages of learning, reduce extrinsic feedback and eliminate guidance.

In effect, instructional methods need to change as progress is made in learning. What is appropriate at one stage of learning may not be appropriate at another. Guidance is especially important in the initial stages, extrinsic feedback in the middle, and intrinsic feedback in the later stages.

THE ACQUISITION OF ATTITUDES

Attitudes are receiving increasing attention in training and education. More and more, it is being recognized that it is not enough to concentrate upon intellectual and motor skills. Attitudes, too, must be learned and changed, if mastery is to be obtained.

At the same time, people's attitudes toward learning and instruction are also important. Instructors and teachers have a responsibility to see that trainees and students enjoy learning. Only then will they put their newfound knowledge and skills to good use. Teachers, in other words, profoundly influence attitudes.

Values, attitudes, and opinions

Attitudes are learned. They are also long-lasting. Sometimes they are acquired consciously. More often, they are obtained gradually, incidentally, and unconsciously. Regardless of how they are acquired, they represent a system of beliefs.

Each attitude causes a person to feel "warm" or "cold" toward an object, idea, person, or situation. It represents a tendency toward or away from something. In effect, attitudes are likes and dislikes, such as a liking for work or a dislike of autocracy. Such feelings have their roots in the emotions but rest upon a foundation of knowledge.

Attitudes and values overlap. They are related to each other. Values, however, are central, as is indicated in Figure 13:6. The major differences between values and attitudes are summarized below:

- *Values*
  (e.g., to value honesty, happiness, truth, justice, equality)
  Values are abstract and general in character. They:
  - Represent an ideal or standard of conduct.
  - Are possessed completely, or not at all.
  - Cannot be observed directly.
  - Do *not* involve specific objects or people.

- *Attitudes*
  (e.g., like or dislike courtesy, cooperation, safety shoes, promptness, answering the telephone)
  Attitudes are specific in character. They:
  - Represent a preference for or against something.
  - Are possessed completely or partially.
  - Can be observed.
  - Do involve specific objects or people.

Values serve as motivation. They determine attitudes, just as attitudes determine behavior.

Attitudes are related not only to values but also to opinions. In fact, there are no sharp differences between them. One grades into the other. For example, if you dislike someone (an attitude), you are likely to expect that they will behave badly (an opinion).

Opinions are really predictions about something or someone. Unlike attitudes, they can always be put into words. For this reason, opinions sometimes seem more concrete and specific. This is why public polls collect opinions; they are easier to obtain with a questionnaire or from an interview.

Components of an attitude

Attitudes have three distinct parts or components. Each one contains:

- *A knowledge component*
  This consists of what a person knows about the subject.

- *An emotional component*
  This consists of what a person likes or dislikes about the subject. There can

FIGURE 13:6. The relationship between values, attitudes and opinions.

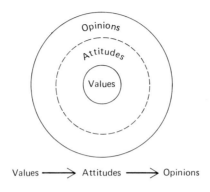

Values ⟶ Attitudes ⟶ Opinions

be different intensities of feeling. Some likes, for instance, may be strong, others weak.

- *An action component*
  This consists of what a person does to express feelings of liking or disliking.

Each component can vary in intensity. A person, for instance, may know little about the subject of sales compensation but may have very strong feelings on the matter.

All attitudes and beliefs are based upon knowledge or information. It may be little; it may be wrong. Nevertheless, as long as it is believed to be true, knowledge supports the attitude. If the knowledge component contradicts it, something has to change—either the attitude or knowledge base. People strive to be consistent in such matters. They hate discord.

The emotional component of an attitude represents positive or negative feelings. Two forces seem to be involved. They are feelings of:

- Attraction or repulsion.
- Liking or disliking.

Usually, attractive things are liked and unattractive ones disliked. But not always. A person, for example, may dislike wearing safety clothing but be attracted to the protection it offers.

The action or behavior component is the most important from a learning point of view. Sometimes there can be a discrepancy between attitudes and behavior. What people say is not what they do. There are two possible explanations for this.

The attitude may be weak or it may be incomplete. Alternatively, the attitude spoken may not reflect the attitude that is held. The person may be paying lip service to an idea and not believe it.

Changing attitudes

Some people believe that if you change someone's attitude, you will change the person's behavior. However, there is very little scientific support for this belief. It is better to change the behavior, for then the attitude is likely to follow. In other words, first change behavior, then attitude. Don't change attitude and then behavior.

Many people who smoke, eat, or drink too much know the hazards to their health. They may even believe that the hazards are real. They want to cut down on their consumption, but they cannot do it. So they continue to smoke, eat, and drink too much. Positive attitudes toward change have not affected what they do. They still overindulge.

Attitude change is better brought about by changing what they do. Their emotions and knowledge will be influenced as their behavior changes. Such change is best brought about in instructional-learning situations which involve:

- Precise objectives, which identify attitude change.
- Small group discussion. The discussion is less important than subsequent commitment to the decisions that are made.
- Participant- rather than leader-centered discussion.
- High levels of individual involvement. Values and attitudes are modified by those around, particularly if you identify with or admire them.
- Role-playing or simulations. Attitudes tend to shift in the direction of the role played.

Above all, the instructional environment must *value* the attitudes desired. This means that people possessing the attitudes must be seen as being rewarded for having them.

Logic is a poor way to change attitudes. It is, however, an excellent way of strengthening them. A more powerful way of changing attitudes is to point out inconsistencies. The inconsistencies may be in what people do and say. They may be in what the task or situation demands.

In either case, inconsistencies are an irritant or stimulus for change. People usually feel a need to bring themselves into line. However, it is important to recognize that there is likely to be:

- Little attitude change when knowledge, emotions, and behavior are consistent.
- Great attitude change when knowledge, emotions, and behavior are inconsistent.

The trick is to exploit opportunity. Change rarely occurs immediately. It takes place over time. For example, most attitude change is best observed after three months.

Some attitudes, of course, are more difficult to change than others. Such resistant attitudes are due to:

- A dramatic experience or trauma.
- Adoption of ready-made attitudes from a home background or peer group.
- Consistent day-to-day experiences which reinforce the attitude.
- Continuance of the attitude over a long period of time.

Personality and group factors are also important.

Some people are more resistant to attitude change than others. Their personalities are less conforming, more outgoing or extroverted, more independent, and more conservative than people who are easier to change. Group membership also has its effect. All groups have social norms. In such circumstances, membership in a work or leisure group affects a person's attitudes. People who belong to a group tend to reflect that group's attitudes and opinions.

Two classes of attitude change

Change in attitudes can occur in many ways. The approaches to change, however, can be classified as involving:

- *Coerced change*
  Coerced change occurs through conformity or compliance. This type of change is:
  - Made with the help of rewards, punishments, sanctions and fear.
  - Fast, sometimes immediate.
  - Short-term, unless the pressure is constantly maintained.
    Often people become hostile. They may set out to sabotage change. Sometimes, instead, they become passive and uninterested.

- *Participative change*
  Participative change occurs through involvement. This type of change is:
  - The result of commitment.
  - Slow and evolutionary.
  - Long-term, as long as the changed attitudes are occasionally reinforced.
    People involved in participative change are likely to be highly committed to the change. They will try to perpetuate it.

From an instructional viewpoint, coerced change raises ethical questions. Participative change, on the other hand, is a mature way of proceeding. It can be tied to both personal and occupational growth.

A strategy for attitude change

Attitude change is more effective when it is carried out on a systematic basis. Poorly organized change strategies are ineffective. People find ways of ignoring or reinterpreting what is happening. It is imperative that attempts to change attitudes be well managed.

Factual approaches can occasionally result in a significant shift in attitudes. Unfortunately, the approach is successful only when people have no prior knowledge or information on the subject and vested interests to protect. If these two conditions are not met, a direct frontal attack should be avoided. It may intensify and solidify the attitudes you want to change. People will ward off the verbal "attack," in order to maintain self-consistency.

Instead of a frontal attack, a gradual approach is preferred. Such a strategy involves:

- *Imitation*
  This is called "modeling." It involves watching others. The instructor is one model, demonstrations are another.

  The person being imitated should be respected. It should be someone with whom people will want to identify themselves.

  The model should be seen exhibiting the required attitudes. Pleasure or satisfaction should be shown. Learners should see the model rewarded for possessing the right attitude.

  Once the desired attitudes (knowledge, emotions, and behavior) have been observed, learners should imitate what they have seen. Role-playing and simulations are useful in such circumstances.

- *Association*
  This is called "contiguity." It involves making certain that the situation is pleasant.

  For example, a lot of safety clothing is unpleasant to wear. As a result, safety clothing is associated with unpleasant feelings. Before long, safety itself begins to be thought of in a negative way.

  Instructors, therefore, should make sure that the circumstances surrounding the desired behavior are pleasant. They should be comfortable, satisfying, interesting. Boredom, fear, discomfort, frustration, embarrassment, humiliation, pain, etc., should be eliminated.

- *Reinforcement*
  This involves feedback. Behavior that is reinforced is likely to be repeated.

  If someone does what is required, but the behavior is ignored, the person will stop doing it. In changing someone's attitude, the same principle holds. It is essential that correct actions be rewarded in some way.

  Noticing is one type of reward, but there are many others. Praise, recognition, and monetary rewards are powerful. So are simple expressions like "Good," and "You are doing well."

All three tactics can be blended together into one strategy for change. Imitation, association, and reinforcement place demands upon instructors and teachers, but the results are worth the effort.

Unfreezing and refreezing

Before a start can be made on changing attitudes, people need to be prepared for change. The process is called "unfreezing." It represents a throwing out, a breaking down of old values, attitudes, and opinions.

Unfreezing usually involves three basic strategies. They are:

- *Inducing anxiety or guilt in the trainees or students*
  Examples: telling them that alcohol and driving kills
  telling them they are breaking the law

- *Demonstrating that their knowledge, emotions, and behavior are out of line*
  In other words, they are not doing what everyone else is doing. They are oddballs.
  Examples: telling them that they are not part of the team
  showing that they are not doing things properly

- *Removing barriers to change*
  Examples: telling them that the company is changing its policy
  removing people from their usual environment

Once the unfreezing process has taken place, learners are ready to accept change.

Once attitudes have been changed, they are notoriously unstable. Steps need to be taken to reinforce *and* maintain them at the new changed level. If this is not done people will slip back into their old patterns of behavior. For this reason, once attitudes have been changed, they must be "frozen" at the new level.

Freezing changed attitudes typically involves integrating new attitudes into a person's belief system. This entails:

- *Reinforcement and feedback*
  Attitudes that have been changed should be recognized and rewarded.

- *Assessment of the beneficial results of the attitude change*
  An assessment should be carried out of the beneficial results that have been obtained as a result of the change in attitudes. These results should show payoffs for the:
  - Organization or institution
  - Work group
  - Individuals whose attitudes have changed
    The results should be made public and communicated to the people involved.

- *Building the changed attitudes into the value structure of the work group*
  If a group accepts the changed attitudes, group members are much more likely to preserve the new behaviors. A work group, like a shift in a factory or a management team, is a more permanent carrier of change than the individuals making up the work group.

Freezing attitudes at the changed level will help prevent them from slipping back to where they were before the change took place.

Message content and attitude change

There has been a great deal of research into the nature of persuasion and good communication. Something of the difficulty can be recognized from a recent study. It was found that:

- Only 10 percent of what managers said was interpreted in the same way by the senders and receivers of the communication.
- More than 50 percent of information reaches its destination by flowing through informal rather than formal lines of communication. Rumor works overtime.
- More than 40 percent of supervisors and subordinates disagreed over what their job responsibilities included.

In other words, the study revealed a serious communication gap. The gap, further study indicated, was not only one of information but also of persuasion and attitude.

Studies by Carl Hovland and his colleagues at Yale University suggest that two factors are important as far as persuasion is concerned. There are a message effect and a communication effect. Some of the findings, as they affect instruction, are outlined in Figure 13:7.

It will be seen that the nature of the group is extremely important. If the group is friendly and accepting, a different tactic can be used than if the group is unfriendly and nonaccepting. The credibility of the instructor is also important. Credibility is not given to someone simply because the person is an instructor. It has to be earned, and it has to be recognized.

CONCLUSION

The ultimate objective of instruction and teaching is *not* learning. Learning is one objective, but more important is mastery of a task, role, or job. Mastery involves learning, but it also entails performance and skill at the level of an experienced person. Only an Experienced Worker Standard makes training and education credible to the world of work and leisure.

FIGURE 13:7. Some rules of effective persuasion.

Presentation effects

- If a group is friendly and accepting, present only one side of the argument.
- If a group is unfriendly and unaccepting, present both sides of the argument.
- If *you* are going to present both sides of the argument, the one presented first is the most persuasive.
- If someone else is going to present the other side, the argument presented last is the most persuasive.
- It is better for an instructor to state the conclusions than allow the group to draw their own.

Instructor effects

- If an instructor is highly credible, there will be greater attitude change.
- An instructor's imagined motives for bringing about the change will affect what is achieved.
- Instructors who demand extreme change are more successful than those who ask for little or medium change.
- An instructor can increase attitude change by having some of the same beliefs and attitudes as the learners.

Much is known about the acquisition of knowledge, skill, and attitudes. Not all of it, however, is always put into effect. Efficiency sometimes wins over effectiveness. Expediency is sometimes valued more than research findings. Effective instruction, however, depends upon a technique that is firmly grounded in good practice and the most recent research.

The acquisition of knowledge, skill, and attitudes demands a great deal from instructors and teachers. Much time, effort, and preparation are involved. In the long term, however, the results achieved make the hard work worthwhile.

Chapter 14
Harnessing Trainee Motivation

FOCUS

"How can an instructor harness student motivation?"

KNOWLEDGE OBJECTIVES

After reading and studying this chapter, you will be able to:

1. recognize the role of motivation in the instructional-learning process;
2. recognize the needs of learners in training and educational programs;
3. question the basic assumptions that are made about human nature;
4. apply the Motivation-Hygiene Theory to the management of learning;
5. decide whether a lesson plan is likely to fulfill basic human needs.

ATTITUDE OBJECTIVES

After reading this chapter, the author hopes that you will:

1. value the importance of motivation in the teaching-learning process;
2. incorporate the principles into your teaching, so that they become characteristic of your instructional style.

Motivation is the force that impels people to work.

Motivating trainees and students to learn is a major concern. Indeed, some people view it as the primary responsibility of an instructor. Unless people are motivated, it is unlikely that they will put out sufficient effort to reach mastery. Without motivated trainees, even well planned and organized training and education programs will fail dismally.

Yet everyone is really motivated already. From the very moment of birth to the time that they die, people are motivated. Motivation is a characteristic of all living creatures. They may not be interested in doing the things that you want them to do. Nevertheless, they are motivated in one way or another.

The role of an instructor, therefore, is less to motivate people than to harness their motivation to the learning task. This means that their attention has to be gained and their energy directed to some new activity. This will occur, however, only if the new activity is seen to be relevant and worthwhile.

THE NATURE OF MOTIVATION

Motivation is a hidden force within us that causes us to behave in a certain way. Sometimes it is instinctive; sometimes it arises from a rational decision. More usually, it is a mixture of both. It is partly instinctive and unthinking, and partly rational and deliberate. Often it is selfish and self-serving.

The role of motivation

Motives are a potent force in the instructional-learning process. Not only is motivation a directing force; it is also a distracting one. If you are motivated toward one thing, you are distracted from something else that you might be doing. A preference has been followed, a choice made.

Motivation has four effects that are important to instruction. They are:

- *Motivation energizes learners*
  It causes them to become active, involved, and concerned. Motivation sustains effort and keeps them going. It makes for persistence.

- *Motivation is goal-directed*
  It directs people to complete a task, to achieve a desired objective. It makes for direction.

274

- *Motivation is selective*
  It selects *what* activity should be undertaken. Motivation also determines *how* the task will be done. It determines priority.

- *Motivation patterns learner behavior*
  It organizes activities. This adds vigor and efficiency to effort. It makes for a plan.

The four effects of persistence, direction, priority, and planned behavior are essential to effective learning. They make for a rich resource that can be tapped by learners and instructors alike.

Anxiety and motivation

As the intensity of motivation increases, there is a build-up in tension and anxiety. Such a build-up affects a person's emotional state and muscular tone. Both states have consequences for instruction. They affect the acquisition of knowledge, skill, and attitudes.

Anxiety, in general, affects human performance in both a positive and a negative way. Most people can adapt to a moderate level of anxiety. Extreme tension, however, is disruptive and often disabling. In other words, you are no longer able to do something that you could do. Anxiety deprives you of skill.

A general lack of tension, on the other hand, is equally weakening. It increases the chances that people will be diverted to something else. All challenge has disappeared, and the activity loses its former attractiveness.

As a general rule, it appears that: *Performance is most efficient when there is a certain amount of anxiety present in the situation.* The tension should not be too high or too low. Performance deteriorates when people either panic or become too placid.

This relationship is illustrated in Figure 14:1. Complicating the matter are the nature of specific tasks and the varying levels of anxiety in particular people. What is optimal in one situation may no longer be optimal in another. Nevertheless, an inverted U-shaped relationship between anxiety and performance seems to be standard for most situations.

The result is of some importance from the point of view of the instructional-learning process. It means that instructors and teachers should be careful to avoid removing all anxiety from an instructional situation. On the other hand, they want to take steps to avoid allowing it to get out of hand.

Maintaining a balance is not an easy thing to do. It involves constantly monitoring a situation. Supplying people with clear objectives helps to reduce anxiety. Assessing them helps to increase it. Briefing trainees on what to expect and what to watch out for helps to decrease tension. Leaving them uninformed is a recipe for disaster. It should also be borne in mind that older people tend to become more anxious than younger ones.

FIGURE 14:1. The relationship between anxiety and performance.

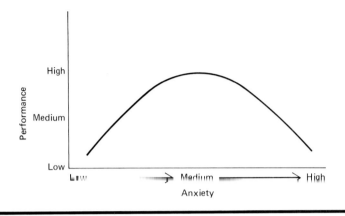

THE NEEDS OF LEARNERS

People have needs that must be met in one way or another. This is as true of instructional situations as it is of other work environments. Unless these needs are attended to by instructors, trainees will not learn. For this reason, motivation is not a matter that should be left to chance.

Meeting learner needs is one of the four functions of an instructor-manager. There is little point to planning, organizing, and evaluating if people are not motivated toward the learning task. In order to obtain this commitment, the task must be designed in such a way as to be satisfying.

Hierarchy of needs

People have many needs. However, it is the need with the greatest strength that dictates what they will do. Once a need has been met, it will decline in importance. However, another need will then become dominant and will demand satisfaction. This idea of need underlies the ideas of Abraham Maslow.

Maslow makes two assumptions about human nature. He argues that:

- *People are wanting animals*
  They are motivated by a desire to fill certain classes of needs. These needs are pursued with varying degrees of intensity. Once a need has been met, it is no longer motivating. People, therefore, turn to another need and again look for satisfaction.

- *Needs are organized*
  Some needs are low-level and basic. Other needs are high-level and are supplemental. As lower-level needs are filled, higher ones come into play.

Needs, as will be seen from Figure 14:2, are arranged in the form of a staircase or hierarchy.

In thinking about needs, it is important to realize that Maslow does not argue that a need must be filled one hundred percent before moving on to the next one. It is a matter of being mainly satisfied or mainly dissatisfied.

A good way of thinking about the hierarchy is to think in terms of decreasing percentages. A person may have 80 percent of the lowest need filled, 50 percent of the next, and only 15 percent of the next. Since the bottommost need is 80 percent met, the need that will look most for satisfaction is the one that is only 50 percent met.

At the base of the staircase are physiological needs. These are concerned with food, drink, sex, sleep, and warmth. In instructional situations, the need for sleep will inhibit learning as much as the need to eat. Overheated instructional areas, sitting still for long periods of time, and an overpowering need for a change of activity will also reduce effectiveness.

If physiological needs are largely met in training, safety needs next come into play. Safety needs involve a desire for security and survival. They include protection from such physical dangers as fire, accident, explosion, chemicals, and noxious fumes. In some situations, a lack of essential safety clothing and equipment will mean that little or no learning takes place.

Trainees who are overanxious are showing a need for safety. Some learners, particularly the less able ones, can feel sufficiently threatened in an instructional setting that little progress is made. Instructors, therefore, must work with them, often on an individual basis. Unless their fear is managed, they will be unlikely to reach mastery.

Social needs make up the next level in the hierarchy. Once physiological and safety needs have been met in training and education, social needs come into play. These include acceptance, friendship, affection, and loyalty. A sense of belonging and caring is also important.

Such needs are of great importance in instruction, since a great deal of learning takes place in group situations. A well integrated and cohesive group

FIGURE 14:2. Maslow's Hierarchy of Human Needs.

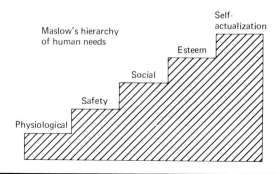

spirit is worth cultivating. Close and friendly relationships are essential. However, they are not dominant needs until physiological and safety needs are satisfied.

Esteem needs become pressing once trainees and students sense that they belong. Everyone has a need for respect. People need to feel important, and they need to feel that other people see them as important. Achievement and recognition are important to all of us. So are freedom and independence.

When training and education programs meet esteem needs, learners feel confident, worthy, adequate, useful, and necessary. Unknowingly, instructors can undermine such feelings in their trainees if, instead of stressing their success and pointing out the progress they have made, they mention only the negative side.

Being supplied with feedback and having their strengths reinforced enables learners to gain a sense of achievement. They develop a sense of worth and importance. Learning takes on a new relevance and becomes a source of recognition. Once the need for esteem is filled, meeting the final need becomes a major driving force.

The final step in the staircase involves the need for self-actualization or fulfillment as a person. The form that this need takes varies from one person to another. In one person it may involve gaining a particular level of skill; in another, achieving an ambition.

Competence, mastery, achievement are all important sources of self-actualization. Meeting challenges is important to some; being the "best" is important to others. Others realize themselves through self-knowledge, and still others through service to society. Sacrifice is one route to self-realization. It is another form of mastery.

ASSUMPTIONS ABOUT HUMAN NATURE

Maslow, of course, is making an assumption when he claims that people are "wanting animals." He is justified, since his ideas seem to make a good deal of sense in the instructional-learning process. However, there are two assumptions that he does not mention. These, too, are important.

These assumptions are also about human nature, and are important to instructors and teachers. Indeed, they determine:

- The character of the instructional environment.
- The instructional style of instructors.
- The way that learners are treated.

Douglas McGregor was the first to draw attention to them.

McGregor points out that people make one of two assumptions about human nature:

- *They* believe that people are naturally lazy, dislike work, and will avoid it if they can.
- *Or* they believe that people find work as natural as rest or play.

The assumptions are important, because each one results in a different set of expectations. The former is called Theory X, and the latter Theory Y.

Figure 14:3 applies the two assumptions to instruction. The Theory X approach, based on the idea that people are lazy, results in either autocracy or permissiveness. It is a stick and carrot approach to teaching.

In Theory X, instructors compensate for learner weakness by adopting one of two styles. They are:

- *An autocratic instructional style*
  As a result:
  - Instruction is instructor- or teacher-centered.
  - Instruction involves direction and control.
  - Interpersonal relationships are likely to be poor.
  - Learners are likely to become resistant and apathetic and put forward minimum effort.

FIGURE 14:3. Theory X and Theory Y instructional styles.

A Theory X instructional style	*A Theory Y instructional style*
Assumption	*Assumption*
The average learner dislikes work and will avoid it if possible.	Work is as natural to the average learner as play or rest.
Consequences of assumption	*Consequences of assumption*

Either a hard line approach.
 	
They must be coerced by:
 	
  • Controls and directions.
  • Threats of punishment.
Only in this way will they put forward an adequate effort to learning.
 	
Or a soft line approach.
 	
They must be coaxed by:
  • Rewards and praises.
  • Permissiveness and blandishments.
Only then will they learn.
	Since learning is natural, a variety of tactics can be used to facilitate learning.
	
	These tactics include:
	
	  • Autocracy
	  • Consultation
	  • Participation
	  • Permissiveness
	
	There will be self-direction and instructor-direction, as appropriate. Instruction will be learner-centered on occasions, and instructor-centered at other times. Decisions have to be made.

- *A permissive instructional style*
  As a result:
  - Instruction is learner-centered.
  - Instruction involves praise and blandishment.
  - Interpersonal relationships are likely to be good.
  - Learners invest minimum effort and have minimum commitment.

Regardless of which of the two styles is adopted, the result is the same. Efficiency and effectiveness are lost.

In Theory Y, instructors are less concerned with learner behavior as it is. They are more concerned with a learner's potential for growth and development. Theory Y teachers and instructors are committed to change. Some people believe that Theory Y represents a soft approach. However, they are wrong. It represents the full range, from soft to hard. Appropriateness is the key issue.

The characteristics of a Theory Y instructional style are:

- Instructors seek to explore the limits of human ability.
- The instructional style is at times autocratic, at times permissive, at times consultative, and at times participative. It depends upon what is appropriate.
- Instructors believe that there is no "one best way." Instructional methods, therefore, depend upon the situation.
- Learners are pushed to realize their potential.

Accordingly, Theory Y instruction tends to be characterized by a great variety of instructional methods, settings, and aids. Such a style demands a great degree of commitment and instructional skill.

From the point of view of motivation, Theory X and Theory Y approaches have one overall effect. They both result in what Douglas McGregor calls the self-fulfilling prophecy. This means that people generally behave in a way that is consistent with the way they are treated.

In other words, if instructors treat learners as lazy and irresponsible, then they are likely to behave in a lazy and irresponsible manner. If they are treated, on the other hand, as responsible and able people, then that is how they will respond. The choice of which instructional style to use affects the way that learners behave.

MAJOR SOURCES OF SATISFACTION AND DISSATISFACTION

In a recent survey, a large number of learners were asked to describe actual incidents in their training. Two incidents were requested. One that made them feel particularly bad, and one that made them feel particularly good, about learning.

On analyzing the data, it was clear that:

- Good feelings were primarily concerned with the things that made them feel they were making progress toward mastery.
- Bad feelings were primarily concerned with the environment in which training was taking place.

Similar results were obtained over twenty years ago by Frederick Herzberg, who interviewed people in industry and the armed services.

Motivation-Hygiene Theory

Herzberg found that people have two sets of needs. He called the factors that led to good feelings "motivators," and the ones that led to bad feelings "hygiene." They work in this manner:

- *Motivators*
  When these are present, a person feels content, happy, fulfilled. Motivators have an uplifting effect. They make a person feel good. People feel satisfied, which leads to greater productivity.

- *Hygiene factors*
  When these are at some low level, a person feels unhappy. Hygiene factors have a depressing or limiting effect on performance. They give rise to feelings of dissatisfaction, which lead to decreased productivity.

In general, feelings of satisfaction are longer lasting than feelings of dissatisfaction.

Numerous investigations have shown that motivators are not the opposites of hygiene factors. When applied to instruction, motivators give rise to feelings of:

- Accomplishment.
- Recognition.
- Responsibility.
- Personal growth.
- Satisfaction from the act of learning.

The motivators have a positive effect on learning. They are illustrated in Figure 14:4.

Hygiene factors, on the other hand, have a negative effect. They involve such things as:

- Training methods.
- Instructor's style of teaching.
- Nature of the instructional setting.
- Security as a learner.
- Status as a learner.
- Instructional policies and administration.
- Interpersonal relationships.

FIGURE 14:4.   The Hygiene-Motivation Theory applied to instruction.

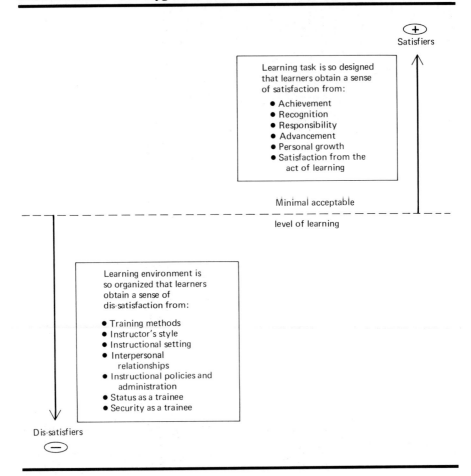

When hygiene factors are not met, learners feel dissatisfied. When they are met, they don't feel satisfied. They are simply no longer dissatisfied.

This distinction between motivators and hygiene factors makes considerable sense in instruction. Obviously, it is pleasant for people to learn in comfortable, well administered instructional settings. Training methods need to be carefully selected, and an instructor's style should be appropriate to the situation. People need to feel secure and experience good interpersonal relationships with fellow learners and instructors.

However, experiencing the effects of good hygiene will not make people happy or satisfied. They are simply no longer unhappy with the environment. The only things that make for satisfaction are the motivators. When they are present, learners feel satisfied. If the motivators are not present in an instructional situation, people will not be happy. Being happy depends upon what they are asked to do.

A checklist for instructors and teachers

Instructors and teachers have an obvious responsibility. They should arrange matters in such a way that trainees and students experience feelings of satisfaction from learning. Many of the factors concerned with the environment lie outside their hands. None of the factors associated with motivation, however, are outside their control.

In order to make certain that trainees and students feel a sense of satisfaction, a number of questions must be asked. As a result of decisions that have been made in lesson planning, will learners experience a sense of:

- Achievement from the learning task?
- Recognition from the learning task?
- Responsibility from the learning task?
- Personal growth from the learning task?
- Satisfaction from the act of learning?

If the answer to all five questions is "Yes!" then the instructional experience is likely to be a motivating one. If the answer is "No!" then the lesson needs to be enriched in some way.

CONCLUSION

Instructors and teachers have a responsibility to design situations that are motivating for their trainees and students. This means that they have to arrange matters so that human needs will be met. People, Abraham Maslow reminds us, are wanting animals. Unless their lower needs are met, meeting the higher ones is of little importance.

The assumptions that we make about people are important. They determine the expectations that we have and influence the responses that we are likely to obtain. A Style X instructor is more limited in options than a Style Y instructor.

Associated with the assumptions that we make are the ways that instructional environments and tasks are designed. The feelings of satisfaction that learners experience are not the opposite of the feelings of dissatisfaction. It is essential that matters be so arranged that learners will feel a sense of achievement, recognition, responsibility, personal growth, and satisfaction from the act of learning. Only then has motivation been harnessed.

Chapter 15
Individual Differences

FOCUS

"How can individual differences be accommodated in the teaching-learning process?"

KNOWLEDGE OBJECTIVES

After reading and studying this chapter, you will be able to:

1. explain the nature of individual differences as far as they affect teaching and learning;
2. take steps in your teaching so as to take into account differences in ability, learning, personality, and age;
3. use individual differences as resources to be exploited, rather than as barriers to effective instruction.

ATTITUDE OBJECTIVES

After reading this chapter, the author hopes that you will:

1. value the significance of individual differences in the teaching-learning process;
2. incorporate the principles into your teaching, so that they become characteristic of your instructional style.

Individual differences are an instructional resource of great value.

People are different; that is their strength. There are similarities between people, and there are also important differences. Were it not for the similarities, *all* instruction would have to be given on an individual basis. Some, of course, is individualized and tailor-made to meet individual needs, but not very much.

Most instruction is given on a group basis. It is not simply a matter of convenience. Similar needs cut across individuals. People, therefore, can be combined in the same instructional group. Any needs not met can then be covered through individual instruction or independent work assignments.

Individual differences, however, must be recognized. It is foolish to ignore them. Similarly, it is foolish to overemphasize their importance. Some differences are notable, others are not. In the same way, some similarities are significant. Others are of little concern.

It is not the existence of similarities and differences that is important. What is important is whether they are significant. Height, weight, and gender, for instance, are of little value from a learning point of view. Personality and experience, on the other hand, are significant. Instructors and teachers would be foolish to ignore their impact. Somehow, provision has to be made for them in the instructional-learning process.

THE NATURE OF INDIVIDUAL DIFFERENCES

The term "individual differences" refers to the way that people differ to a great enough extent to affect their performance on a learning task. Sometimes performance is affected in a positive manner, sometimes negatively. In most instances, however, industriousness and motivation overcome deficiencies in ability, aptitude, and experience.

Most people differ, from a learning viewpoint, in a limited number of ways. They can differ in:

- Aptitude and ability.
- Knowledge, skill, and attitude.
- Personality and style of learning.
- Age and experience.

Nevertheless, people are more gifted than some teachers and instructors recognize.

286

Stereotypes, particularly negative ones, must be avoided at all costs. The aim of instruction is to recognize individual differences, and then to build on the strengths. There is little point in identifying all the reasons why someone cannot do a particular task. There is every reason for thinking positively and constructively.

Some people have many talents and do little with them. They fail to realize their very high potential. Others, who are less gifted, work hard and surpass themselves. Potential is important. Lack of imagination sets limits to what can be achieved.

APTITUDE AND ABILITY

People possess different aptitudes and abilities. Some are good at one thing; some are good at another. Genetics undoubtedly has some influence, but opportunity is probably more important. For instance, recent research indicates that women are often better than men at verbal tasks, but poorer than men at spatial ones like reading drawings, diagrams, and maps.

Training, however, removes the differences between the two groups. It may be that, as children, males have traditionally played with building blocks, made models, and tackled spatially based tasks. Females, on the other hand, have characteristically played with dolls, sat quietly reading and drawing, and joined their mothers in domestic chores. Now all of that is rapidly changing.

Opportunity, however, determines ability. When differences are recognized, steps need to be taken to remove them. An instructor or teacher should minimize the negative effects of individual differences in aptitude and ability. There is no point in maximizing them.

Ability, in its broadest sense, is the product of two things:

● Ability on intellectual tasks, *and*
● Ability on motor ones.

Figure 15:1 illustrates how the two are organized. Some people, for example, are good with their hands but poor at intellectual tasks like writing reports. In other words, they have an ability for motor tasks but not for intellectual ones. Practice, of course, could change this.

Intellectual tasks

Intellectual ability is largely made up of five specific skills. They are:

● *Verbal ability*
This involves skill with words. The ability is largely composed of:

FIGURE 15:1. An organization of abilities.

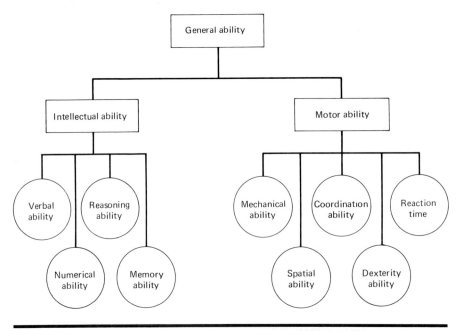

- Fluency with words.
- Understanding of words.

- *Numerical ability*
  This involves skill with numbers. It involves a mental agility in dealing with problems according to well learned rules like addition and multiplication.

- *Reasoning ability*
  This involves skill in solving problems and dealing with difficult situations.

- *Memory ability*
  This involves both recall and recognition. Some people remember what they hear, some need to see *and* hear.

- *Creativity*
  This involves an ability to come up with an original solution to problems. It involves two skills:
  - Flexibility.
  - Originality.

People vary greatly in the intellectual skills they have developed, but all of them improve with practice.

Motor tasks

Motor ability is largely a product of five specific skills. They are:

- *Mechanical ability*
  This involves skill with mechanical things, such as working with an engine or a component.

- *Dexterity*
  This involves skill associated with the movement of fingers, hands, arms, and legs. Speed and precision are especially important.

- *Coordination*
  This involves ability to fix, grasp, and manipulate items smoothly and care fully.

- *Reactions*
  This involves ability to respond quickly to a changed situation.

- *Spatial ability*
  This involves ability to deal with relationships in two or three dimensions..

The importance of these abilities depends upon the nature of the task or job that has to be done, and the degree of skill achieved.

For example, in a task like distinguishing between different types of aircraft or qualities of meat, it has been found that:

- Verbal and spatial ability are of:
  - Greater importance in the early stages of skill acquisition.
  - Lesser importance in the latter stages of skill acquisition.
- Reasoning and reaction time are of;
  - Lesser importance in the early stages of skill acquisition.
  - Greater importance in the latter stages of skill acquisition.

As skill develops, so the abilities needed change in importance.

Instruction and ability

Learning involves intellectual and motor abilities, but in different degrees. In skill acquisition, intellectual abilities play a dominant role in the early stages of learning. Later on, abilities involving reaction time, coordination, dexterity, and mechanical ability become increasingly important. Since so many abilities are involved in the final stages, they must be organized into a coherent way of behaving. This is done through practice and rehearsal.

Practice, therefore, is important as far as many abilities are concerned. Indeed, with practice and guidance, people who lack some abilities can still acquire a satisfactory level of intellectual and motor skills. Their progress may be slow and inaccurate at first, but learning takes place over time.

Instruction has to take account of people's needs. When learners are lacking in certain abilities, instructors and teachers should:

- Take steps to gain learner attention. Tap their motivation through a growing sense of achievement and recognition.
- See that there is immediate feedback. People must have a sense of progress.
- Break down the task into stages. Teach each stage separately, but in the correct sequence.
- Use distributed, rather than massed, practice. Make sure that the skill is overlearned.
- Place emphasis on accuracy, not on speed. Speed can be built up during the later stages of learning.

In this way, instruction, based upon clear objectives, helps people of varied ability achieve mastery.

KNOWLEDGE, SKILL, AND ATTITUDES

People vary not only in ability and aptitude but also in knowledge, skill, and attitudes. Some people are more knowledgeable than others, some more skilled. There are many reasons for this. Most of them, however, arise out of different experiences, opportunities, and abilities. Sometimes, they are associated with education, and sometimes with job history.

Before instruction takes place, it is important that instructors and teachers find out what trainees and learners can do. What do they know that is relevant to mastery? What skills do they already possess? What attitudes do they have that are essential to job mastery? Effective instruction recognizes prior learning and experience and builds upon them. It is insulting not to make use of them.

Information about what people know and can do can be obtained in many ways. These include:

- Interviewing the learners' supervisors.
- Finding out about their education and training.
- Identifying their previous job history and work experience.
- Determining why they have been nominated for additional training or education.
- Interviewing each learner, and finding out his or her learning needs.
- Testing them for knowledge, skill, and attitudes.
- Observing their knowledge, skill, and attitudes during the first few days of instruction.

In this way, it is possible to build up a fairly accurate profile of each trainee and student. Always bear in mind that information from a number of sources is better than information from one source.

Increasing numbers of instructors and teachers prefer not to give formal tests and examinations prior to instruction. They feel that it is anxiety-provoking.

There are also problems of reliability and validity. Many people also feel that it is a poor way to start a course of instruction. They argue that it is preferable to determine knowledge and skill levels during instruction.

Trainability testing

Despite the problem that some instructors have with pre-testing, there is an alternative. Instead of using a written test or examination, under formal conditions, a work sample approach can be used. This can be used to select people for training, on the basis of their aptitude for both the job and the instruction.

It involves making an inventory of tasks that describe a job or role. A sample of these is then used in the test. For example, in jobs involving motor skills the sample might include: adjusting a carburator, throwing a bead with a welding torch, or laying some bricks. In jobs involving intellectual skills the sample might include: memorizing a paragraph, writing a memorandum, dealing with a complaint, or interviewing a customer.

Once the samples have been obtained, a brief videotape lesson is prepared for each one. The length of each lesson varies with the nature of the task. Usually it will be about ten to fifteen minutes in duration. Sometimes a five-minute lesson might be sufficient, if the task is small and self-contained.

A trainability test consists of four steps. These involve:

- A group of trainees watching a videotaped lesson demonstrating a procedure or skill.
- Each trainee independently imitating what he or she has observed.
- An instructor observing each imitation, using a checklist to identify significant errors.
- An instructor awarding a grade or score on the basis of the information collected.

In this way, it is possible to select people who are most likely to benefit from instruction.

In selecting samples, only critical tasks should be used. Furthermore, it should be possible for the tasks to be taught and imitated in a reasonable amount of time. They must also be complex enough for a reasonable number of errors to be made. If they are too demanding, people won't be able to imitate them.

Figure 15:2 shows some examples of tasks that have been used. Bear in mind that the task has to be selected, as does the instructional method. The method should be typical of those used in training.

This method of work sampling, as a measure of trainability, can be used to select people who are applying for jobs elsewhere in their own company or organization, or applying for jobs in a company or organization other than their own. The procedure is particularly useful when decisions are being made about the possibility of retraining.

FIGURE 15:2. Examples of tasks used in trainability tests.

Bricklaying	: laying bricks in missing portions of a partly built wall.
Carpentry	: making a half-lap T-joint.
Welding	: making a straight run on mild steel.
Hotel receptionist	: taking a telephone reservation, guaranteed with a credit card.
Fork lift operator	: picking up a pallet and setting it down in a marked area.
Salesperson	: dealing with a customer objection.
Sewing machine	: joining two pieces of fabric.
Dentistry	: preparing a cavity in casein teeth.

Trainability tests have high face validity. People do the kind of work that they will be doing during and after training. They also get a good idea of what the job involves. In this way, they find out whether it appeals to them.

The tests have good predictive power. People who have done well on a trainability test, in other words, usually do well both in training and subsequently on the job. Those who do badly on the test normally do badly in training.

One reason for the success of the procedure is to be found in the way that the test is constructed. People are not only being assessed for their skill, but also for their ability to benefit from the instructional method used.

PERSONALITY AND LEARNING STYLE

Personality is an important factor in the instructional-learning process. Its effects, however, have been little studied in any formal way. Nevertheless, personality influences the process in a number of ways. Sometimes it assists learning and teaching; sometimes it hinders them.

Personality affects the individual learning styles of the learners themselves and the work style of the instructional groups to which the learners belong. Hardworking and responsible groups have a different attitude toward instruction and learning than lazy and irresponsible ones.

Personality and individual style

Personality describes a person's unique disposition or character. It involves two types of statements:

- A summary of a person's *past* behavior.
- A prediction of how the same person will behave in the future.

If we say that someone is reliable, two separate points are being made. It implies that the person has been reliable in the past, and will be reliable in the future.

In order to summarize past and future behavior, labels of one kind or another are normally used. Sometimes the labels are complimentary, like "hardworking," "trustworthy," and "conscientious." At other times, they are not complimentary: "lazy," "difficult," and "argumentative."

All labels are applied to someone after an assessment. Such an evaluation is usually carried out informally on the basis of our knowledge of a person. Occasionally, it is carried out on the basis of a professional assessment. Regardless of how the assessment is carried out, great care needs to be taken to insure that the labels are reliable and valid.

Since labels stick, it is essential that they be used with caution. Personality is one area where the self-fulfilling prophecy seems to work overtime. People who are labeled lazy tend to behave that way. People who are labeled irresponsible tend to fulfill that prophecy, too.

So it is with instructional groups. Reputations become common knowledge. A hardworking, conscientious group generates a reputation that it tries to live up to somehow. In fact, it will often try to surpass its reputation, regardless of whether it was originally deserved. Reputation and style go hand in hand.

Mature personality

Maturity is the objective of all adults. Yet a mature personality is a difficult thing to describe. Most people recognize mature and immature people but have problems describing the characteristics involved. Nevertheless, an underlying goal of most training and educational programs is to help people become well rounded. Mastery and maturity are complementary terms.

Immature trainees and students are characterized by three distinct tendencies. They constantly:

- Demand attention from both instructors and fellow trainees.
- Refuse to undertake learning tasks on their own initiative.
- Avoid responsibility at all costs.

An immature person is someone who wants to be at the center of things; someone who is unwilling to take on the responsibilities of adult people. Unless they are supported by others, they refuse to take action on any matters that are not routine.

Mature persons, on the other hand, have four essential qualities. They have an ability to:

- *Live their life to the fullest.* Mature people are interested in many things. They are curious and active. They have great resilience.
- *See themselves objectively.* Mature people recognize their own strengths and weaknesses. They have a sense of humor and can laugh at themselves.

- *Believe in themselves.* Mature people accept responsibility. They have a sense of their worth. This gives them dignity and standing.
- *Behave in a consistent manner.* Mature people are predictable. Their actions are based upon a well developed sense of values and beliefs.

These four qualities, E.A. Peel argues, provide the ingredients of a mature personality.

By themselves these qualities do not describe a mature person. Added together, however, they make for maturity. Yet, there must be balance. A student who is overly objective cannot lead a full life. Someone who is painfully consistent, and has a highly developed sense of belief in self, will not be able to see himself or herself objectively. Maturity is a matter of balance, and instructors can help learners to obtain it.

Instructional situations need to be planned and organized so that learners are encouraged to adopt mature behavior. This can be done if instructors plan learning tasks so that trainees and students are:

- Active in the instructional process.
- Interested and motivated toward the task.
- Responsible for their own learning.
- Accountable for their own actions.
- Concerned about the future, as well as the immediate present.

Unless situations are designed in this way, learners are likely to behave immaturely. Self-knowledge and self-awareness come from a healthy environment for mature people.

Style and maturity

Gifted trainees and students have many of the characteristics of mature people. When comparisons have been made of gifted and average learners, gifted people have been found to possess a distinctive learning style.

FIGURE 15:3. A sociogram of an instructional group.

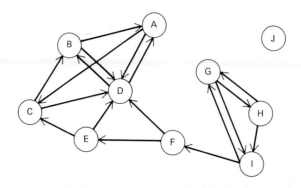

Gifted learners, compared to less able ones, tend to be:

- Self-motivated, rather than instructor-motivated.
- Persistent, with a strong sense of goal.
- Independent in their approach. They prefer to learn alone, rather than with others.
- People who learn through all the senses, rather than just the sense of hearing.

For these reasons, it is important that instructors recognize their needs and make arrangements to meet them. More time can then be spent with less able trainees, who may require greater help and encouragement.

Interpersonal attractiveness

Some people are more popular than others. Some exercise a leadership role, and some a follower one. Such matters affect the cohesiveness of a group, as well as its effectiveness. Cohesive groups not only work harder but have a better sense of purpose. They also possess high morale.

Most experienced instructors and teachers are able to recognize such matters with little difficulty. However, there is a useful technique for mapping the relationships in an instructional group. It is called "sociometry."

In effect, people are asked to name two people whom they would work with on a task like a project. They may like them; they may dislike them. Liking and disliking are not important. What is important is their willingness to work with them on a joint task.

Once the information has been gained, it can be illustrated in a sociogram. An example is shown in Figure 15:3. Learners are represented by circles and letters, and choices by solid lines. The direction of an arrow indicates the choice made.

In a cohesive group, there will be an interlocking of arrows. Everyone should receive at least one choice. A few people will receive a large number of choices, indicating their leadership role. Subgroups or cliques are represented by breakaways from the main grouping.

The typical patterns that will be found on a sociogram include such differences as:

- *Star leaders*
  These are people who have been selected by an unusually high number of individuals. An example is person D.

- *Isolates*
  These are people who have not been chosen by anyone. Sometimes their role is made even more dramatic by their own refusal or inability to choose someone. An example is person J.

- *Islands or cliques*
  These are small groups of people, separated from the larger pattern. They

have chosen each other, but have not been chosen by anyone outside their own group. An example would be the clique made up of people G, H, and I.

- *Mutual pairs*
  These are people who select each other, indicating some dependency. An example would be persons G and H.

Such patterns not only help to identify the character of a group; they also identify the roles played by the individuals involved. It is another way of looking at individual needs for acceptance and belonging.

AGE AND EXPERIENCE

Age and experience cannot be ignored in the instructional process. They demand not only better prepared instructors and teachers, but also more efficiently organized ones. Since experience is largely, although not always, a product of age, the two can be dealt with together.

The aging process begins around the age of nineteen. It shows itself in two ways:

- *A decrease in certain skills and abilities*
  For example:
  - Coil-winding skills begin to show the effects of aging around the age of nineteen.
  - Punch press operators begin to show the effects of aging around the age of twenty-five.
  - Performance on tasks involving creative and flexible solutions to problems begin to show the effects of aging around the age of thirty-five.

- *An increase in other skills and abilities*
  For example:
  - Ability to make skilled judgments and decisions increases with age up to the age of thirty five. It then levels off for the remainder of the normal working life.
  - Certain abilities develop and increase with age. Among them are boldness, will power, and feelings of independence of action.

In some tasks, aging does not appear to be a significant factor. For example, young people do not appear to be any better, or any worse, at solving problems than much older people.

In the past, a great deal of instruction has involved younger people. The scope of training and education, however, is now changing. All age groups are beginning to be involved on an increasing scale. Training, retraining and cross-training are becoming a way of life.

Jobs are changing, automation spreads, and rationalization in business continues to grow. All of this increases the need for people to acquire new skills. Mergers between companies, too, are having an effect. As a result of all these changes, instructors and teachers need to become increasingly sensitive to the needs of "older" people as learners.

Characteristics of "older" people

As compared with "younger" people, those past their mid-thirties increasingly possess a number of qualities that affect the teaching-learning process. "Older" people, compared with "younger" ones, are:

- More easily discouraged.
- More anxious, tense, and lacking in confidence.
- More fearful of failure and of the unknown.
- More resistant to change and innovation.
- More self-conscious, embarrassed, and cautious.
- More careful. They take greater pains, and place greater emphasis on accuracy. They downplay speed.
- More troubled with problems of unlearning. Casting off errors and mistakes is much more difficult.

These characteristics make it difficult for "older" people to find new jobs. Prospective employers think that they will have too many problems if they try to change their skills.

The same characteristics can make it difficult to instruct "older" people compared with "younger" ones. Older people demand good instruction. In fact, with appropriate instruction, older people acquire new skills easily and enthusiastically. The teaching, however, has to be right.

Teaching "older" learners

Despite all difficulties, real and imagined, the evidence clearly indicates that "older" people can be successfully trained and retrained. Success, however, depends upon motivation, good lesson preparation, and recognition of the human aspect. With good teaching the success rate is as high as with younger people.

Some of the changes that have to be made in instruction are indicated in Figure 15:4. It will be seen that four factors have to be attended to: organizational, instructional, learning, and personal. Many of these factors are also relevant to teaching younger people. They are essential as far as older ones are concerned.

In teaching "older" people, keep the following points in mind. It is better to:

FIGURE 15:4.   Adapting instruction to suit "older" learners.

- *Organizational factors*
  - Arrange for training periods of about 60 to 90 minutes duration.
  - Make instruction purposeful and job-related.
  - Mix young and old in the same instructional group.
  - Match instructors to learners, and learners to instructors.
  - Respect adult status and experience.
  - Give strong emotional support and encouragement.

- *Instructional factors*
  - Use discovery methods of learning.
  - Arrange for longer orientation sessions.
  - Restrict the range and content of lessons to essentials.
  - Demonstrate the whole, then the parts, and then the whole again.
  - Use written instructions rather than verbal ones for projects and assignments.
  - Avoid audiovisual aids that use a different logic or sequence.
  - Avoid formal tests and examinations. Use continuous assessment.
  - Vary instructional methods and work assignments. Provide variety.

- *Learning factors*
  - Reduce the need for verbal information, and for memorization.
  - Avoid abstract and irrelevant information.
  - Employ a great deal of practice, review, and consolidation, so that over-learning takes place.
  - Reduce interference and distractions.
  - Insure that material is meaningful and relevant.

- *Personal factors*
  - Allow learners to participate in the planning process.
  - Avoid any sense of competition.
  - Allow learners to proceed at their own pace.
  - Encourage learners to set their own goals, and to beat their own targets.
  - Make sure that learners feel a sense of achievement and recognition.
  - See that learners learn correctly from the start.
  - Promote group feelings and identity.

- Mix older and younger people together, rather than to keep them apart. It is especially effective to have a group of older people in the instructional group who know each other.
- If people are going to be trained on the job, it is preferable to do it on the evening rather than the day shift if they are shift workers. In the evening, pressures are less, and there is more time for practice and review.

- Avoid error and failure. They are discouraging. A warm, supportive atmosphere is essential. Independent study, case studies, programmed instruction, simulators, slide-tape etc., are useful. Emphasize accuracy, downplay the importance of speed.
- Introduce new knowledge and skills gradually. Review, practice, and consolidation are essential. Have learners overlearn the task; reduce the chance of forgetting.
- Avoid traditional "school room" type settings. Older people are fearful of answering questions, taking notes (some may be illiterate), working by themselves on a problem. Use group situations, group assignments, help them to learn how to learn.

It is important to build on strengths. Guidance and feedback, in a gentle and encouraging manner, are necessary tactics in the instructional process.

Discovery is an essential characteristic of the instructional process, as far as "older" people are concerned. They prefer not to be told. They like to find out for themselves. In such a process, an instructor or teacher's role revolves around: providing objectives, giving guidance and feedback, acting as a resource, organizing learning situations, and offering encouragement when needed. It is a management situation rather than an operating one.

To a large extent, the strategy consists of a variation of management by objectives. In this case, however, it involves learning by objectives. It entails the realization of objectives that are understood and have been mutually agreed upon as necessary. Expectations must be made clear. Once this has been done, it is up to individual learners to accept responsibility for their own learning. They must then take steps to find out for themselves. This is what is meant by discovery.

CONCLUSION

Individual differences are an important resource in the instructional-learning process. They offer a springboard for positive action. Some differences are significant, others are not important. Many are the result of differing opportunities, and they should be recognized as such.

The aim of all instruction is mastery. Individual differences, therefore, should not be used as an excuse for failure. The self-fulfilling prophecy is especially powerful in this area. Provided teachers and instructors recognize the need to vary instruction, differences in ability, personality, learning style, and experience will assist learning and teaching.

Differences in learners, in other words, demand a degree of sensitivity and flexibility in instructors and teachers. They must be sensitive to the needs of the people involved and to the needs of the learning task. At the same time, they must be flexible enough to vary their instructional technique so as to accommodate the needs of the situation. Without such flexibility, much will be lost, and talent will be wasted.

Chapter 16

Discussion Technique

FOCUS

"What are the most effective discussion techniques?"

KNOWLEDGE OBJECTIVES

After reading and studying this chapter, you will be able to:

1. recognize the purpose and role of discussion in the teaching-learning process;
2. manage a discussion group in an efficient and effective manner;
3. encourage and control the flow of discussion;
4. recognize the characteristics of an effective discussion group;
5. select a group discussion method most likely to realize the objectives of the situation.

ATTITUDE OBJECTIVES

After reading this chapter, the author hopes that you will:

1. value the importance of discussion in the teaching-learning process;
2. incorporate the principles into your teaching, so that they become characteristic of your instructional style.

Discussion is the basis of understanding.

Discussion is as natural as work and play. It is a learner-centered activity. Ideas and experience are shared; involvement and participation are reinforced. Most people find it a highly motivating activity. They enjoy the cut and thrust of debate, the challenging of attitudes, beliefs, and values.

Discussion takes place under formal and informal circumstances. Often it is part of an instructional strategy, either in the context of a case study or perhaps a small group discussion. At other times, it occurs spontaneously and informally during a work break. Regardless of when and how it happens, discussion is essential to understanding and mental health.

THE PURPOSE AND ROLE OF DISCUSSION

The discussion method is probably the oldest instructional strategy. It does not involve a solo performance from an instructor, like the lecture, but rather a joint exploration with the learners of a problem or situation. Argument and debate are free-flowing. The experience can be an interesting, exciting, and creative undertaking.

The purpose of discussion

Discussion serves a number of purposes in the teaching-learning process. Some of these are concerned with the acquisition of knowledge, skill, and attitudes. Others are concerned with motivation and personal satisfaction arising from the experience itself.

As an instructional strategy, discussion serves the following purposes. It:

- Informs the people taking part.
- Stimulates and motivate them.
- Encourages critical analysis of assumptions and attitudes.
- Stimulates creative solutions.
- Develops sharing and cooperative skills.

However, none of this will occur if discussion lacks a clear objective, and knowledge, skill, and attitudes.

Purpose is all-important to discussion. There is little worse in instruction than a debate that seems to wander like a tired and sluggish river before drying up on the salt flats. Discussion should be spirited and exciting, relevant and purposeful. For this reason, objectives must be not only clear but worthy of time and effort.

Participation in discussion, too, has to be informed. Unless people are informed, discussion loses steam. Participants must have something to say or something to share. Prejudice and ignorance make for poor discussion. People who are well prepared, and who are clear about the purpose of the activity, are able *collectively* to contribute to an efficient and effective learning experience.

Leader-led and leader-less groups

There are many different types of discussion groups. Some have a definite leader, who chairs the discussion. Sometimes the leader is an instructor. At other times, it is one of the participants appointed by the instructor or group. In still other situations, a group may be leaderless.

Leaderless groups are used extensively in stress type situations. The method involves a group of people who are given a topic to discuss, but no leader is assigned. If the group works effectively, someone will emerge and occupy the role. Unless this happens, it is unlikely that the task will be accomplished.

Discussion groups without nominated leaders are also used to demonstrate group dynamics. In this sense, they act as simulations or case studies. Leaderless groups are sometimes used in selection procedures, as a means of identifying "natural leaders."

The role of a discussion group leader

Although discussion should be participant-centered, this in no way implies that there should be no leader or chairperson. The efficient working of a group demands that someone exercise a leadership role. It can be an instructor or trainee.

The responsibilities of a discussion leader are not large, yet they are important and need to be exercised carefully. Leaders who are too dominant, and make too many interventions, disrupt the free flow of discussion. On the other hand, leaders who fail to exercise their role preside over ineffective groups.

Generally speaking, a discussion leader should make procedural decisions and occasionally act as a subject matter consultant or resource. Problems related to the content of the discussion should be left to the discussion group members. Discussion group leaders, furthermore, must insure that minority opinion is given sufficient time to be heard.

The main responsibilities of a group discussion leader are to:

- Make arrangements for the discussion. This usually includes making certain that a room is reserved, group membership identified, a topic decided, seating patterns organized, and a time limit set.
- Announce the objectives of the discussion, and the procedures that are to be followed. This includes information about reporting back the conclusions reached.
- Get the discussion started, and then keep it moving along. It should also be relevant to the objectives. It may involve facilitating discussion and giving directions.
- Deal with difficult situations, like members who are too talkative or argumentative. It also involves encouraging everyone to take part.
- Summarize the discussion, or get someone else to do this. The group may also need help to make a decision or draw a conclusion.

By and large, a discussion group leader has more to do with the success of the group than any other person. Such a person, however, should aim to do the least amount of talking.

Since discussion groups are a learning process in group dynamics, an instructor or teacher should brief and debrief the group on working effectively. In this way, people taking part can obtain generalizable discussion skills, useful to them in both their jobs and personal lives.

MANAGING A DISCUSSION GROUP

Discussion tends to make people more tolerant and understanding. Participants learn, however, according to their degree of participation and active involvement. Those who actively take part, by and large, learn more than those who simply sit and listen.

In order to make for an efficient and effective learning experience, a discussion has to be managed. Planning, organizing, leading, and evaluating are all essential activities. In addition, an instructor may need to operate as a resource to the group. This means that, on occasion, a teacher will take part in the debate itself.

In managing a discussion group, a number of topics are of special importance:

- Identifying the size of the group.
- Organizing optimal seating arrangements.
- Making a seating chart and participation checklist.
- Handling difficult situations.
- Dealing with controversial issues.

Maximum participation is the ultimate goal. Unless issues are dealt with in a businesslike manner, participation will be diluted and undermined.

Discussion group size

The optimal size for a discussion group is seven. A lower limit of not less than three is workable, as is an upper limit of ten participants. In groups of between five and seven, all discussion group members participate and speak to each other. Even those who are shy and retiring generally take a part in discussion.

As the group gets larger than seven, a number of things begin to happen:

- Quiet people speak less and less often.
- Discussion begins to be dominated by a few people.
- The quality and quantity of group interaction begins to decline.
- The development of cliques and subgroups begins to occur.

The quality of a learning experience is affected by group size.

Seating arrangements

Seating arrangements play an important part in the dynamics of a discussion group. People feel much friendlier when they sit in a relaxed atmosphere and face each other. Illumination should be soft. The room should be well ventilated and not stuffy.

In general, the following arrangements are optimal:

- A small room, for intimacy, is better than a large one.
- Everyone should be able to see each other's face.
- Chairs should be comfortable, and arranged in a circle or horseshoe.
- A round table is preferable to a rectangular one. (Square and rectangular tables have a top and bottom. They make for greater formality, and more dominant leadership.)

A flip chart should be provided for each group, together with an assortment of colored pens. Masking tape can be used to attach charts to the walls of the room, as they are torn from the pad.

Making a seating chart

If the group members are unknown to you, learn their names as quickly as possible. Most groups generally sit in a circle or around a table. One way to familiarize yourself with their names is to ask them to write their names on a piece of paper. This can then be folded, like an inverted-V, and placed in front of them on the table or floor.

Another way is to draw a seating chart. An example is shown in Figure 16:1. The chart shows the names of people in the discussion group, according to where they sit. Writing out the names in this way also helps you to remember them.

FIGURE 16:1.   Example of a seating chart with checkmarks indicating number of interactions.

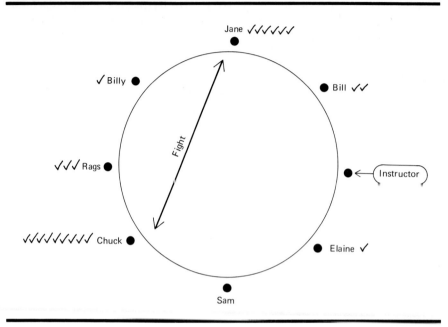

Seating charts have a number of uses other than as a plan of seating. They help instructors and other discussion leaders to:

- Ask people direct questions by calling on them by name. This personalizes the process. It also helps in the management of the questions, as well as with the management of the group.
- Keep a check on who has participated and who has not. As each person speaks, place a check mark alongside his or her name. People who speak too much and those who speak too little will then be recognized. Try and arrange matters so that everyone participates at least two or three times.
- Identify those people who are in "fight" or "flight." Sometimes two or more participants will constantly be arguing with each other. Other people are not attending to what is going on. They are deep in their own thoughts. The chart helps identify these occurrences before too much time has been lost.

Charts of where people sit are very quick to draw. They are a useful management tool.

Handling difficult situations

Three situations often arise in discussions that necessitate a great deal of tact from group leaders. If they are not dealt with, they undermine the effectiveness of group processes. They dilute the value of discussion.

The three difficult situations involve:

- *Someone who is too talkative*
  They monopolize discussion time. People can be dealt with by:
  - Summarizing the major points that have been made. This has the effect of moving the discussion into a new phase. It shuts off a talkative person.
  - Asking the talkative person a factual question. When they answer, ask someone else what he or she thinks or feels about the response.
  - Ask a question that demands a yes/no answer, and then ask someone else for his or her views.

- *Someone who is not taking an active part in the discussion*
  Shy and retiring people can be brought into a discussion by asking them:
  - A factual question to draw them out.
  - An interpretive or evaluative question.
    They should not be asked questions that can be answered with a yes or no.

- *Two or more people who are in conflict*
  There are a number of things that can be done in this type of situation. They include:
  - Don't take sides.
  - Remind people of the areas of agreement.
  - Draw attention to the objectives of the discussion.
  - Use humor to release tension and defuse the situation.

If someone asks you, as discussion leader, what you think, don't answer. In most cases, it is better to turn to someone in the group and ask "Jean, what do you think?" or "John, help me out?"

Dealing with controversial issues

When the subject of a discussion involves a controversial issue—for instance, abortion—adopt a neutral position. Anything that involves values and beliefs is a personal matter. Let the group deal with it.

Adopting a neutral position, however, is not easy. When matters of value or belief are involved, it is wise for an instructor or teacher to:

- Renounce the role of subject matter expert.
- Maintain the agreed procedures for group discussion.
- Avoid participating in the discussion, other than as chairperson.

- Be sure that minority opinions are given a fair hearing.
- Protect the privacy and rights of group members.
- Assist people to understand viewpoints different from their own; they need to come to terms with them.

The natural authority of an instructor or teacher should not be used to indoctrinate. Nothing should be done that causes people to adopt premature opinions. These will only harden into prejudice later.

In matters of conscience, objectives should not be concerned with changing people's values or beliefs. It is important, though, that people clarify their positions. They should be able to verbalize them and defend them in an intelligent manner. People need to understand their feelings about controversial matters. They need to identify the assumptions on which they are based, and accept responsibility for them. Change is not important; understanding is important.

ENCOURAGING AND CONTROLLING THE FLOW OF DISCUSSION

Sometimes discussion will start with little encouragement from an instructor or group leader. It gets going on its own. At other times, a great deal of prodding is necessary. Even when things have started well, discussion can slow down. It has to be refueled; otherwise momentum is lost.

Four techniques are useful. They can be used to start a discussion or to refuel it. They are:

- Questions.
- Probes.
- Expectant body language.
- Silence.

Of the four, silence is the most powerful. It is also the most difficult to handle.

Questions

Broadly speaking, three types of questions are employed in discussion groups:

- *Factual questions*
  These questions have only one right answer. They involve recall. Answers depend either on the memory or on reference material. No explanation is necessary. Once a correct answer has been given, the matter is settled.

  Question of fact: How much production time was lost last year due to worker stress? *Answer:* One quarter.

- *Evaluative questions*
  These questions involve an opinion. There is no right or wrong answer. People are asked whether they agree or disagree. Opinions are based upon belief, values, attitudes, likes and dislikes. There is no way of settling these matters. As a result, they are controversial.

  Question of evaluation: Why has it taken so long for people to recognize the effects of stress on the worker? *Answer:* I think that it is because . . .

- *Interpretive questions*
  These questions involve an explanation. People are asked to explain the meaning of something. Although there is no one right answer, some answers fit the facts better than others. People have to draw conclusions, and work things out for themselves.

  Question of interpretation: Middle managers have the most stressful jobs. How do you explain this fact? *Answer:* They must produce, but cannot always affect policy.

Most discussion groups are characterized by all three types of question.

However, questions of fact should be restricted. They have little role in discussion. They bring debate to a halt. If a question can be answered satisfactorily with a fact, there is nothing to discuss.

A question like: "How does the idea that stress-prone people compulsively push to capacity fit in with your thought that . . . ?" will stimulate discussion. The question "What are the characteristics of stress-prone people?" will be less effective.

Evaluative and interpretive questions should make up the bulk of questions in discussion groups. Interpretive questions are especially valuable. Instead of being asked for an opinion, people are required to explain. They are involved in a search for meaning.

An easy way to begin a discussion is to start with some factual questions. Then ask questions of interpretation. Finally, bring the discussion to an end with questions of evaluation. Such a sequence of factual, interpretive, and then evaluative questions is a good way of managing a discussion group.

Probes

Once an answer is given or a point made in a discussion group, it should not be just accepted. It should be probed, questioned, explored, and challenged. Particular attention should be placed on relationships, applications, agreement, defense, and contradictions.

Be careful, though, about challenging things yourself as discussion leader. Try to get someone else in the group to challenge them. This can be done by saying "Do you agree, Jim?" particularly if you have good reason to believe that Jim most certainly does not agree. Ask someone "If you had said that, how would you defend it?" Alternatively, ask "What is the other side of the picture?"

Most probes consist of:

- *Follow-up questions*
  These obtain additional opinions. They are designed to find out what other people think.
  "Bill, do you agree?"

- *Repeating a question*
  This technique is good when someone fails to respond to a question, or you ask the same question of someone else in the group.
  "I asked Jane what she would do to master stress. What would you do, Dick?"

- *Prompting a participant*
  Prompting involves giving people hints to help them think through the consequences of what they have said. It is very effective with hesitant people or those who are shy and retiring.
  "But, isn't there more to it than that?"

- *Tapping higher levels of thinking*
  These techniques were discussed in detail in Chapter Eight. They involve:
    - Asking for further information: "What do you mean?"
    - Asking people to be more critical in their replies: "How would you defend that?"
    - Refocusing an answer or statement: "What would this mean if . . . ?"

The better a remark, the more useful it is to probe.

To start with, probing can appear artificial or contrived. However, it soon becomes a way of life, and members within the discussion group adopt it themselves. They pick up the technique and challenge the remarks of other people in the group.

Expectant body language

Body language, as we have seen, is one of the more effective ways of communicating. Sometimes more is said with a glance than with a multitude of words. Furthermore, body language does not interrupt the flow of discussion. It refuels it and keeps it going.

Discussion can be encouraged by such tactics as:

- Leaning forward in an expectant manner.
- Raising an eyebrow in a questioning manner.
- Fixing someone with an expectant look. Then they feel obliged to say something.

- Looking around the group while someone is talking. This encourages others to participate.
- Gently pointing to someone, while someone else is talking (perhaps too verbosely), encourages them to interrupt.

Keep things going. Make sure that no one person hogs the discussion.

Use of silence

Silence identifies a change in the dynamics of the situation. A shift is occurring in the subject matter of the discussion, or a change is occurring in the relationships of the people taking part.

At first, silence is ignored, particularly if it occupies only a reasonable amount of time. Most people express tension by talking too much or talking too little. If silence is prolonged, the pressure to break it becomes enormous. Few people can cope with silence that lasts more than ten seconds.

For this reason, silence can be used to encourage further discussion. Most instructors, however, intervene in a group whenever silence occurs. They, rather than the group members, break it. This is unfortunate and should be resisted. It is better to sit through it. Allow one of the group to feel compelled to say something.

Keeping the discussion on track

Encouraging and controlling the flow of discussion are essential skills for discussion leaders to develop. One further skill is to keep discussion on track. This is not applicable to all discussion groups. Some should be encouraged to wander, as in brainstorming.

However, if discussion is tied to the realization of a clear set of objectives, attention needs to be paid to this matter. Relevance is important; otherwise dissatisfaction sets in. People soon begin to feel that the discussion is going nowhere and that valuable time is being lost.

Some of the techniques for keeping a discussion group on track include:

- The use of follow-up questions.
- Asking a question of fact.
- Asking an interpretive question.
- Drawing attention to the objectives of the session.
- Reviewing the major points that have been made in the discussion.

It is easy for a group to lose its way. Priorities shift. Threads of an argument are lost. Instructors need constantly to be on the watch for such occurrences. Corrective action should be taken as soon as possible.

312 INSTRUCTIONAL CONCERNS

THE CHARACTERISTICS OF AN EFFECTIVE DISCUSSION GROUP

Effective discussion groups do not happen by chance. They are the result of a great deal of planning, organizing, leading, and evaluating. They are the products of good management. Sensitivity to people is also essential. People must be protected from the harm that is possible in a group situation.

Briefing and debriefing

As with so much of instruction, preparation is important. Such preparation involves both self-preparation and preparation of the discussion group. Briefing, prior to discussion, is essential.

In briefing a discussion group, the following matters should be included:

- Explain why the group has been brought together.
- Inform the participants what they are to accomplish.
- Inform them of their methods of working.
- Tell them what your expectations are of the situation.
- Explain what resources are available to them.

Since most group discussions involve reporting back, make certain that they spend time preparing a presentation. Flip charts are invaluable.

Once discussions are complete and presentations made, debriefing is advisable. Sometimes, debriefing will take less than a couple of minutes. At other times, it might occupy a substantial period of time. Debrief the group on the content of the discussion, as well as on their working as an effective group.

Debriefing a discussion group should normally include the following matters:

- Summarize the major points that have been made by the groups.
- Reinforce the most significant elements when they are appropriate to the objectives.
- Point out the learning that has been gained. This might include learning that is both job-related and personal.
- Mention, if appropriate, their effectiveness as a work group. Such remarks should include how they might increase their skills.

Briefing and debriefing groups insures that the maximum learning is extracted from the situation. Since discussion takes time, it is important that it be used wisely.

Issues in most group discussions

If a group of learners is to work effectively together in a discussion group, a number of issues arise. Unless these concerns are dealt with, the effective working of the group will be affected. The concerns are characteristic of all groups (including family, church, club, and work groups). Accordingly, learning can be generalized outside the immediate instructional situation.

The issues involve five things. These make up a "hidden agenda":

- *A problem of identity*
  Who am I in relation to this group?
  What resources do I bring that the group will find useful?
  How will the group use me?

- *A problem of objectives*
  What will we do?
  How will our goals be decided?
  How will my needs be met?

- *A problem of acceptance*
  Will I be wanted?
  What are the limits for expressing feelings?
  Can I trust them?

- *A problem of control and influence*
  How will the decisions get made?
  How will directions be established?
  Will they listen to my ideas?

- *A problem of collaboration and competition*
  How will the group deal with dissent?
  How will conflict be handled?
  Can I rock the boat?

These issues are often unspoken. Yet they will be present within the group. An attempt should be made to deal with them in a low-keyed manner. Learners will simply play it safe, and the hidden agenda will never be discussed.

In some situations, a group should be encouraged to deal with the issues. They should decide their own manner of working. On other occasions, an instructor or teacher may wish to deal with the issues as part of the briefing. Sometimes, it is best to let the participants work things out for themselves. This is particularly important, if the group is going to spend a considerable amount of time working together.

Characteristics of an effective discussion group

One characteristic of an effective discussion group is unity of purpose. Such a group is closely knit as a social unit. There is a great deal of fun, as well as a great deal of hard work. Fun and work go hand in hand in most learning situations.

An effective discussion group has a number of characteristics. They can be used by instructors as a checklist. If the group is not working well, it is important to find what is wrong. Perhaps they don't understand the assignment. Perhaps they are working at a "play it safe level."

Effective discussion groups pay:

- *Attention to the task side of the discussion*
  This includes making certain that:
  - Objectives are accepted and understood.
  - Individual assignments to group members are understood and accepted.
  - Group procedures and methods of working are understood and accepted.
  - Tasks and not people dominate the discussion.

- *Attention to the people side of the discussion*
  This includes making certain that there is:
  - An informal and relaxed atmosphere.
  - A great deal of participation and involvement.
  - An expression of feelings as well as ideas.
  - Frank, yet comfortable, criticism of ideas and not of people.
  - Listening, as well as talking.

Above all, as Douglas McGregor loved to point out, an effective work group is self-conscious about itself. It feels shy about having other people observe its inner workings.

Once an instructor or discussion leader has helped people reach this level of working, they can be left alone. Only an occasional intervention is necessary. This will insure continued working together in an effective, as well as an efficient, manner.

SELECTING AN APPROPRIATE GROUP DISCUSSION METHOD

There is a wide range of different group methods for use with discussion groups. Over two dozen are recognized. From the point of view of most teaching and instruction, however, only a few discussion methods are in common use.

Generally speaking, there are three classes of discussion objectives. These are discussion methods that are concerned with:

- Sharing, reacting, and valuing.
- Analyzing, judging, and deciding.
- Gathering, classifying, and summarizing.

Each one has a characteristic pattern of communication. These are illustrated in Figure 16:2.

FIGURE 16:2. Communication patterns in discussion groups.

Sharing, reacting and discussing

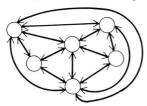

Analyzing, judging and deciding

Gathering, classifying and summarizing

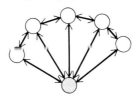

It will be seen that sharing, reacting, and valuing involves an interactive communication network. Everyone interacts with everyone else, without a general focus. A discussion leader, in such circumstances, acts as a facilitator. The leader is not a focus of the discussion.

In the case of the analyzing, judging, and deciding mode, there is a definite focus. The communication network, however, still involves everyone interacting with each other. The communication network associated with gathering, classifying, and summarizing, on the other hand, is dominated by the instructor or discussion group leader. The leader serves as a dominant focus for all group activity.

Sharing, reacting, and valuing groups

Discussion group methods that use this format are case study, buzz groups, free discussion, brainstorming, T-groups, and square root groups. In each one of these groups, size is somewhere between five and seven. Anything smaller or larger limits the character of the interaction.

The case study method is a problem-solving group, in which participants are well prepared. First, they study a case history beforehand. Then, they discuss it in the light of their knowledge and experience. In the case of free discussion groups, both topic and objectives are controlled by the participants.

Buzz groups and huddles are informal groups. They discuss matters for a short period. They normally occur in the course of a lecture or lesson. People are directed to "huddle" together and share or react for a few moments.

Brainstorming involves people offering spontaneous, creative solutions to a problem. The solutions are received uncritically. It is a freewheeling, suspend judgment type of format. T-groups, on the other hand, are used for self-aware-ness and sensitivity training. They are therapeutic, and should be used with caution.

Square root groups, sometimes called cross-over groups, occur when a class is organized into a number of subgroups for discussion purposes. They get their name from the fact that the number in each group approximates the square root of the class total. For instance, if there are twenty-five in the class, the class is divided into five groups of five people. The resulting discussion is brief and informal.

Analyzing, judging, and deciding groups

Analyzing, judging, and deciding groups can be a little larger than seven and somewhat smaller than five. The usual range is from three to twelve people. The method includes: seminars, tutorials, role-playing, games, simulations, and syndicate work.

Seminars are usually subject-centered. The participants usually prepare beforehand. Sometimes they follow a lecture or a demonstration; sometimes they follow a reading or assignment. Tutorials are given on both an individual and group basis. They are useful for remedial work and for monitoring trainee or student progress.

Syndicates and task forces are assigned a definite task or problem. The task usually involves a fair amount of time for its completion. This may range from half a day to a week or more. They are problem-centered, and a report is normally required. Sometimes the report is given orally as a formal presen-tation; at other times it is written.

Games, simulations, and role-playing also involve group discussion. This takes place either beforehand or as part of a general debriefing.

Gathering, classifying, and summarizing groups

Gathering, classifying, and summarizing groups are generally instructor- or leader-centered. Since they are structured, it is possible to deal with larger numbers of people. Seven to twenty-four people is normally regarded as a manageable group.

The discussion methods that fall into this grouping include: horseshoe groups, step-by-step groups, controlled groups, and question and answer groups. Horseshoe groups sit in the form of a horseshoe. An instructor moves from one group to another. There is always a place left for the instructor to occupy.

Step-by-step groups deal with issues in sequence as a lesson proceeds. When the moment arrives for discussion, the lesson is interrupted for a short while. Controlled groups are autocratically handled. The instructor controls matters in such a way that it is really a variant of a question and answer period at the end of a lecture.

Question and answer group discussions occur at the end of other instructional strategies. Often, they occur at the end of a lecture. Members of the audience ask questions of the lecturer. Q and A discussion groups also occur at the end of most lessons and demonstrations, as well as before and after most instruction.

CONCLUSION

Group discussion offers learners an opportunity to come together and interact with each other. Although one of the oldest of the instructional methods, it is one of the most effective. There is a strong demand, among trainees and students alike, for such experiences. They are motivating and pleasurable, as well as effective as a learning strategy.

Although, to a casual observer, they involve little instructional skill, a great deal of preparation, organization, leadership, and evaluation are involved. Good group discussion rarely occurs by chance. A lot of hard work has taken place behind the scenes. If learning is to be reinforced, work still remains to be done after the discussion has finished.

Chapter 17
Managing Time and Paper

FOCUS

"How can time be managed and paperwork be controlled?"

KNOWLEDGE OBJECTIVES

After reading and studying this chapter, you will be able to:
1. manage and allocate time in the teaching-learning process;
2. control the flow of paperwork in the teaching-learning process.

ATTITUDE OBJECTIVES

After reading this chapter, the author hopes that you will:
1. value the importance of managing time and controlling paperwork in the teaching-learning process;
2. incorporate the principles into your teaching, so that they become characteristic of your instructional style.

Time is the most precious instructional resource.

Effectiveness is the main responsibility of teachers and instructors. Nothing is more central to the teaching-learning process. Efficiency, as we have seen, is important, but it does not guarantee effectiveness. Effectiveness comes from doing the right things.

Fortunately, it can be learned. To apply Peter Drucker's thoughts, effectiveness requires that instructors build upon their trainees' strengths and not upon their weaknesses. It requires that instructors make the right decisions. They must focus upon opportunities and not upon difficulties. Every problem is a new opportunity. Effectiveness also involves concentrating upon the few key areas that produce outstanding results.

MANAGING AND ALLOCATING TIME

However, one skill of effectiveness remains. Effective instructors and effective teachers know where their time goes. They can account for every minute of it. Time, after all, is the only limiting factor to teaching and learning.

All other resources can be expanded. Money, people, materials, equipment can be increased, or at least stretched. Time, however, is limited. You have what you have. All you can do is to make the best use of it. For this reason, it is the scarcest resource that instructors and trainees possess. It must never be wasted.

Finding out where time goes

Effective instructors and teachers learn to manage time. They resist allowing time to manage them. They learn to include it in lesson planning and to monitor it during their teaching. Unless they know where it goes, it is impossible to do much about it.

An instructor-manager makes time available for:

- Planning instruction and learning.
- Organizing instruction and learning.
- Leading instruction and learning.
- Evaluating instruction and learning.

What is left over should be used for the operating duties of the role. But time has first to be found for planning, organizing, leading, and evaluating functions.

320

For this reason, effective instructors do not start out with planning. They start out by finding where their time goes. This means making an inventory. Simply keeping a record of each instructional day, for a week or two, will serve the purpose.

Most teachers and instructors refuse to believe the record. By and large, they find that less than one third of their day is spent on things *directly* concerned with teaching and learning. Most of it is consumed in necessary but trivial activities.

Planning the use of time

Once you have found out where your time goes, it is possible to start thinking about how you can manage it. Instructors and teachers need to ask themselves a number of questions whenever they plan a lesson. Answering the questions allows better use of their own as well as their trainees' time.

In order to manage time, decide four things:

- *What are the things that must be done, and what are the things that need not be done?*
  It is important to identify the objective of the instructional situation. It is equally important to maintain it. This can be done only if there is a clear sense of priorities. Must, could, and should is a start; "A," "B," and "C" categories are another.

- *What are the things that must be done by an instructor, and what are the things that must be done by the trainees?*
  It is easy to fall into the trap of underestimating trainees. Furthermore, every time we do underestimate them, the self-fulfilling prophecy comes into being. Expectations are unwittingly met.

- *What are the things that must be done in the training room, and what are the things that can be done in unsupervised settings?*
  Some work has to be undertaken in settings appropriate to close supervision. Other things are best done away from the workroom and instructor. The trap of thinking that instruction is always essential to learning has to be resisted.

- *What steps can instructors take to avoid wasting trainee time?*
  This is a common problem. Trainees are often given too much busywork. It contributes little to student effectiveness. Instructors must prune back the work they do in instructional situations, so that learners have an opportunity to do things for themselves.

As with so many things, effective time management involves *resisting* the human temptation of overestimating our own importance.

A great deal of detail can be given to students and trainees by means other than the instructor's voice. In this way, the instructor can be freed to do those things that can only be achieved through direct instruction.

Identifying time wasters, however, requires foresight and planning. Figure 17:1 summarizes the major steps that can be taken. In effect, it can be used as a checklist. In this way, some of the more significant questions can be asked, so that instructors and teachers can manage time effectively.

Allocating time

Prior experience and intuition are invaluable sources of information. Deciding what time should be allocated to different parts of the lesson demands a somewhat more disciplined approach.

This involves taking into account:

- The nature of the objectives to be achieved.
- The abilities, aptitudes, and knowledge of the trainees.
- The nature of the tasks to be mastered.

FIGURE 17:1. Checklist for managing instructor and trainee time effectively.

Effective management of an instructor's time involves:

- Identifying what the role of an instructor entails.
- Identifying your own objectives as an instructor.
- Analyzing how you spend your time in instructional situations.
- Planning ahead for time, as well as for the content of your instruction.
- Obtaining a clearer sense of the objectives in your scheme of work.
- Identifying priorities, and managing them accordingly.
- Resisting spending time on tasks that trainees can do just as well by themselves.
- Spending time on material that is best covered by an instructor. Resist spending time on material that can be gotten from other sources.

Effective management of the trainee's time involves:

- Eliminating busywork.
- Communicating a sense of priority to trainees. This will help them to allocate their own time more effectively.
- Giving trainees the quantity and quality of the information they need for *them* to learn efficiently.
- Letting trainees concentrate on one particular learning task long enough for them to master it.
- Informing trainees of your expectations. In this way, they will know where to put their effort to obtain the results that you want.
- Listening to trainees, and evaluating what they say.
- Teaching trainees how to learn, and how to manage learning situations.

As a rule of thumb, most of the objectives should be achieved most of the time, by the majority of the trainees. The 90/90/90 criterion is a key feature of mastery learning.

A useful way of calculating the time needed for particular parts of a lesson has been suggested by Desmond Cook. He has applied program evaluation and review techniques to instruction (Cook, 1971). As a result, Cook has identified a formula that is useful to instructors and teachers trying to determine how much time should be spent on particular tasks.

The Cook formula involves three steps. They are:

- Estimating the time you would expect each instructional-learning activity to take under normal circumstances.

  This expected time is referred to as "E."
- Estimating the time you would expect each instructional-learning activity to take if everything went wrong

  This pessimistic time is referred to as "P."
- Calculating the mean time that is likely to be taken to complete the instructional-learning activity 90 percent of the time.

  This is referred to as allocated time. It involves using the formula $\left(\dfrac{E + P}{2}\right)$.

Calculating the time needed in this way gives a useful estimate of time for the purposes of lesson planning.

For example, imagine that the expected times for three instructional tasks are 2, 3, and 2 minutes respectively. This yields a mean expected time of 2.3 minutes. Now let us suppose that the pessimistic times for the three activities are 3, 8, and 4 minutes respectively. The mean pessimistic time is 5.0 minutes. Using the formula the allocated time should be around 4 minutes (actually 3.65).

MANAGING INSTRUCTIONAL PAPERWORK

A great deal of instructional time is taken up with paperwork. Lesson plans, identifying objectives, needs analyses, organizing instructional activities, assessing trainee performance, keeping records all involve paper. Most instructors and teachers, in fact, feel that paperwork often gets in the way of instruction.

A recent survey of paperwork in the instructional setting estimates that the cost of a single page, typewritten, exceeds $15. For this reason something has to be done to control it. A further reason is that any unnecessary time spent on paperwork reduces the amount of time spent on essential instructional activities.

Managing paperwork

Paperwork can be controlled. But it entails attacking it at every stage of the instructional-learning process. The most effective area to hit is the creation stage. Instructors are natural producers of paper materials. They create paper to help not only with instruction but also with learning.

In order to reduce the amount of paper produced, a number of things should be considered. These include:

- The purpose of the paper that has been produced.
  What are you going to do with it?
- The importance of the paper produced.
  Is it really important to the teaching-learning process?
- The timing of the paper produced.
  What is the right time for using it?
- The aptness of the paper produced.
  Can the same result be obtained by other means?
- The need for the paper produced.
  What would be the effect if the paper were not available?
- The use of the paper produced.
  How will supervisors, you, or the trainees use the paper?

Once these six questions have been answered, instructors can decide whether or not it is necessary.

There is simply no point in producing class handouts, reports, documents assessing trainees, etc., unless they are necessary. Once a need has been identified, the next stage is to use as little paper as possible. This is an obvious instructional tactic, but it is also an important one.

Most people tend to get carried away. They produce far too much, with the result that costs are increased. A good rule of thumb is to use as little paper as necessary, as long as the job gets done. This also increases the chances that the paper will be used. Controlling paperwork in instruction requires constant attention, but the results are worthwhile.

CONCLUSION

Time is the most precious resource. It is the one commodity that instructors and teachers cannot increase. It sets a limit to effectiveness. Unless time is managed carefully, teaching and learning will be undermined. For this reason alone, instructors and trainees should master time, rather than allow time to master them.

Instruction, like many activities, involves a great deal of paperwork. Lesson plans, implementing instruction, assessing the progress of trainees, handouts, and reports all take a great deal of time. In order to save themselves from a flood of paper, instructors must take steps to control the problem.

Periodically reviewing the paper that is distributed is one way. Another is to control, on a systematic basis, the creation stage. This involves identifying what paperwork is essential and what can be eliminated. Only toughness will save the day.

Chapter 18
Out-of-Class Assignments

FOCUS
"What is the role of out-of-class assignments?"

KNOWLEDGE OBJECTIVES
After reading and studying this chapter, you will be able to:
1. state the role of out-of-class assignments in the teaching-learning process;
2. recognize opportunities when out-of-class assignments facilitate learning;
3. manage out-of-class assignments, so that they enhance the teaching-learning process.

ATTITUDE OBJECTIVES
After reading this chapter, the author hopes that you will:
1. value the importance of out-of-class assignments in the teaching-learning process;
2. incorporate the principles into your teaching, so that they become characteristic of your instructional style.

Out-of-class assignments have a role in the teaching-learning process.

Homework has become a way of life for children. It also has a role in adult education and training programs. Rarely is it possible for students and trainees to cover all the material in class. It is even less likely that they will have enough time to practice and rehearse the skills they have gained.

Certain assignments, therefore, have to be completed outside of "class." Indeed, many training programs are designed on the understanding that work will be done at home or in one's room in the training center during the evening hours.

Unfortunately, evening is often a time when students and trainees are jaded and tired. It is also a time when people become frustrated and discouraged. This happens particularly if they feel that the assignment is little more than busywork.

THE ROLE OF OUT-OF-CLASS ASSIGNMENTS

Busywork, in the context of instruction, was largely the invention of the one-room schoolhouse. It was a means of coping with people of widely different backgrounds, experience, and ability. Most importantly, it was a means of coping with different age groups. The work kept some learners occupied while the teacher gave attention to those requiring specialized instruction or remedial assistance.

Unfortunately, this practice has spread to adult situations. It continues in the form of homework, or what some prefer to call "out-of-class assignments." Another name is independent study. Oddly enough, the justification for busywork, based on keeping some of the brighter learners occupied while slower ones receive remedial instruction, hardly applies. Yet busywork is often given for out-of-class work assignments.

The purposes of out-of-class assignments

Out-of-class assignments fill a number of personal and task needs. They give trainees and students an opportunity to:

- Practice skills, as well as increase speed and accuracy.

328

- Read, absorb, and summarize what they have learned.
- Accept responsibility and be accountable for their actions.
- Act in an honest and persevering manner.
- Manage time effectively.
- Develop confidence in their own ability.

None of these objectives, however, will be realized unless instructors and teachers check the work that is done and note its accuracy and completeness. Immediate feedback of results is essential.

Types of assignments

There are two types of out-of-class assignments:

- *Preparatory assignments*
  These are usually referred to as "prep." They consist of activities that *prepare* for work that will be undertaken in class. An example would be reading and studying a case study prior to its discussion in class.

- *Further assignments*
  These consist of activities that are completed after instruction. They rehearse and consolidate what has been learned in class. An example would be solving a group of problems or making a component.

Preparatory and further assignments, of course, do not have to be done at home or in a hotel room. Many of them, depending upon the circumstances, need to be carried out at work in the factory or office or wherever the job is performed.

Advantages and disdvantages

Out-of-class assignments have a role in the teaching-learning process. However, their advantages and disadvantages need to be clearly recognized. Otherwise, the tactic fails to realize its potential as an aid to learning.
  In general, the following characteristics can be identified:

- *Advantages of out-of-class assignments*
  - They are usually done on an individual basis.
  - They are done under circumstances where self-reliance and independence are necessary.
  - They allow trainees and students to work at their own speed.
  - They allow teachers and instructors to delegate work to students and trainees.
  - Some work is better done under real life conditions away from the instructional setting.

- *Disadvantages of out-of-class assignments*
    - They may involve knowledge and skill beyond the capabilities of the students and trainees.
    - There is no immediate knowledge of results. There can be a lengthy period of time between completing the work and getting it assessed.
    - It is often done when trainees and students are tired, if not exhausted.
    - It eats into a trainee's and student's time for relaxation and rest, if it is done at home or in a hotel room.

Unless out-of-class assignments are used or graded soon after completion, they should not be assigned.

Some home assignments are made because of poor time management. Unless care is taken, instructors and teachers run out of time in the classroom. As a result, essential consolidation is not carried out.

Teachers attempt to redeem the situation by giving learners work assignments. These are meant to be carried out in their own time. However, since they were originally meant to be done under supervised conditions, trainees may find them difficult to complete. The instructions may not be clear, or an essential piece of information may be missing. As a result, because of poor time management, the learner's confidence is undermined.

Planning out-of-class assignments

Independent study or work assignments must be carefully planned and organized. If they are to be successful, such assignments should be:

- A necessary part of the course.
- Clearly assigned, with clear instructions for their completion.
- Definite and limited in scope.
- Limited in length. A definite time limit should be placed for their completion.
- Planned in such a way that they can be completed without the help of colleagues, friends, and relations.
- Used or assessed soon after they have been completed.

If trainees or students experience difficulties, similar work should be included in later assignments.

Just as planning is necessary from an instructor's point of view, so planning is important from a trainee's. It is unreasonable to expect assignments to be completed by the next day. Students and trainees may have other activities planned for that evening. Common courtesy indicates that a reasonable time period should be given for completing the task.

Something also needs to be said about the virtues of *not* assigning independent work for completion at home. An evening is not a void to be filled. It is a time for relaxation and for a change of pace. "All work and no play, make Jack and Jill dull people." Even more worrying from a learning point of view, it makes them tired and jaded ones.

OUT-OF-CLASS ASSIGNMENTS AND THEIR RELATIONSHIP TO LEARNING

Although good instruction aids learning, it cannot guarantee it. For learning to take place in an efficient and effective manner, a number of conditions must be filled. Learning, for instance, is an active process. It occurs when people respond to stimuli that have caught their attention and interest.

Learners need to be motivated toward the task. If they find it dissatisfying they will tend to avoid the situation. Time and the conditions under which learning is taking place also have to be right. A noisy and distracting environment is not conducive to learning.

Sequencing, too, is important. Certain things need to be learned before others. At the same time, progress in learning is rarely uniform. It is related to rapid periods of growth followed by periods of little or no progress. Interference is a common cause of forgetting. Above all, practice is essential in both verbal and physical skills.

Once these principles are accepted, the relevance of out-of-class assignments can be understood. Trainees need to be provided with opportunities to learn. Such opportunities, however, must give them a sense of responsibility and achievement. Uninterested students rarely learn.

Thus, independent assignments should be satisfying experiences. They should be worthwhile and relevant to the learner's needs. The activities, too, need to be logically arranged. Sufficient opportunities for practice and rehearsal must be planned; otherwise the skill may not be acquired. For all of these reasons, out-of-class assignments need to be carefully planned ahead of time.

Rehearsal and repetition in some tasks aid memory. They also reduce the possibilities of forgetting. Since forgetting is initially rapid, and then proceeds less rapidly as time goes on, independent work is essential. Early assignments provide students with an early opportunity to practice soon after instruction.

Feedback or knowledge of results is also important. It can be more effective than practice in reducing or eliminating error. This means that promptly correcting out-of-class assignments is doubly important. Not only is uncorrected or unused work dissatisfying, but feedback helps reduce the chances of errors being made.

GIVING OUT-OF-CLASS ASSIGNMENTS

Out-of-class assignments should be varied and worthwhile. Telling students and trainees only to complete problems like 1 to 24 on page 93 of some textbook is unimaginative. Giving them an unvaried diet of case studies is as bad.

It is equally bad to give learners an assignment on the spur of the moment. In such circumstances, they can only feel that they are being given tasks to keep them occupied.

Placing assignments within an instructional plan

Assignments are best conceived within the framework of an overall instructional plan. They should be set out within the scheme of work, and referred to in the lesson plan as an integral part of the program. Trainees should also be informed of:

- The assignments that will be allocated.
- The dates that they are due.
- Instructions and procedures that are to be used in their completion.
- How their assignments will be used or assessed.

This information should be written down and distributed at the beginning of each phase of the training or education program.

It is a good idea for instructors and teachers to complete the assignments themselves. In this way they will be able to see what difficulties emerge. Perhaps the instructions were not clear. Perhaps the assignment was trivial and meaningless.

Types of assignments

The range of out-of-class assignments is limited only by the imagination of instructors and teachers. Figure 18:1 illustrates some of the possibilities. They run from pen and paper tasks carried out in private to tasks involving performance in work situations.

In every case, the identification of a problem should be involved. If there is no problem, there is little point in making the assignment. Trainees need to be briefed on the task beforehand, and debriefed once it has been completed. Briefing and debriefing are essential steps in the process. If they are forgotten or skimped, some of the impact is lost.

Out-of-class assignments can include such activities, for example, as:

- Making a component or balancing a ledger
- Drawing up an Affirmative Action Plan or defining the role of an "Assistant to" a senior executive position.
- Constructing flow diagrams, writing procedures, or keeping a diary of activities.
- Tracing pipelines, identifying faults, collecting reliability data.
- Establishing corporate travel and expense policies and procedures.
- Preparing presentations, studying case studies, reading and interpreting cash flow reports.

The work might involve building more effective work teams. In this way, the out-of-class assignment can "make it happen" in the workplace. Successful people skills are best obtained by practicing skills in job situations.

Out-of-class assignments, of course, do not always have to be carried out on an individual basis. They can also be done by students and trainees working together. Sometimes the groups can be put in competition with each other.

FIGURE 18:1.   The range of out-of-class assignments.

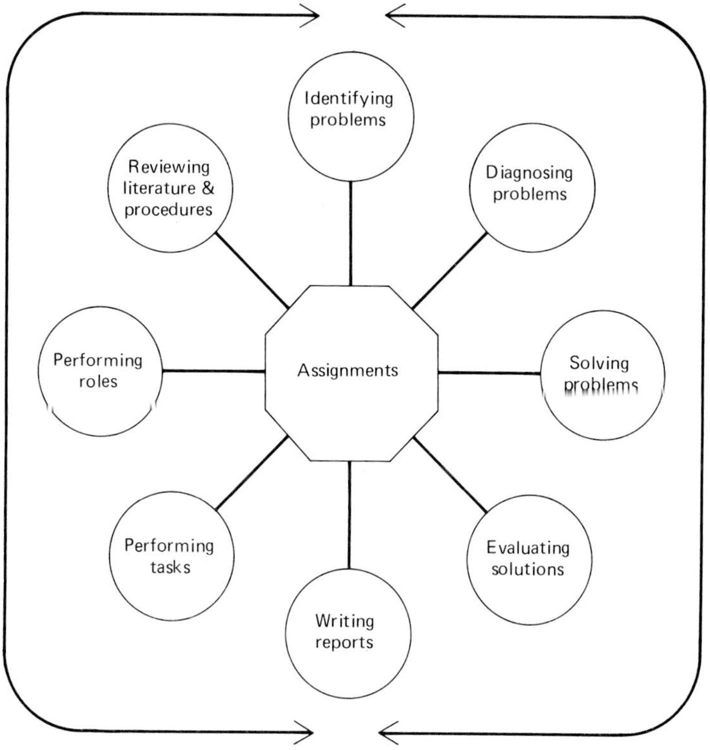

On other occasions, it is useful to get trainees to work alone making some independent judgments. They then move into small groups, where they discuss what they have done and reach consensus. All of this is done as an out-of-class assignment. Their reports, however, are given as formal presentations to the class as a whole.

CONCLUSION

Out-of-class assignments are an important part of the teaching-learning process. However, assignments must be relevant and worthwhile to the needs of trainees and students. Busywork should be avoided.

If assignments are going to be given, they should form part of the scheme of work and be written into the lesson plan. Trainees should be informed in advance of what is required, the dates the assignments are due, and the manner in which they will be used or assessed. It is important that tasks be work related. For this reason, many of the assignments are best done in the context of the job.

Chapter 19
The Personality of the Instructor

FOCUS

"What is the personality of an effective instructor or teacher?"

KNOWLEDGE OBJECTIVES

After reading and studying this chapter, you will be able to:

1. identify the three approaches to analyzing the personality of effective teachers and instructors;
2. recognize the factors in your personality that you can use to realize your potential as teacher or instructor.

ATTITUDE OBJECTIVES

After reading this chapter, the author hopes that you will:

1. value the importance of realizing your potential as an effective instructor or teacher;
2. incorporate the principles into your teaching, so that they become characteristic of your instructional style.

Personality is a resource to be used as an aid to instruction.

Most people have strong views about the personality of the "ideal" teacher. Profiles usually include such characteristics as sincerity, resoluteness, courage, efficiency, energy, and tact. People with such qualities, it is thought, are most likely to be successful in the art of instruction.

However, the simple fact remains that many quite successful instructors have few of these characteristics. They are ordinary people, with all the imperfections and faults of humanity at large. There is little going for them, other than their knowledge, enthusiasm, and love of people. But, when you come down to it, those are the only qualities that are essential.

THREE APPROACHES TO INSTRUCTORS

There are many ways of looking at instructors and teachers. However, from the point of view of the instructor as a manager of learning, three approaches seem to make sense. Each is quite different from the others.

The three ways of looking at instructors are:

- *A qualities approach*

- *A situational approach*

- *A functional approach*

Each perspective represents a different way of looking at the same problem. It is not that one approach is right and the others wrong. Rather, each adds another dimension to the age-old problem of what makes for a good teacher.

THE QUALITIES APPROACH

The qualities approach focuses on the *qualities* of a "good" instructor. These characteristics are usually identified by asking instructors and teachers for their views, and trainees and students for theirs. In this way, key qualities are described.

336

Qualities identified by instructors

There is little agreement in the list of qualities mentioned by instructors and teachers. Among the most common ones are: intelligence, good speaking voice, clear writing, above average height, neat and tidy appearance, well organized manner, ready command of words, enthusiasm, etc.

This list seems endless. There also appears to be little agreement on what is the most important. Furthermore, when the list is applied to quite competent instructors and teachers, there are some who fail on almost every count.

What makes matters worse is that it is possible to identify people who possess most of the above characteristics and yet they are poor instructors. It is obvious that there is no watertight list which can be used for all people in all instructional situations.

While there does not appear to be much agreement on what makes for a good instructor, there is more agreement on what makes for a poor one. Included in the list of don'ts are:

- Don't be pompous.
- Don't bring your personal problems into the workroom.
- Don't ridicule learners.
- Don't start late or finish late.
- Don't lose your trainees' respect.
- Don't be too familiar with your trainees.
- Don't waste time.

Above all, don't be autocratic all the time. There is a place for autocracy, just as there is a place for a more consultative style.

Qualities identified by trainees

Trainees and students tend to identify rather different characteristics than instructors. Included in their list are such qualities as: patience, good communication, caring, organization, fun, humor, hard work, thinking about trainees and their problems, and making sure that they get it right.

What comes through is a concern for people. The instructor's list is very much oriented toward the task, toward achieving the objectives that have been set. Trainees, on the other hand, emphasize skills with people. To them warm, human relationships are essential.

The list of don'ts is also revealing. Trainees and students seem to stress that teaching is:

- Not talking.
- Not an ego trip.
- Not fancy accommodation and equipment.

- Not faking it.
- Not monopolizing class time and discussion.
- Not reading material.
- Not wasting time.

Above all, teaching is *not* never having to say "I'm sorry." Instruction is learning, listening, and sharing together. It is a quickness to say, "I'm sorry. I made a mistake. You are right, and I am wrong."

Some common points

When speaking to instructors and trainees, there appear to be two qualities that almost everyone agrees on. Both groups speak of them as being among the essential traits of efficient and effective instructors and teachers.

They are:

- An instructor *must* know the subject matter.
- An instructor *must* believe in the value of the subject matter.

Instruction is inseparable from mastery. It is not possible for an instructor to know "well enough." Teachers must know more than they are required to teach.

Students and trainees are not fools. Any attempt to bluff them is seen for what it is. The instructional-learning process is a fragile one. For this reason alone, it is essential that it be founded upon mutual respect and understanding.

At the same time, instructors must truly believe in the value of what they teach. If teachers dislike what they instruct, that feeling will be readily communicated to trainees. Instruction will lack the vitality that comes only from a deep and abiding interest. Dislike merely results in an instructor doing what has to be done in a mean and grudging manner.

Few people can go on, time after time, teaching the same material. If they are not interested, it will bore them. If they are interested, they will take steps to change it, so that freshness can be maintained.

Teaching is a people activity. It involves dealing with, associating with, and working with people. Unless you like them, there is little point in being an instructor. Teachers are dedicated to the idea of assisting trainees to achieve mastery. This involves working very closely with people of widely varying ability and experience. Instructors cannot pick and choose.

Establishing a proper relationship with learners is fundamental. An effective instructor will know the name of everyone in the group. Good eye contact is also important, not with just one or two trainees but with everyone in class. By watching and observing trainee expressions, a teacher knows whether a point has been made.

Above everything else, an instructor should cultivate a sense of humor. Humor, Gilbert Highet reminds us, is a bridge between experience and inexperience. It takes the sting out of the most critical remark. At the same time, it furthers a relationship that might be threatened by failure and frustration.

THE SITUATIONAL APPROACH

The situational approach focuses on the technical skills appropriate to teaching-learning situations. This perspective emphasizes mastery of:

- The technical skills of instruction.
- The technical skills of the subject matter.

Once instructors and teachers become proficient in teaching and in the subject matter, they are ready to take on the role of instruction. They are equipped, in other words, to deal with the situation.

There is, of course, some overlap between this and the qualities approach. The major difference is to be found in the belief that enthusiasm, humor, liking people are of subsidiary importance. Technical skills are the most important.

The approach, in many ways, is a simplistic one. Research suggests that ineffective instructors use similar instructional strategies and tactics to effective ones. They use them, though, in a more rigid and authoritarian manner. Little or no accommodation is made to the varying needs of different instructional situations.

Effective instructors, on the other hand, spontaneously vary their approach. They move from a dominating one to a supportive one, depending upon the needs of the task and the people involved. Sensitive to needs, they have sufficient flexibility to be able to change their style to meet the circumstances of the moment.

THE FUNCTIONAL APPROACH

It is certainly true that efficient and effective instructors seem to have slightly above average intelligence. It is also true that they tend to be good at communication. They also appear to like people, are well motivated, and have maturity and breadth of vision. Above all, they think well of people.

Figure 19:1, using information from Coombs & McGregor, summarizes some of the distinguishing features of good teachers. It will be seen that the people orientation looms large. Not so obvious, but indicated in the figure, is the ability to change role and style.

Flexibility, as we have seen, is important. In other words, successful teachers and instructors have a functional approach to their craft. Such an approach emphasizes accommodating, in some way, to three sets of competing needs.

FIGURE 19:1.   Characteristics of good instructors.

Good instructors are often distinguished from poor ones by their ability to:

- Understand how things seem to trainees.
- Orient themselves to people rather than to things.
- Deal with both subjective and objective experiences.
- Trust people and believe in them.
- Assume that people are friendly and cooperative, rather than hostile and uncooperative.
- Believe that people are worthy rather than unworthy
- Assume that people are active and motivated, rather than passive and uninterested.

These are:

- The needs of the learning task.
- The individual needs of the students and trainees.
- The needs of the group as a whole.

The successful instructor is able to meet all three, one way or another.

Needs of the learning task

The needs of the learning task are many and varied. However, an effective instructor or teacher must:

- Analyze the learning need.
- Identify learning objectives.
- Prepare a lesson plan.
- Organize resources and activities.
- Motivate the trainees.
- Evaluate the success of instruction.

These are some of the responsibilities of the instructor-manager. But there are others. These arise from the needs of the people involved in the teaching-learning process.

Needs of the group

The group has needs that must be met. If they are ignored, the effectiveness of the teaching-learning situation will be reduced. In order to meet these needs, an effective instructor or teacher must:

- Set standards to be achieved.
- Maintain good order and housekeeping.
- Build class spirit and identity.
- Praise and motivate the class as a whole.
- Insure good communication within the group.
- Utilize the class as a whole on some tasks.

The class is a work group. As such, it has an integrity and existence of its own. This sense of being should be encouraged. It is a resource in the instructional process.

Needs of the individual trainees

Although there are task needs and group needs, the needs of the individual learners are also important. They, too, expect they will be met. Accordingly, effective teachers and instructors must:

- Attend to trainees and students as individuals.
- Reward them when they learn.
- Encourage and motivate them in their learning tasks.
- Provide them with opportunities for independent action.
- Recognize, and use, individual differences as a resource.
- Insure that trainees experience a sense of achievement and personal growth.

Only if these needs are met will trainees and students be willing to invest the individual effort necessary for effective learning.

Harmonizing all three needs

The functional approach identifies three sets of needs. It also emphasizes that all three must be met. This is not an easy task for most instructors and teachers to accomplish. In some situations, one or other of the needs will have to be sacrificed. They don't all have the same priority.

If a task becomes excessively difficult, some trainees may experience excessive frustration and anxiety. This, in its turn, will undoubtedly affect the efficient working of the group as a whole. Breakdown of class spirit and morale, similarly, will affect the ability of individual trainees to realize the task.

Since all needs do not have the same priority, much will depend upon the specific situation. In some circumstances, the needs of the task must dominate over all else, pushing group and individual needs into the background. Such a situation might arise when a safety procedure has to be mastered or an abnormal condition rectified.

At other times, the needs of the group or the individual trainees might be allowed to dominate. The needs of the task then assume a lower priority.

FIGURE 19:2.   The three functions to be met by an instructor.

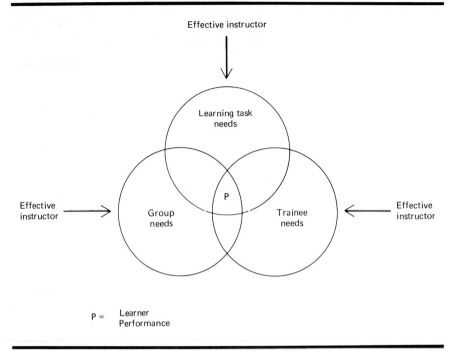

Excessively long periods of either task or people priority, however, can be disruptive. Instructors and teachers, therefore, should seize every opportunity to redress the balance. That is the essence of good instructional technique.

CONCLUSION

There is much for an instructor or teacher to do. Sensitivity is necessary, and diagnostic ability. There must also be a willingness to experiment and to reflect. Flexibility of instructional style is of paramount importance. But so is a capacity to reflect upon and to reassess a situation.

There is no one right way, and there are lots of ruts. Fortunately, there are rules to indicate paths that might be worth following—at least for a time. Try them for yourself, and see.

Epilogue

Effectiveness and Competence

Teachers and instructors are a bridge between experience and inexperience. As a bridge, they serve learners on the one hand and a company or institution on the other. In this sense, they are oriented toward the future, never to the past. Such an orientation is both challenging and humbling. Change is the essence of their craft.

Although instruction is a serious business, there is another side to it. A wise old teacher once remarked, "I consider a day's teaching wasted if we don't all have a good laugh." When people laugh together, they become one. Differences of age, ability, and experience merge momentarily, so that they all become colleagues sharing a common experience.

Enjoyment and change, after all, are the essence of education and training. One is possible without the other. The two together, however, make for a powerful combination. Trainees and students expect to get more out of instruction than knowledge and skill. They expect to acquire worthy performance, as well as a satisfying experience.

In order to arrange for all of this, much is expected of teachers and instructors. Effectiveness is the name of the game. It is their sole responsibility. In order to be effective, instructors must certainly possess the techniques of successful instruction. They should also be good managers of learning. Above all, they must know and like people. This is why good teachers are, themselves, such interesting and competent people.

Bibliography

Introduction

Allen, LA (1964). *The management profession.* McGraw-Hill.

Davies, IK (1973). *Competency based learning.* McGraw-Hill (Published in the UK as *The management of learning*).

Davies, IK (1973). *The organization of training.* McGraw-Hill.

Drucker, PF (1967). *The effective executive.* Harper & Row.

Gage, NL (1978). *The scientific basis of the art of teaching.* Teachers College, Columbia University.

Gane, C (1972). *Managing the training function.* George Allen & Unwin.

Gilbert, TF (1978). *Human competence: engineering worthy performance.* McGraw-Hill.

Goffman, E (1959). *The presentation of everyday life.* Doubleday.

Harless, JH (1975). *An ounce of analysis (is worth a pound of objectives).* Harless Performance Guild.

Highet, G (1963). *The art of teaching.* Methuen.

Highet, G (1976). *The immortal profession.* Weybright & Talley.

Lessinger, LM & Gillis, D (1976). *Teaching as a performing art.* Crescendo Publications.

Mager, RF & Beach, KM (1967). *Developing vocational instruction.* Fearon.

Mager, RF & Pipe, P (1970). *Analyzing performance problems.* Fearon.

Michalak, DF & Yager, EG (1979). *Making the training process work.* Harper & Row.

Pullias, EV & Young, JD (1977). *A teacher is many things.* Indiana University Press.

Warren, MW (1979). *Training for results: a systems approach to the development of human resources in industry.* Addison-Wesley (2nd edition).

Chapter 1

Davies, IK (1973). *The organization of training.* McGraw-Hill.

Davies, IK (1976). *Objectives in curriculum design.* McGraw-Hill.

Drucker, PF (1967). *The effective executive.* Harper & Row.

Drucker, PF (1973). *Management: tasks, responsibilities, practices.* McGraw-Hill.

Humble, JW (1973). *How to manage by objectives.* Amacom.

Chapter 2

Allen, LA (1964). *The management profession.* McGraw-Hill.
Anon (1976). *Instructional methods.* Ministry of Defence, JSP 345.
Anon (1971). *Glossary of training terms.* HMSO.
Beard, R (1976). *Teaching and learning in higher education.* Penguin (3rd edition).
Bligh, D et al (1975). *Teaching students.* Exeter University Teaching Services.
Bligh, D (1972). *What's the use of lectures?* Penguin.
Carpenter, WL (1967). *Twenty-four group methods and techniques in adult education.* Tallahassee, Florida: Florida State University, Department of Adult Education.
Cooper, C & Bowles, D (1977). *Hurt or helped? A study of the personal impact on managers of experiential, small group training programmes.* HMSO. Training Information Paper Number 10.
Cruikshank, DR & Teffler, RA (1978). *Simulations and games.* Washington, DC: ERIC Clearinghouse.
Curzon, LB (1976). *Teaching in further education.* Cassell.
Davies, IK (1973). *Competency based learning.* McGraw-Hill (Published in the UK as *The management of learning*).
Davies, IK (1966). *Training methods: an analysis of the research findings.* HQ Royal Air Force Training Command, Research Branch Report Number 234.
Keller, FS & Sherman, JG (1974). *The Keller plan handbook.* WA Benjamin.
Lancaster, OE (1974). *Effective teaching and learning.* Gordon and Breach.
McLeish, J (1968). *The lecture method.* Cambridge Institute of Education.
Michalak, DE & Yager, EG (1979). *Making the training process work.* Harper & Row.
Mills, HR (1977). *Teaching and training.* Macmillan.
Newstrom, JW and Scannell, EE (1980). *Games trainers play.* McGraw-Hill.
Powell, L (1973). *Lecturing.* Pitman.

Chapter 3

Cenci, L & Weaver, GG (1968). *Teaching occupational skills.* Pitman.
Curzon, LB (1976). *Teaching in further education: an outline of principles and practice.* Cassell.
Davies, IK (1973). *The organization of training.* McGraw-Hill.
Gagné, RM (1974). *Essentials of learning for instruction.* Dryden.
Gagné, RM (1977). *The conditions of learning.* Holt, Rinehart & Winston (third edition).
Gilbert, TF (1978). *Human competence: engineering worthy performance.* McGraw-Hill.
Lancaster, OE (1974). *Effective teaching and learning.* Gordon & Breach.
Mills, HR (1977). *Teaching and training: a handbook for instructors.* Harrap.
Pinsent, A (1969). *The principles of teaching method.* Harrap.
Taba, H (1956). *Teaching strategies and cognitive functioning.* San Francisco State College.
Verduin, J, Miller, H & Greer, C (1978). *Adults teaching adults.* Wiley.

Chapter 4

Ackoff, RL (1970). *A concept of corporate planning.* John Wiley.

Bligh, D et al (1975). *Teaching students.* Exeter University Teaching Services.

Cook, DL (1971). *Program evaluation and review techniques: applications in education.* USOE.

Davies, IK (1976). *Objectives in curriculum design.* McGraw-Hill.

Drucker, PF (1967). *The effective executive.* Harper & Row.

Mossman, LC (1938). *The activity concept: an interpretation.* Macmillan.

Chapter 5

Anon (1975). *Acoustics in educational buildings.* HMSO.

Bell, G (1979). Six tips on how to remember trainee names. *Training:* 16, 1, 14.

Birren, F (1958). *New horizons in color.* Reinhold.

Broadbent, DE (1958). Effect of noise on an 'intellectual' task. *Journal of Acoustical Society of America,* 30:824–827.

Davies, IK (1973). *Competency based learning.* McGraw-Hill. (Published in the UK as *The management of learning.*)

Drew, CJ (1971). Review of the psychological and behavioral effects of the physical environment. *Review of Educational Research,* 41:447–465.

Goffman, E (1959). *The presentation of self in everyday life.* Doubleday.

Gilliland, JW (1969). How environment affects learning. *American School and University,* 42:48–49.

Glass, G (1979). Newsfront. *Kappan,* 60:6, 411.

Hall, E (1961). *The hidden dimension.* Premier Books.

House, ER & Lapan, SD (1978). *Survival in the classroom.* Allyn & Bacon.

Howells, LT & Becker, SW (1962). Seating arrangements and leadership emergence. *Journal of Abnormal and Social Psychology,* 64:148–150.

Lipman, A (1967). Chairs are territory. *New Society,* 9:283, 564–566.

Marland, M (1975). *The craft of the classroom.* Heinemann.

McVey, GF (1971). *Sensory factors in the school learning environment.* National Education Association.

McVey, GF (1975). *Environments for effective media utilization.* Unpublished paper, Boston University.

Russo, NF (1967). Connotations of seating arrangements. *Cornell Journal of Social Relations,* 2:37–44.

Shaw, ME (1971). *Group dynamics, the psychology of small group behavior.* McGraw-Hill.

Sommer, R (1965). Further studies of small group ecology. *Sociometry,* 28:337–348.

Sommer, R (1969). *Personal space: the behavior basis of design.* Prentice-Hall.

Sommer, R (1974). *Tight spaces: hard architecture and how to humanize it.* Prentice-Hall.

Tinker, MA (1948). Trends in illuminating standards. *Illuminating Engineer,* 43: 866–881.

Vredevoe, LE (1971). *Discipline.* Hunt Publishing.

Wadd, K (1973). Classroom power. In B Turner (ed) *Discipline in schools.* Ward Lock.

Chapter 6

Bloom, BS, ed (1956). *Taxonomy of educational objectives. Handbook I: Cognitive Domain.* McKay.

Davies, IK (1976). *Objectives in curriculum design.* McGraw-Hill.

Harrow, AJ (1972). *A taxonomy of the psycho-motor domain.* McKay.

Kaulman, R (1975). *Needs assessment.* Florida State University, University Consortium for Instructional Development and Technology.

Mager, RF (1973). *Measuring instructional intent.* Fearon.

Mager, RF (1974). *Criterion-referenced instruction.* RF Mager Associates.

Mager, RF (1975). *Preparing instructional objectives.* Fearon (2nd edition).

Michalak, DF & Yager, EG (1979). *Making the training process work.* Harper & Row.

Steele, H (1979). Why training programs succeed and fail: the advice of Scott Parry. *Training: The Magazine of Human Resources Development.* 16:8, 9 and 12.

Wilson, V (1969). *Setting precise performance objectives.* Brandon Systems.

Chapter 7

Argyle, M (1967). *The psychology of interpersonal behavior.* Penguin.

Birdwhistell, RL (1974). The language of the body. In A. Silverstein (ed) *Human communication: theoretical exploration.* Wiley.

Blubaugh, J (1969). Effects of positive and negative audience feedback on selected variables of speech behavior. *Speech Monographs,* 36:131–137.

Danziger, K (1976). *Interpersonal communication.* Pergamon.

Darwin, C (1872). The expression of the emotions of man and animals. Reprinted in BJ Loewenberg (ed) *Evolution and natural selection.* Beacon.

Eckman, P (1965). *Communication through non-verbal behavior.* Langley Porter Institute Progress Report.

Eckman, P & Friesen, WV (1971). Constants across cultures in the face of body cues. *Journal of Personality and Social Psychology,* 17:124–129.

Fast, J (1970). *Body language.* Pocket Books.

Fessenden, SA, Johnson, RI & Larson, PM (1954). *The teacher speaks.* Prentice-Hall.

Hall, ET (1969). *The hidden dimension.* Doubleday.

Izard, CE (1971). *The face of emotion.* Appleton-Century-Crofts.

Jay, A (1971). *The new oratory.* American Management Association.

Keltner, JW (1970). *Interpersonal speech-communication: elements and structure.* Wadsworth.

McBurney, JH & Wrage, EJ (1975). *Guide to good speech.* Prentice-Hall (4th edition).

Mehrabian, A (1968). Communication without words. *Psychology Today,* 2:53–56.

Parry, J (1967). *The psychology of human communication.* University of London Press.

Schelflen, AE (1964). The significance of posture in communication systems. *Psychiatry,* 27:4.

Sheflen, AS (1968). Human communication. *Behavioral Science,* 13.

Tubbs, SL & Moss, S (1978). *Interpersonal communication.* Random House.

Chapter 8

Anon (1969). *Glossary of training terms.* HMSO, Department of Employment and Productivity, Training Division.

Austin, FM (1949). *The art of questioning.* University of London.

Hamilton, ER (1929). *The art of interrogation.* Kegan Paul.

Robinson, WP & Rackstraw, SJ (1972). *A question of answers.* Routledge & Kegan Paul.

Taba, H (1956). *Teaching strategies and cognitive functioning.* San Francisco State College.

Verduin, JR (1967). *Conceptual models in teacher education.* American Association of Colleges for Teacher Education.

Ward, RF (1970). *A survey of micro-teaching.* Stanford Center For Research and Development in Teaching. Memorandum Number 70.

Chapter 9

Allen, S (1979). *A manager's guide to audiovisuals.* McGraw-Hill.

Bothan, CN (1975). *Audio-visual aids for co-operative education.* UNO. FAO Development Paper Number 86.

Brown, J, Lewis, RB & Harcleroad, FF (1977). *AV instruction: technology, media and methods.* McGraw-Hill.

Davies, IK (1972). Presentation techniques. In J. Hartley (ed) *Strategies for programmed instruction.* Butterworths.

Foster, J (1968). A note on the visibility of black-on-white and white-on-black photographic slides. *Psychological Society Bulletin,* 21:72.

Michalak, DF & Yager, EG (1979). *Making the training process work.* Harper & Row.

Seymour, WD (1937). An experiment showing the superiority of a light colored 'blackboard.' *Journal of Educational Psychology,* 7:259–268.

Chapter 10

Allen, S (1979). *A manager's guide to audiovisuals.* McGraw-Hill.

Anderson, RH (1976). *Selecting and developing media for instruction.* VanNostrand Reinhold.

Botham, CN (1967). *Audio-visual aids for cooperative education.* FAO Paper 86.

Brown, J, Lewis, RB & Harcleroad, FF (1977). *AV instruction: technology, media and methods.* McGraw-Hill.

Cable, R (1972). *Audio-visual handbook.* University of London Press.

Davies, IK (1973). *Competency based learning.* McGraw-Hill. (Published as the *management of learning* in the UK).

Jay, A (1971). *The new oratory.* American Management Association.

Kemp, JE (1975). *Planning and producing audiovisual materials.* Thomas Crowell.

McCloud, LA (1979). Flying without wings. *US Air Magazine.* October, 1979, 46–50.

Michales, W (1979). *Business games and management systems.* Education Research.

Minor, E & Frye, HR (1977). *Techniques for producing visual instructional media.* McGraw-Hill.

Powell, LS (1961). *A guide for the use of visual aids.* BACIE.

Powell, LS (1969). *Communication and learning.* Pitman.

Rigg, RP (1969). *Audio-visual techniques in managerial and supervisory training.* Hamish Hamilton.

Robinson, J & Barnes, N (1968). *New media and methods in industrial training.* BBC.

Romiszowski, AJ (1968). *The selection and use of training aids.* Kogan Page.

Taylor, EA (1966). *Visual presentation in education and training.* Pergamon.

Winman, RV (1972). *Instructional materials.* Charles Jones.

Wittich, WA & Schuller, A (1976). *Audio-visual materials.* Harper & Row.

Zuckerman, DW & Horn, RE (1979). *The guide to simulation and games for education and training.* Information Resources.

Chapter 11

Buzan, T (1974). *Use your head.* BBC.

Cenci, L & Weaver, GG (1968). *Teaching occupational skills.* Pitman.

Davies, IK (1973). *Competency based learning.* McGraw-Hill. (Published in the UK as *The management of learning*).

Hartley, J & Davies, IK (1978). Note-taking: a critical review. *Journal of the Association for Programmed Learning and Educational Technology,* a15:3, 207–224.

Heim, A (1976). *Teaching and learning in higher education.* National Foundation for Educational Research.

Horn, RE (1976). *How to write information mapping.* Information Resources Inc.

Mills, HR (1977). *Teaching and training: a handbook for instructors.* Macmillan.

Chapter 12

Anon (1979). Making your tests effective and legal. *Training: The Magazine of Human Resources Development.* 16:4, 80–81.

Anon (1974). *Examinations and assessment methods.* MOD (RAF).

Bissell, J, White, S & Zivin, G (1971). Sensory modalities. In GS Lesser (ed) *Psychology and educational practice.* Scott Foresman.

Davies, IK & Davis, RW (1975). *Measurement and testing for developers and evaluators.* Far West Regional Laboratory.

Feder, B (1979). *The complete guide to taking tests.* Prentice-Hall.

Heywood, J (1977). *Assessment in higher education.* John Wiley.

Jessup, G & Jessup, H (1975). *Selection and assessment at work.* Methuen.

Levin, J (1977). *Learner differences: diagnosis and prescription.* Holt, Rinehart & Winston.

Lewis, DG (1974). *Assessment in education.* University of London Press.

Lindahl, LG (1949). How to build a training program. *Personnel Journal,* 27:417–419.

Michalak, DF & Yager, EG (1979). *Making the training process work.* Harper & Row.

Pask, G & Scott, BCE (1972). Learning strategies and individual competence. *International Journal of Man-Machine Studies,* 4:217–253.

Rowntree, D (1977). *Assessing students: how shall we know them?* Harper & Row.
Tyler, LE & Walsh, WB (1979). *Tests and measurement.* Prentice-Hall.
Wood, DA (1960). *Test construction: development and interpretation of achievement tests.* Charles E. Merrill.

Chapter 13

Ammons, RB (1947). Acquisition of motor skill. *Journal of Experimental Psychology,* 37:393–411.
Annet, J (1969). *Feedback and human performance.* Penguin.
Blakemore, C (1977). *Mechanics of the mind.* Cambridge University Press.
Buzan, T (1974). *Use your head.* BBC Publications.
Davies, IK (1973). *Competency based learning* McGraw-Hill. (Published in the UK as *The management of learning.*)
Davis, IK (1973). *The organization of training.* McGraw-Hill.
Fitts, PM & Posner, MI (1967). *Human performance.* Brooks Cole.
Gregg, V (1975). *Human memory.* Methuen.
Hergenhahn, BR (1976). *An introduction to theories of learning.* Prentice-Hall.
Hilgard, ER & Bowers, GH (1975). *Theories of learning.* Prentice-Hall.
Hovland, CI (1957). *The order of presentation in persuasion.* Yale University Press.
Hultman, KE (1980). Identifying and dealing with resistance to change. *Training and Development Journal,* February, 28–33.
Legge, D & Barber, PJ (1976). *Information and skill.* Methuen.
Ludwig, E (1968). Memory and program construction. In L. Bung (ed) *Programmed learning and the language laboratory.* Volume I. Longmac.
Mager, RF (1968). *Developing attitude toward learning.* Fearon.
Morris, P (1977). Practical strategies for human learning and remembering. In MJA Howe (ed) *Adult learning: psychological research and applications.* Wiley.
Penfield, W & Rasmussen, T (1957). *The cerebral cortex of man.* Macmillan.
Reason, J (1977). Skill and error in everyday life. In MJA Howe (ed) *Adult learning: psychological research and application.* Wiley.
Reich, B & Adcock, C (1976). *Values, attitudes and behavior change.* Methuen.
Salvendy, G & Seymour, WD (1973). *Prediction and development of industrial work performance.* Wiley.
Seymour, WD (1970). *Skills analysis training.* Pitman.
Singleton, WT (1978). *The analysis of practical skills.* University Park Press.
Stammers, R & Patrick J (1975). *The psychology of training.* Methuen.
Welford, AT (1976). *Skilled performance: perceptual and motor skills.* Scott, Foresman.

Chapter 14

Beck, RC (1978). *Motivation: theories and principles.* Prentice-Hall.
Birch, D & Veroff, J (1969). *Motivation: a study of action.* Brooks Cole.
Cofer, CN & Appley, HM (1964). *Motivation: theory and research.* John Wiley.
Davies, IK (1973). *Competency based learning.* McGraw-Hill. (Published as *The management of learning* in the UK).

Davies, IK (1973). *The organization of training.* McGraw-Hill.

Gellerman, SW (1963). *Motivation and productivity.* American Management Association.

Grollman, WK (1974). Hygiene factors in professional education programs. *The Journal of Accountancy,* 137, 1, 85–88.

Herzberg, F (1966). *Work and the nature of man.* World.

Herzberg, F, Mausner, B & Snyderman, B (1959). *The motivation to work.* John Wiley.

Hodgetts, RM (1975). *Management: theory, process and practice.* WB Saunders.

Maslow, AH (1954). *Motivation and personality.* Harper.

McGregor, D (1960). *The human side of enterprise.* McGraw-Hill.

Porter, LW & Lawler, EE (1968). *Managerial attitudes and performance.* Richard Irwin.

Steers, RM & Porter, LW (1975). *Motivation and work behavior.* McGraw-Hill.

Vernon, MD (1969). *Human motivation.* Cambridge University Press.

Chapter 15

Anon (1957). *How to construct a sociogram.* Teachers College, Columbia University.

Belbin, E & Belbin, RM (1974). *Problems in adult retraining.* Heinemann.

Bischoff, LJ (1976). *Adult psychology.* Harper & Row.

Davies, IK (1973). *Competency based learning.* McGraw-Hill. (Published in the UK as *The Management of Learning*).

Downs, S (1977). *Trainability testing: a practical approach to selection.* HMSO, Training Information Paper Number 11.

Dunn, R, Dunn, K & Price, G (1975). *Learning style inventory.* Price Systems.

Ferguson, GA (1954). On learning and human ability. *Canadian Journal of Psychology,* 8, 95–112.

Fleishman, EA & Hempel, WE (1955). The relation between abilities and improvement with practice in a visual discrimination reaction task. *Journal of Experimental Psychology,* 49:301–312.

Newsham, OB (1969). *The challenge of change to the adult trainee.* HMSO, Training Information Paper Number 3.

Peel, EA (1956). *The psychological basis of education.* Oliver & Boyd.

Robertson, I & Downs, S (1979). Learning and the prediction of performance. *Journal of Applied Psychology,* 64, 1, 42–50.

Thurstone, LL (1938). *Primary mental abilities.* University of Chicago Press.

Vernon, PE (1950). *The structure of human abilities.* Methuen.

Welford, AT (1958). *Ageing and human skill.* Oxford University Press.

Chapter 16

Bion, WR (1959). *Experiences with groups.* Ballantine Books.

Bormann, EG (1975). *Discussion and group methods.* Harper & Row (2nd edition).

Curzon, LB (1978). *Teaching in further education.* Cassell.

Dyer, WG (1977). *Team building: issues and alternatives.* Addison-Wesley.

Flynn, EW & La Faso, JF (1972). *Group discussion as a learning process.* Paulist Press.

Fordyce, JK & Weil, R (1971). *Managing with people.* Addison-Wesley.

Hon, D (1980). How to hold productive meetings with your peers. *Training: The Magazine of Human Resources Development,* 17:5, 53–63.

Klein, J (1963). *Working with groups.* Hutchinson.

Luft, J (1969). *Of human interaction.* National Press.
Luft, J (1970). *Group processes: an introduction to group dynamics.* National Press.
McGregor, D (1960). *The human side of enterprise.* McGraw-Hill.
McKeachie, WJ (1969). *Teaching tips.* DC Heath.
Mills, HR (1977). *Teaching and training: a handbook for instructors.* Macmillan.
Morgan, B, Holmes, GE & Bundy, CE (1976). *Methods in adult education.* Interstate (3rd edition).
Schmuck, RA & Schmuck, PA (1971). *Group processes in the classroom.* WC Brown.
Stenhouse, L (1969). Handling controversial issues in the classroom. *Education Canada,* 9:4, 12–21.

Chapter 17

Cook, DI (1971). *Program evaluation and review techniques: applications in education.* United States Office of Education.
Davies, IK (1976). *Objectives in curriculum design.* McGraw-Hill.
Drucker, PF (1967). *The effective executive.* Harper & Row.
Pasierb, B (1979). *Methods in management.* Price Waterhouse.

Chapter 18

Bischoff, LJ (1976). *Adult psychology.* Harper & Row (2nd edition).
Cole, PR (1935). *The method and technique of teaching.* Oxford University Press.
Hill, LA (1969). Homework for theory and practice. *Engineering Education,* 60:1, 120.
Hudson, JA (1965). *A pilot study of the influence of homework in mathematics and attitude towards homework.* (Doctoral dissertation, University of Arkansas). University Microfilms, Number 65-8456.
Lancaster, OE (1974). *Effective teaching and learning.* Gordon and Breach.
Milligan, MW & Reid, RL (1973). Homework: its relationship to learning. *Engineering Education,* 64:1, 32–33.
Seligman, J (1979). The decline of homework. *Newsweek,* January 1979: 32.
Small, DE, Holtan, BD, & Davis, EJ (1967). A study of two methods of checking homework. *The Mathematics Teacher,* 60:149–152.
Ten Brinke, DP (1967). *Homework: an experimental evaluation of the effect on achievement.* (Doctoral dissertation, University of Minnesota). Ann Arbor, Michigan: University Microfilms, Number 65-15.

Chapter 19

Adair, J (1968). *Training for leadership.* Macdonald.
Adamson, W (1969). *Functional leadership.* MOD RAF.
Coombs, A (1965). *The professional education of teachers.* Allyn & Bacon.
Highet, G (1974). *The art of teaching.* Methuen.
Highet, G (1976). *The immortal profession.* Weybright & Talley.
McGregor, D (1960). *The human side of enterprise.* McGraw-Hill.
Michalak, DF & Yager, EG (1979). *Making the training process work.* Harper & Row.
Wiemann, JM & Backlund, P (1980). Current theory and research in communicative competence. *Review of Educational Research,* 50, 1, 185–199.

Author Index

357

Subject Index